"*Family Conscience* is an extraordinary memoir. Tracing the various manifestations of conscience in his Protestant mid-western family over several generations, Barbour illuminates the way in which 'family values,' whether adopted or resisted, can persist and shape behavior for decades. At the same time, his book is an acute inquiry into—and demonstration of—the ethics of writing about one's relatives. It is an impressive achievement."

—G. THOMAS COUSER,
Professor emeritus of English, Hofstra University

"'The unexamined life is not worth living'—so said Socrates. In *Family Conscience*, John D. Barbour re-examines several of his long-standing intellectual concerns—solitude, ethics, spirituality and its precarity—in light of his most intimate personal relations. The nature and challenges of conscience hold his narrative together, and the result is a memoir that draws readers deeply into personal reflection on the meaning of their own lives and those of others. Socrates would approve."

—CRAIG HOWES,
Professor of English, University of Hawaii

"Drawing on detailed interviews, journal entries, letters, and photographs, John Barbour intricately mines his family's past for clues about how moral conscience develops. From host homes in India to work camps in Germany, this generational memoir investigates the places, events, conversations, and relationships that form our personal understanding of right and wrong. With compassion and curiosity, Barbour eloquently investigates how war, marriage, parenting, suicide, religion, community, and vocation affect the moral dimensions of one family. But Barbour is also acutely aware of the mutability of memory; woven through the book are his interrogations of his own writerly motives and his family's mixed response to his observations. The result is a lucid, wise, and engaging memoir that offers a moving example of why searching for truth is both a fraught and necessary endeavor."

—KAETHE SCHWEHN,
Associate Professor of Practice in English, St. Olaf College

"Meticulously researched and elegantly written, *Family Conscience* provides a genealogy of the values of four generations of an accomplished and morally aspiring clan. As honest as it is tender, Barbour's study is rife with illuminating reflections on the nature of conscience considered as an amalgam of reason, desire, and history. Life's moral complexity is brought home with engaging stories and the author's willingness to give voice to relatives with conflicting perspectives on family history."

—**GORDON MARINO,**
Professor Emeritus of Philosophy, St. Olaf College

FAMILY CONSCIENCE

Family Conscience

A Memoir of Four Generations

JOHN D. BARBOUR

CASCADE *Books* • Eugene, Oregon

FAMILY CONSCIENCE
A Memoir of Four Generations

Copyright © 2025 John D. Barbour. All rights reserved. Except for brief quotations in critical publications or reviews, no part of this book may be reproduced in any manner without prior written permission from the publisher. Write: Permissions, Wipf and Stock Publishers, 199 W. 8th Ave., Suite 3, Eugene, OR 97401.

Cascade Books
An Imprint of Wipf and Stock Publishers
199 W. 8th Ave., Suite 3
Eugene, OR 97401
www.wipfandstock.com

PAPERBACK ISBN: 978-1-5326-3637-0
HARDCOVER ISBN: 978-1-5326-3639-4
EBOOK ISBN: 978-1-5326-3638-7

Cataloging-in-Publication data:

Names: Barbour, John D., author.

Title: Family conscience : a memoir of four generations / John D. Barbour.

Description: Eugene, OR: Cascade Books, 2025.

Identifiers: ISBN: 978-1-5326-3637-0 (PAPERBACK). | ISBN: 978-1-5326-3639-4 (HARDCOVER). | ISBN: 978-1-5326-3638-7 (EBOOK).

Subjects: LCSH: Autobiography—Moral and ethical aspects. | Conscience. | Suicide victims—Family relationships. | Fathers—Death—Psychological aspects. | Dickinson, Robert Latou, 1861–1950. | Barbour, George B. (George Brown), 1890–1977. | Barbour, Dorothy Dickinson. | Barbour, Ian G. | Barbour, Hugh. | Barbour, John D.

Classification: CT28 B28 2025 (print). | CT28 (epub).

VERSION NUMBER 06/16/25

For Edgar and Esme

Contents

Acknowledgments | *ix*

Preface | *xiii*

Chapter 1   The Afterlife of Suicide | 1

Chapter 2   "I think I shall call you Honor" | 24

Chapter 3   Not Passing by on the Other Side | 41

Chapter 4   A Scot and a Dragon-Saint | 64

Chapter 5   Finding Them in the Archives | 83

Chapter 6   Pros and Cons, Regrets and Grace | 112

Chapter 7   Another Elder Brother | 140

Chapter 8   Early Scruples and Quandaries | 157

Chapter 9   Choosing a Life: Work, Marriage, Money, and Buddha | 184

Chapter 10 Professing Religion and Traveling with Students | 208

Chapter 11 A Father's Questions | 223

Chapter 12 When the Memoired Protest: My Story and Their Privacy | 255

Epilogue: Who Is Speaking? | 280

Acknowledgments

I could never have written this book without the collaboration and support of the family members I portray here. It was often difficult for them to understand what I was doing or to accept how I put things. I am deeply grateful for their patience, honesty, and forthright challenges as I sought to depict my own take on a very murky subject, family conscience. The insight, courage, and compassion of my parents, Ian and Deane, were an enormous gift. I am indebted in countless ways to my siblings, Blair, David, and Heather; to my former spouse, Meg Ojala; and to my sons, Graham and Reed. My uncle and aunt, Hugh and Sirkka Barbour, were thoughtful, frank, and supportive in responding to my questions about the family. Over the past twenty years, friends and colleagues have expressed interest in this project, even when it was not clear to them or to me exactly what I was doing. Thanks especially to Judith Nelson and two dear friends who have died: Rick Fairbanks and Jere Chapman.

I first thought about writing a family memoir when Richard Freadman invited me to a conference on "Life Writing and the Generations" at La Trobe University in Melbourne, Australia, in 2002. An early snippet was presented at Indiana University in 2004, and I'm grateful to Richard B. Miller for inviting me to contribute to his faculty seminar on childhood. A conference of life writing scholars at the University of Hawaii in 2005 was very helpful, especially the comments of Richard Freadman, Craig Howes, Gene Stelzig, the late David Parker, Roger Porter, Margaretta Jolly, Paul John Eakin, and Thomas Couser, whose writings about the ethics of life writing also influenced me. John and Tom responded to an early draft of the manuscript.

I benefited from a group of poets and novelists gathered for two summer workshops in 2006 and 2007 at the Collegeville Institute for Ecumenical and Cultural Research at St. John's University in Minnesota, especially Todd Maitland and our astute and inspiring teacher, Michael Dennis

Acknowledgments

Browne. Cathie Brettschneider, then at the University of Virginia Press, was enthusiastic about this project from the outset, encouraging me.

I began work on this project while I served for four years as St. Olaf College's first Martin Marty Chair of Religion and the Academy, and I am grateful for that gift of released time and freedom to explore a topic and approach that were not traditional scholarship.

Chapter 10 revises two earlier publications: "Tourist Traps and Guilt Trips," *St Olaf Magazine* 52 (2005) 13–14, 47–49; and "Professing Religion," in *Claiming Our Callings: Toward a New Understanding of Vocation in the Liberal Arts*, edited by Kaethe Schwehn and L. DeAne Lagerquist (New York: Oxford University Press, 2014), 175–84.

I'm grateful for the good work of the staff at Cascade Books, especially to the editor in chief at Wipf and Stock Publishers, K. C. Hanson, and to Jeremy Funk, whose careful copyediting greatly improved my writing.

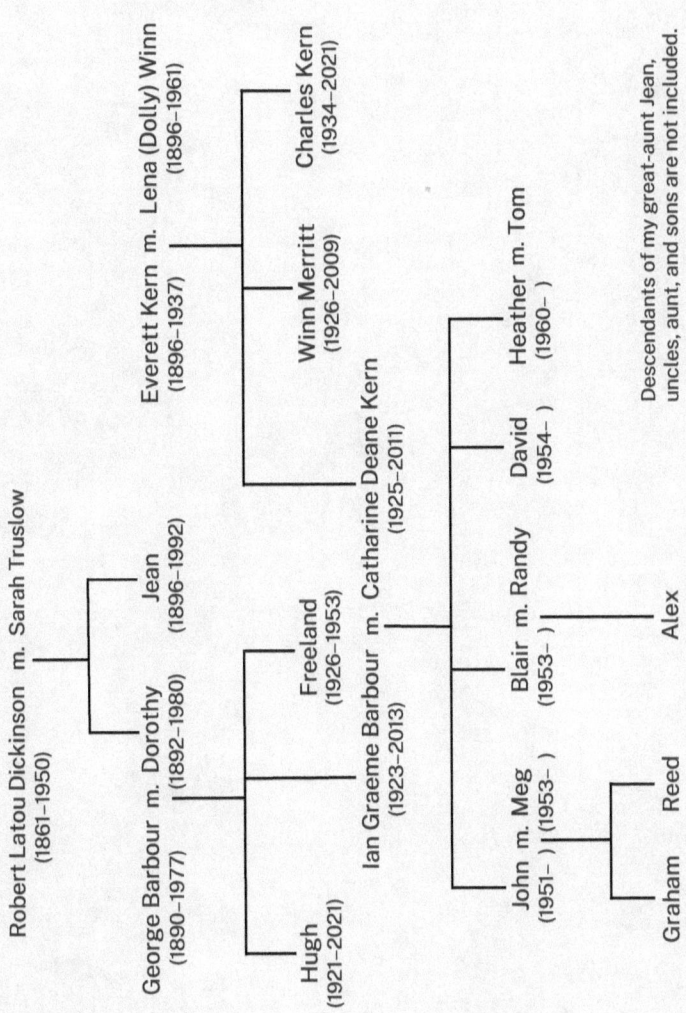

Preface

My grandfather's suicide had a huge effect on my mother and remains a hidden influence on the entire family. I began writing this family memoir in 2002 by trying to understand this traumatic event and its aftermath. The inquiry expanded to include nearly a century of family history, and my focus shifted to how moral values were passed on and transformed through the generations. Conscience—the ways we judge ourselves—reveals who we are as individuals and as a family.

Conscience means moral self-assessment: how I appraise and evaluate my actions and character. In my family, conscience has led individuals to acts of generosity and courage, to penetrating insights, and to periods of depression, paralyzing guilt, or anxious scrupulosity. Family conscience, as I understand it, encompasses the common values and patterns of self-judgment that members of my family share, and also the ways our differing moral views have been influenced by interactions with each other.

Family voices echo in many of the ethical questions I ask myself. Should I trust reason or emotion? Should I follow my immediate intuition or what I decide after lengthy consideration? How do work, relationships, and religious faith give meaning to my life, and what should I do when their demands conflict? Does God speak to me through my conscience? Sometimes when I'm making a decision, an impulse, scruple, or insight comes, and it sounds like what a family member said or what I imagine they would tell me. In a biblical passage, an ethical theory, or the words of a Shakespearean character, familiar voices may resonate. Conscience is where ancestors live on, sometimes haunting or confusing me like threatening ghosts, sometimes empowering me to seek the good or do what I know is right.

My family left me a moral inheritance that shapes the ways I assess and judge my actions and character. This legacy is different from a sum of money, a lock of hair, or a piece of furniture. Even if rejected, it comes with strings attached, bonds that influence me in ways I don't always fully comprehend. I am trying to understand my moral inheritance, criticize and appreciate it, and discern how it burdens and empowers me.

The individuals in my family have certain things in common in terms of moral values and concerns, yet we differ in significant ways. Like a physical family resemblance, conscience is not identical in every individual, but expresses itself in various ways: in shared ways of thinking and feeling, in recurring motifs, and in concerns shaped by religious and cultural values. What themes and patterns of ethical scrutiny and judgment are repeated through the generations? What are the sources of these recurring tendencies, in terms of cultural influences, individual and family psychology, religious beliefs, and the basic nature of conscience? How did our relationships with each other shape the different ways each of us developed a moral orientation? How did belonging to this particular family affect our fundamental values? To answer these questions, I consider how family members have understood work and vocation, religious commitments, political and economic values, choices about marriage and raising children, conflicts within the family, and other moral situations and decisions.

I describe my interactions with four generations: my grandparents, parents and two uncles, my own generation (brother, two sisters, former spouse), and two sons. I don't tell anyone's whole story, including my own, but only what illuminates the role of conscience in this family. I see relatives from my own peculiar angle, trying to discern how their lives shed light on mine. A net is spread for a certain kind of fish, and others escape. I simplify complex lives, omit large parts of each person's experience, and ignore many facets of individual character.

My sources are memories, journals, written documents, photographs, conversations, and tape-recorded oral interviews. In the first seven chapters, my interpretations of ancestors elicit comparisons and insights into my life. I quote copiously so that the distinct voices of these individuals are heard. Starting in chapter 8, I turn more directly to my own life. This thematic family memoir thus blends the genres of biography, oral interview, autobiography, and essay as I depict and reflect on how conscience has been transmitted and transformed through several generations.

I have had what by any account is a very happy and privileged life. The ethical issues explored here may seem microscopically trivial when compared with problems of international conflict, global warming, racism, medical dilemmas, and other pressing challenges. Whatever the weight of various moral problems on some imaginary scales, my capacity to be concerned about any of them is deeply influenced by how a specific family context shaped me. My family mediated cultural values and moral traditions regarding religion, money, work, sexuality, social justice, pleasure, the

Preface

use of time and energy, and other matters. A family context also shaped my capacities to be self-critical, to revise my values, and to seek a fuller understanding of the good than what I first learned. My people both stamped me with a particular character and culture and nurtured my limited but crucial capacity for self-transcendence.

I made many decisions about disclosing or withholding information and interpreting other people's experience. This memoir is not a confession of all my sins or those of others; it is not a tell-all exposé of anyone's shameful past or guilty secrets. Because the writing process is subject to ethical scrutiny, this book is itself an expression of family conscience as I navigate the issues involved in telling a story that touches on several kinds of vulnerability in ancestors and living persons I respect and love. The last chapter tells the story of the story, focusing on ethical questions that arose in writing it. I portray dialogues with others about how to reconcile care for vulnerable loved ones with benefits that might come from a book like this, including self-expression and insights that others may find in it. I hope that readers are moved to think about how their own conscience was formed in the context of a particular family.

I gave family members early drafts of this manuscript for reaction and I deleted statements that they thought were misleading or just plain wrong. Rather than trying to portray some harmonized version of family history that everyone agrees on, however, I present other voices arguing with mine. My version of things is sometimes challenged by contrasting interpretations offered by a parent, sibling, or son. In the end, of course, this is my take on family conscience.

Writing a memoir is in many ways like writing fiction. I select incidents and arrange them in an order, characterize others and myself, and interpret everything in terms of a theme, conscience. I connect diverse human experiences to create a pattern. At the same time, a memoirist's concern for historical accuracy constrains and guides this story. The distinctive truth of memoir is at once imaginative, personal, and the author's best attempt to describe "what really happened." A memoir's veracity, like memory itself, is a version of the past that is both limited and revealing—and sometimes revealing in its very limitations. This may be especially the case as I portray the workings of conscience, which can idealize, censor, and rationalize even as it seeks to know the truth.

Chapter 1

The Afterlife of Suicide

My mother, Deane, rarely spoke about her father when I was growing up. If she did it was always in very positive terms, as a loving and devoted parent. But I sensed a painful underside of this version of the past. It was difficult for Deane to talk about her father, Everett Deane Kern (1896–1937). She fought back tears and became tense or turned away. Memories of her mother, too, were often painful. Deane's mother, named Lena and called Dolly by her friends and husband, was killed suddenly in a car accident in 1961, when I was nine. Both of my mother's parents died suddenly, and these unexpected losses were so traumatic that even good memories sometimes seemed to bring her excruciating grief. Not wanting to hurt her, I learned not to ask questions about her family background. Shortly after I turned eighteen, on the evening before I left home to go to college, my mother asked me to sit with her in the living room. She told me that her father had committed suicide. I was stunned by this disclosure and not sure how to react or what I was feeling, yet some of the mysteries of my childhood started to make sense.

Her father's suicide, which happened just before Deane's twelfth birthday, had a decisive effect on her life. Both certain recurring psychological struggles and her deepest moral concerns were influenced by patterns of thinking I trace back to Everett's death. (My grandfather was sometimes known as Deane, but I will call him Everett to distinguish him from my mother.) The afterlife of Everett's suicide continues to shape the lives of his descendants. At least half of his grandchildren struggled with depression, several attempted suicide, and one succeeded, although it was an ambiguous death related to alcohol abuse. There were also positive things that came out of the way my mother responded to losing her father. Like the

Family Conscience

ripples caused by a stone thrown in a lake, the effects of Everett's life and death become weaker as time goes on and harder to distinguish from other influences.

When my mother told me about her father's suicide, she gave me a newspaper clipping that reported his death. These are the facts about his suicide as reported in the Washington, DC newspaper the *Evening Star* on August 26, 1937:

> Motive Lacking in Kern Suicide
> Former Naval Officer Had Been Depressed, Family Discloses
>
> A motive for taking his own life was still lacking today in the death of Everett Deane Kern, 40, Maritime Commission engineer, former naval officer and member of a prominent Washington family, as Coroner A. Magruder MacDonald closed the case with a certificate of suicide.
>
> Kern was married and the father of three children. Only the statement of his mother, Mrs. Charles E. Kern, 2632 Woodley Place, that he had been depressed lately offered a possible reason for his act.
>
> The body was recovered yesterday afternoon from Chesapeake Canal, off of Canal Road, a short time after two notes written by Kern had been found. One note, addressed to his brother, Wells B. Kern, was left at the Woodley Place address. It said, "I'll be somewhere in the canal."
>
> Wells Kern and another brother, Willis F., led police to the canal bank and there was found Kern's hat and coat and a second note which read "No one is to blame but myself." Within an hour his body was recovered.
>
> In recent weeks Kern had been living with his mother while his wife, Mrs. Lena Winn Kern, and their children were spending their summer vacation in Norfolk, Va.
>
> Kern was graduated from the Naval Academy at Annapolis in 1918 and served for a short time during the World War aboard a destroyer off the coast of Brest, France. He remained in the Navy until 1927, when he had attained the rank of lieutenant. He resigned in that year to join the U. S. Shipping Board, which was superseded by the Maritime Commission.
>
> His father, the late Charles Kern, was a prominent Washington attorney and newspaper man.

Accompanying the article is a picture of Everett wearing the uniform of a lieutenant in the United States Navy. An obituary in the *Washington Post* adds that "he was in excellent health, but had been despondent for several weeks, his brother said."

Everett in naval uniform.

Although the newspaper reported that a motive was lacking, there are several ways I understand why Everett took his own life. The most immediate reason for Everett's suicide is grief over the breakup of his family. During the summer of 1937, Dolly took her three children from Washington to live in Norfolk, Virginia, near her relatives. Deane was eleven, her sister, Winn, was ten, and her brother, Charles, was three. Everett stayed in Washington, living with his mother and brother, and considered selling the family home. According to Deane, Dolly had planned to return to her husband at the end of the summer, but in August she told Everett that for the present she would be staying in Norfolk with the children. I think that Everett's despair at the loss of his wife and children was the primary reason why he killed himself: he did not want to go on living without them.

Why did Dolly leave her home and husband? Everett had a problem with alcohol. When Deane described her father's drinking, she emphasized that he never became abusive or violent; rather, he was quiet, sad, downcast, or despondent. He did not walk steadily, and Deane remembered her mother twice telling him that he was driving too fast. The effects of his drinking became more noticeable after Everett's father died in December 1934. At that time there were no Alcoholics Anonymous groups to turn to and few resources to help an alcoholic recover. Alcoholism was seen as a moral failing, a recurring lapse of willpower. I think Everett struggled with what he saw as weakness of character and condemned himself.

As we talked about family history in March 2003, Deane described her mental image of a bottle of alcohol lying on Everett's coat by the Chesapeake and Ohio Canal where he drowned. She was not sure whether she imagined this image or was told about it by Everett's brother Wells. She believed that her father quit drinking during that final summer. She also thought that he would have needed the help of alcohol "to numb his conscience" when he took his life. Using the present tense, she asked: "Is there a bottle there or not?"

I think that some of Everett's despondency is related to his father's death and the related problem of vocation. Charles E. Kern was an influential Washington journalist and attorney. With the endorsement of his friends in the Senate, three of his four sons received appointments to the Naval Academy at Annapolis. While Willis thrived in the Navy and eventually became a professor of mathematics at Annapolis, the third son, Miles, did not. According to Deane, Miles said "I'd rather sell apples than be an admiral." He deliberately failed an examination so that he could leave the Naval Academy. Miles, too, developed a problem with alcohol, suffered from depression and, in accord with medical theory in the 1920s, was subjected to a lobotomy. There are probably genetic factors in my mother's family that make some of us prone to depression, exacerbating negative judgments of self-worth.

Everett's response to the Navy was more ambivalent than that of his brothers. He did well, graduated from the Naval Academy in 1918, and served off the coast of France until the war ended. A letter Everett wrote to his father from the U.S.S. McCalla in New York on August 15, 1919, describes his decision to leave the Navy:

> I have finally and definitely made up my mind to get out of the Navy and I intend to begin work toward this end immediately. ... I have done my best to get interested in the work and work up a spark of ambition for a naval career, but it has been in vain. When one does not like his work he is very unhappy, unless he is absolutely worthless and lazy. I am unfitted both in temperament and instinct for this kind of life and I honestly feel that to delay making this step will be one of the greatest mistakes and one which I will look back upon all my life with regret. I am beginning to look upon dissipation as a mere joke, a means to

while away the time when I am lucky enough to be away from the ship and an existence which I detest. I have no insane idea that I can step out of the service into a job which will pay me anything like the money I am getting now, but I feel confident that in ten years' time I shall be making very much more than would be the case if I remain in the Navy. Money cuts no figure anyway. I wouldn't stay in the Navy if my pay were tripled. To wait longer is simply foolish. My determination to get out will only be strengthened by time and the longer I wait the harder it will be for me when I do finally make these steps. I am not the first man who has found out that he has found himself in the wrong career. God pity him who doesn't find that out until too late. I have no sympathy with a man who shrinks from giving up a dead sure thing for something he is not sure of. Witness the case of hundreds of grey-haired office clerks in the Government Departments in Washington. One of the many reasons why I admire you is that you gave up your job on the Star, practically a dead sure thing, and took a chance on something else that wasn't dead sure and won. There is no argument which can be advanced which will tend in the slightest degree to change my decision in this matter. Frankly I would rather sell peanuts on the streets than be an admiral in this outfit.

The rest of the letter is alternately humorous and desperate, and firmly determined while pleading for his father's approval. He concludes: "I don't intend to sacrifice myself to this slow grinding machine. Remember Dad we live *only once.*" Everett was working up his nerve, steeling himself to act on his deepest desires yet afraid to do so.

What Everett found most onerous about the Navy and what work he would have preferred are unclear. I think his reference to "dissipation" means that he had taken to drinking to escape the drudgery of routine duty and shipboard life. He says that he could eventually make more money in another career, yet also that "money cuts no figure." He appeals to his father's own history of career changes: Charles Everett Kern had been a journalist with the *Washington Post*, the *Washington Star*, and the Associated Press. He went to law school and graduated in 1917, when he was fifty-five. He became an expert on American petroleum laws and policies and knew prominent politicians. Everett lived in the shadow of this powerful and influential father. His negative view of a secure government position, a "dead sure thing," must have weighed heavily on him when he found himself working in a Washington bureaucracy fifteen years later. We live only once, he had said: *carpe diem*. But he let it slip from his grasp.

Family Conscience

In spite of his desperate wish to get out of the Navy as soon as possible, a few months later, on January 24, 1920, Everett wrote to the Navy Department from the Philadelphia Navy Yard to withdraw his resignation: "At the time I put in my resignation my mind was very unsettled and I now realize that I acted too hastily. I feel that, with my short Naval career, I am not properly fitted to judge on this matter until I have had more experience." He settled for an unhappy career in the Navy, perhaps because he could find no alternative.

Soon Everett was serving in China on a naval vessel that protected American interests during a period of clashing warlords. In October 1921, he wrote to his parents that his gunship was guarding a shipment of opium that had come under the jurisdiction of the American consul through a complicated chain of events. Everett was anchored on a river near the consulate for several weeks, waiting for the water level to go down so that the ship could safely navigate. He vividly describes the scene:

> Over on the beach a great dark Chinese village or rather city. It seems utterly deserted tonight, but no—the silence is disturbed at irregular intervals by a wild sputter of fire crackers set off by some of the superstitious natives and intended to drive away evil spirits. That muffled beating of drums issues from some secluded joss house where reside terrible and awe-inspiring gods. At these times the spell is broken. I awaken from my reverie and realize that there are hundreds of thousands of humans huddled together in the dark over there; humans like ourselves in form and yet so different in their manner of life and thought that I am prone at times to imagine myself on another planet.

He may have been reading Conrad's *Heart of Darkness*. Wending his way up the Congo River, Marlow described a similar moral dislocation in an exotic setting. Although Everett was fascinated by the mysterious otherness of Chinese culture, he found the enforced isolation and waiting to be a strain: "After dinner, back to de Ballar's again for poker which we played till 6:30 a. m. If it were not for these stag parties I suppose we would all go crazy in a few months. In a place like this where there are comparatively so few foreigners, we are thrown back on ourselves to furnish our own amusement." The naval officers played tennis, laid out a golf course, and watched horse races in Hankow. It sounds harmless, boring, and a temptation to slow dissipation. Everett tried not to succumb to sloth: "I must do something to keep in condition as I find I am taking on too much weight." I think he yearned for a vocation: work that would fully engage his mind, call forth a deeper commitment, and provide a moral tether.

The Afterlife of Suicide

In 1927 he resigned from the Navy and worked thereafter as an electrical engineer for the US Maritime Commission. This was a difficult decision for him, for it was against the wishes of his father as well as Dolly, whom he had married in 1924. It may have been another reason why he was estranged from his wife; Deane said that her mother found it hard to give up their naval life. The nature of his duties at the Maritime Commission are not clear to me, but I think the lack of meaningful work played a significant role in his final unhappy years. After his father died in 1934, Everett did not work as hard at keeping up appearances or being a worthy son. So many conflicts between fathers and sons revolve around work, and often involve a father's high and specific ambitions for a son who needs to find his own way in the world or can't settle on a path. When his father died, Everett may have looked at his job and asked himself: "Why am I doing this?" By then he was nearly forty, with three children to support, and America was in an economic depression; changing careers would not have been easy. A vocation that challenged and absorbed him would have helped fill the emptiness when his family was absent. Deane told me: "I think he must have asked himself: Is this all there is? There must be something more. He loved to study literature and would have been happier as a teacher."

During the last summer of his life, Everett wrote letters to his children in Norfolk. Desperately missing his wife and children, he seems a lost soul as he describes his life in Washington without them. He pretends to speak as the toys they left behind. A toy soldier says he has a right to know whether the family will return soon. If it will be long, he may die rather than eat his heart out. These letters are also messages to his estranged wife, who would be reading them to the children. Everett promises to reform, pours out his grief and loneliness, imagines dying, and expresses remorse and repentance. Empty time weighed heavily on his weekends: "Don't know what I'll do tomorrow. Sundays seem a week long to me and in a way I wish I could skip them." Reading these heartbreaking avowals of love for his family, I can better understand why he decided to take his life when he heard that they would not be coming back to Washington at the end of the summer.

At the start of his final summer, Everett returned to the Episcopal Church. In July he writes: "I find that my memory serves me quite well and I am able to follow the service and make all of the moves expected from the congregation. The catechism has all come back to me." He looks forward to attending church with his family. I wonder if he would have gone on living, surviving separation from his wife and children, if his faith had been stronger or different. Did he think his failings were unforgivable?

On July 8 he told Catharine Deane, his eleven-year-old daughter: "I want you to know that I never take anything to drink now, except milk, water, coffee, and lemon juice and I am resolved never to take any beer or other alcoholic drinks as long as I live. You can depend absolutely on this." He is certain that "everything is going to come out right," that the five of them "shall be a united family again," and that "Daddy will be a nicer more considerate man than he ever was." Interspersed with avowals of character reform are confessions of despair: "I am lonesome and homesick for the four of you. There doesn't seem to be any fun or real happiness in anything now without my family." Everett encourages Deane to work hard and play hard at summer camp, and "never worry about things you can't help." His last two letters, quite brief, reveal his disappointment that the family will not be returning to Washington. Everett advises his daughters how they can play a positive role: "The way you girls can help most of all is to accept things as they are and make a point of being cheerful and as happy as you can be."

In his final letter, two days before his suicide, Everett tells Deane that he will not be able to come to Norfolk for her twelfth birthday celebration because he has used up all of his sick leave. These are my grandfather's last words to his daughter: "I hope you have at least eighty-eight more birthdays after the one to come next month, that will make you one hundred years old won't it? I know you will enjoy Margaret's visit, she is such a fine girl for you to have for a friend. It is very important to have fine people for friends because they help you to form your own character. Best love to you and twelve kisses—your Dad." Throughout her life, Deane was keenly interested in how friends influence a person.

Everett searched for a physical cause of his deepening melancholy and gloom, hoping for a diagnosis that would lead to help. In July 1937, a month before he took his life, he had a comprehensive physical and psychological examination at the Mount Alto Veterans Hospital. After two weeks of tests and examinations, the doctors said that he was in good condition. In 1960, Deane obtained the examining psychiatrist's report. In the summer of 2002, I asked to see any documents related to her father that she was willing to share. Handing me the letters her father had written to her, she said: "You are one of the very few people I would trust with these documents." She also gave me the psychiatrist's report, placing it in the folder with the letters and saying: "I don't think I want you to read this yet." I immediately read the report, telling myself that she is ambivalent, but finally she wants me to know.

> Clinical Report of Neuropsychiatric Examination (made 7-28-37)
> This 40-year-old veteran was admitted to this hospital on July 16 for treatment of urinary urgency and frequency, cause undetermined. He is a graduate of Annapolis, resigned from the

Navy after the war and has been working at the United States Shipping Board. He has had no financial difficulties, has been drinking somewhat excessively for the past three years but none for two months ... He has been of a nervous temperament all of his life, has had a tendency to make decisions very rapidly without due consideration for the future and as the result has made some mistakes. For the past two or three years he has been increasingly irritable, easily upset, easily excited, and had a feeling as though he wanted to throw things. He has been under a great deal of tension, had difficulty in relaxing, has not slept very well, realizes that he has been apprehensive, somewhat suspicious even without foundation and at this time states that he is suffering from remorse ...

This patient is above the average in intelligence. He gives a very clear history of his present condition. His statements are well connected, coherent and no speech defect is noted. His attention is good. He is oriented in all fields. His memory is well retained for both recent and remote events. Emotionally he becomes tearful during the examination, rather critical of himself and blaming himself for his wife leaving him and for his indiscretions and he states that as he looks back now he seems to be an entirely different individual from what he used to be although he feels that if he can conduct himself properly that his wife will return to him. He shows no signs of delusion or hallucinations but he does appear anxious and somewhat depressed. During his conversation he became very much agitated and his eyes filled with tears. His reasoning appears clear and logical and his judgment very good at this time.

Discussion: Physical examination is essentially negative. The neurological examination is within normal limits. From his history and reactions during the examination there is evidence of a moderate neurosis of the mixed type.

Diagnosis: Psychoneurosis, mixed type, moderate.

Recommendations: Symptomatic treatment.

(Signed) G. T. Sheffield, M.D., Neuropsychiatrist

The psychiatrist's clinical language suggests the depths of inner pain in Everett: depression, impulsivity, anger, paranoia, guilt, and grief. My grandfather took his own life when he realized that he was not going to find any medical or psychological help. In the days before depression could be treated pharmaceutically, it was considered a moral failing, another reason to judge oneself negatively, and a further impetus to a downward spiral of melancholy gloom. Deane recalls several of Everett's letters from his period of naval service that referred to individuals who had "gone rhino," that is, suffered unmanageable depression. I think today my grandfather would be treated with a combination of antidepressant drugs and therapy. Would this have helped him? Did he feel moral guilt that is untreatable by medical means? The doctor's diagnosis refers enigmatically to his patient's "indiscretions." Whatever Everett considered these to be, he suffered from crippling remorse.

Among the papers Deane gave me in 2002 was a poem her father copied out and sent to Dolly. Titled "Alone with my Conscience," with no author given, it is handwritten on Everett's father's personal stationery. That my grandfather identified with this poem reveals his desperate state of mind, the weight of his guilt, and the centrality of conscience in his identity:

Alone with My Conscience

I sat alone with my conscience in a place where time had
   ceased,
And we talked of my former living
In the land where the years increased
And I felt I should have to answer
The question it put to me,
And to face the answers and questions
Through all eternity . . .

And I thought of a far-away warning
Of a sorrow that was to be mine,
In a land that then was the future,
But now is the present time.
And I thought of my former thinking
Of the judgment day to be;
But sitting alone with my conscience
Seemed judgment enough for me.

And I wondered if there was a future
To this land beyond the grave;
But no one gave me an answer
And no one came to save.
Then I felt that the future judgment
and the present would never go by
For it was but the thought of my past life
Going into eternity.

Then I woke from my timely dreaming

And the vision passed away
And I knew that the far-off morning
Was a warning of yesterday;
And I pray that I may not forget it
In that land before the grave
That I may not cry in the future
And no one come to save.

And so I have learned a lesson
Which I ought to have known before;
And which, though I learned it dreaming,
I hope to forget no more.
As I sit alone with my conscience
In the place where the years increase
And I try to remember the future
In the land where time will cease.

And I know of the future judgment
How dreadful soe'er it be,
That to sit alone with my conscience
Will be judgment enough for me.[1]

    These haunting verses capture the eerie sense of temporality of a guilty conscience as the speaker tries to "remember the future" and foresees contemplating past deeds interminably. There is a ghastly claustrophobic quality about this ordeal of guilt with no prospect of release from an eternity of remorse and no escape from an endless succession of lonely moments. Yet paradoxically, the speaker is grandiose, self-important, omnipotent in his power to judge. The speaker's solitary consciousness displaces any other perspective. The judgment of God, "how dreadful soe'er it be," would be merciful compared with the unrelenting judgment of the poet's own conscience. I wonder whether this line expresses my grandfather's lack of faith in the possibility of forgiveness: "No one came to save."

    I had a strange sense of self-recognition as I read "Alone with My Conscience." My grandfather's harsh conscience and search for self-knowledge in literature prefigured aspects of my own life. It suddenly struck me as significant that I had spent so many years doing academic work about themes that echo my grandfather's death. My graduate school dissertation and first book were about the ambiguity of virtue in tragedy, that is, the ways in which the protagonists' most admirable qualities contribute to their deaths.

---

    1. An internet search reveals that the author is Charles William Stubbs (1845–1912), an English poet and bishop of Truro.

Family Conscience

I had written three scholarly books about autobiography that examine the themes of conscience, deconversion (the loss of faith), and solitude. I wrote an essay about suicide in William Styron's *Sophie's Choice* at a time when I was depressed and briefly fantasized about taking my life.[2] It struck me that much of my intellectual work was, among other things, an indirect attempt to understand from several perspectives my grandfather's suicide. Everett's demanding conscience was a tragic flaw that was partly responsible for his self-destruction, for he could not go on living with harsh self-recrimination. His inability to forgive himself may have reflected a lack or loss of faith in a forgiving God. During that final summer, his solitude turned into depression, introspective self-assessment endlessly circling upon itself, and agonizing loneliness. My scholarly writings, whatever their merits and limitations as intellectual studies of ethical issues related to conscience, deconversion, and solitude, were also unconscious attempts to come to terms with family trauma. This seems clear to me now, but as a young scholar I was not aware of how the afterlife of Everett's suicide influenced my academic focus and motivation. It is as if the inner work that I had to do could only happen indirectly as I first explored ethical questions in literature, rather than through direct confrontation with family history and its effects on me.

* * *

IN JANUARY 2005, I asked Deane whether she had any documents that reveal her mother's character. She gave me several packets of letters to read. Warm and tender messages to Deane and to her grandchildren reinforce my dim memories of Dolly's generous, affectionate, and playful nature. She died when I was nine, and I only saw her a few times. My sole memory is of her coming to my room at bedtime to kiss me goodnight. How very different she was from my other grandmother, the stern, demanding, and judgmental Dorothy Dickinson Barbour. I have always felt that Dorothy played a large role in shaping my moral orientation, and that Dolly (or Gam, as we

---

2. These publications are John D. Barbour, *Tragedy as a Critique of Virtue: The Novel and Ethical Reflection*, Scholars Press Studies in the Humanities Series (Chico, CA: Scholars, 1984); John D. Barbour, *The Conscience of the Autobiographer: Ethical and Religious Dimensions of Autobiography* (copublished—London: Macmillan; and New York: St. Martin's, 1992); John D. Barbour, *Versions of Deconversion: Autobiography and the Loss of Faith*, Studies in Religion and Culture (Charlottesville: University Press of Virginia, 1994); John D. Barbour, *The Value of Solitude: The Ethics and Spirituality of Aloneness in Autobiography*, Studies in Religion and Culture (Charlottesville: University of Virginia Press, 2004); and John D. Barbour, "Suicide, Tragedy, and Theology in *Sophie's Choice* and Gustafson's Theocentric Ethics," *Literature and Theology* 8.1 (1994) 80–93.

called her) did not. But Gam's steady, loving presence in my mother's life must have influenced me, too.

Lena Maud Winn, called Dolly (1896–1961), grew up in Mathews County, Virginia, in the Tidewater area where several generations of her family had lived. Her father, Alexander, was a landscaper, and he and his sons owned nurseries near Norfolk. Several members of the Winn family served in the Confederate army. According to Deane, the family continued to feel deeply the tragedy of the Civil War. Dolly was the fourth of seven children who lived to adulthood. She was interested in literature, especially Shakespeare, and was the class poet at Richmond Women's College. Dolly was teaching school in Norfolk in 1924 when she met US Navy Lieutenant Everett Deane Kern.

An excerpt from Dolly's diary in July 1924 considers Everett's offer of marriage. A quotation haunted her all night long: "O, I am sure of my body's faith. But what if my soul broke faith with you?" She had doubts about marrying a man whom she had only known for three months. Then the diary entry goes on confidently: "Deane [Everett] came this afternoon, and it seemed quite easy then to say 'yes' to him. He has been so precious and sweet ever since . . . The two of us loving each other and dreaming dreams together. I wonder if we'll do the things we say. Stay in the Navy a year and then start out in business. Go to church every Sunday. Always look nice in my clothes. Laugh a lot. [Everett] says he will laugh a great deal more with me. He smiles often but laughs seldom." Dolly quoted this phrase several times: "Peace shall thatch the roof and love shall latch the door." Deane asserted that her mother loved Everett but did not know him very well before they were married and was surprised and disappointed when he became despondent and began drinking.

As I pore over the papers that Deane gave me, I am struck by the roles played by literary quotations in Dolly's family—as forms of moral instruction and inspiration, as coded allusions, and signs of the thoughts and feelings of the person doing the quoting. I have many poems and passages of literature that Dolly gave her daughter. When Deane graduated from Duke in 1947, her mother sent her "A Christmas Wish" by Delia Thompson Lutes. The poet wishes she could hope for nothing but joy in the lives of those she loves, but she cannot. Yet "disappointment often hides a richer gift / Than we had prayed for." The poem affirms that "deprivation and withheld desires all serve / Their purpose, leaving one / Who is not weak, but resolute to fight, stronger for the fray." Dolly hoped that Deane would have the perseverance, courage, and faith to find meaning in experiences of suffering.

When she was in Washington, DC, for her mother's funeral, Deane copied a set of quotations she found in Dolly's writing desk. A poem called

"Send Flowers, Dear Friends" by Galbraith (no first name) is a eulogy for a woman with many faults who:

> ... Loved joy and pain and existence whole;
> Loved dreams and women and men ...
> Loved life so much she'd give all but her soul
> To live it over again!

For Dolly, soul is closely related to conscience, integrity, and honor. Several other quotations describe or praise selfless giving to others. To many people, this kind of writing seems sentimental, abstract, or didactic. But Dolly, Deane, and I cherished literature about the meaning of particular virtues, and this became the focus of my work in graduate school.

Dolly in later years.

Often when Deane gave me a book, she inscribed a quotation on the first page. Or on the card accompanying a gift would be a poem or short quotation that expressed her hope for how the gift would be used or make a difference. In conversations, Deane often recalled some significant literary fragment, such as King Lear's "Sharper than a serpent's tooth it is / to have a thankless child." Or "O what a tangled web we weave / when first we practice to deceive" (from Sir Walter Scott's *Marmion*). These quotations were sometimes the most memorable part of a conversation, putting into a nutshell its essential point. This is a characteristic of Dolly's and Deane's moral orientation: ethical values are transmitted not in the form of rules, commandments, or principles, but in literary examples, lines of poetry, and pithy descriptions of virtues or moral ideals. Sometimes one must use imagination and intuition to discern the relevance of a quotation, and sometimes it is obvious. This way of thinking about moral questions is very different than my father's family's logical approach, reliance on principles, and weighing of pros and cons. I share Dolly's and Deane's love of literature, their belief that it presents a moral vision or ideal, their appreciation of choice quotations, and their trust in the imagination.

Deane discerned a strange fissure between Dolly's keen sensitivity to human suffering as depicted in literature and her seeming inability to face it in her own family. In her notes for a journaling workshop in 1984, Deane described how her mother loved poetry that was introspective, melancholy, and sometimes desperately sad. Yet with her family Dolly avoided such feelings and was determined to be cheerful:

> She shied away from anyone who expressed or embodied that sadness and conflict in real life. It scared her. She would try to "cheer" the person up. True of Daddy. True of me. It came too close. Did she feel it in herself, too? Was she combatting sorrow in herself? She would even make fun of something "too serious." Especially about death, whereas in her own earlier writing she often wrote about death, sometimes the sad part, sometimes rays of hope. Did she feel that instead of being able to share insights, or learning from someone she loved who spoke of these things, she would be tempting them down a dangerous street? What would be at the end of the street? Suicide had been there for EDK. Suicide might be there for me. But death thoughts had seemed beautiful to her in Keats and other poets. Now they seemed, if not self-indulgent, precariously near a kind of insanity.

In this questioning way, Deane explored a limitation of her mother with painful consequences when Deane felt that her own sadness, grief, and depression were denied.

I see in this reflection, and in Deane's observations of a few other people she knew well, a profound question about the effect of literature. Does imagination and appreciation of other lives in literature carry over into a reader's life? I have wanted to believe that in teaching novels by Dostoevsky, George Eliot, or Toni Morrison I am nurturing my students' moral imagination and capacity for wise discernment. Yet reading does not necessarily affect a reader's own moral life. In graduate school, my humanistic ideals were chastened when I read the Preface of George Steiner's *Language and Silence*, which calls into radical doubt the humanistic faith that the classics of Western civilization necessarily have a positive ethical effect. Many of the masterminds and foot soldiers of Auschwitz went home to listen to Beethoven and read Goethe and Rilke. The Holocaust arose from within a center of European civilization and was engineered or passively accepted by men who appreciated the arts, books, and the life of the mind. The failure to translate the insights of a humanistic education into one's society is hardly an exclusively German one: "Ten years after the Gestapo quit Paris, the countrymen of Voltaire were torturing Algerians and each other in some of the same police cellars."[3] Steiner addressed a crisis of confidence about Western culture; Deane focused on individuals she knew. I, too, want to believe in the morally transformative value of literature, yet sometimes it is hard not to be skeptical about this classic humanistic ideal.

* * *

TWO PASSAGES IN DOLLY's letters comfort Deane at a difficult moment and hint at her own suffering after Everett's death. In July 1946, her fiancé, Ian, was hospitalized with acute meningitis and mumps. Dolly wrote about how a frightening moment can look so different in retrospect, and yet stay with one: "I hope that by the time this reaches you that Ian will be feeling fine and you will be smiling together over fear that is so very large and dark when someone we love so much more than ourselves is in danger. And later, when the sun is shining again, you will relegate the memory to some surreal corner of your mind, never quite forgetting. And this is a part of *loving*, darling. 'As witnesseth the living I!'" Dolly felt that way about Everett's death: it was consigned to the distant past like a bad dream, yet sometimes emerged as a continuing grief.

In January 1953, Ian's brother Freeland died suddenly of a brain tumor at the age of twenty-six. Deane was very close to Freeland. Dolly wrote to console her, affirming that in Freeland's single year of marriage, he and his wife "had one whole beautiful year of happiness together. More than many persons *ever* know in a long lifetime." Dolly said that Deane's having to take care of her two-year-old son was a blessing and alluded to her own care for her son, Charles, after Everett's death: "It was fine that you had Johnny to take you through those sad dark days. I'll never forget how a gay laughing

---

3. George Steiner, *Language and Silence: Essays on Language, Literature, and the Inhuman* (New York: Atheneum, 1967), ix.

little three-year-old kept me believing that God was good and the world a beautiful one with sunshine, music, and children in it." Everett's suicide left a deep wound that Dolly rarely spoke of, Deane said, and "only knowing what I was going through evoked that admission." I see Dolly as undaunted by grief or guilt: resilient, cheerful, and affectionate. I think suffering made her compassionate. Although a shadow fell on her, she moved on, into and out of the light, again and again. That's what I want to believe about my grandmother, but I don't really know.

* * *

IN OCTOBER 2005, I went with Deane, Ian, and my sister Blair to a family reunion in Virginia. This was a gathering of the Hudgins and Winn families from whom Dolly was descended. We met in Mathews County, on the tip of one of the Tidewater peninsulas on the Chesapeake Bay, about an hour north of Norfolk.

I learned a lot about Deane's ancestors on her mother's side. My forebears participated inf many varieties of Protestantism. Dolly was baptized in the Christian Church, which was founded by Campbellite "restorers" of the primitive apostolic church and later became the Disciples of Christ. When she married Everett, she became an Episcopalian. At the reunion were an architect and a taxi-driving blues guitarist, a real estate agent, several teachers and professors, businessmen, and a family that researches Colonial music and plays it at Williamsburg. One side of the family owns orchards, nurseries, and a landscaping business in Norfolk. Like most family trees, its branches include just about every human virtue and failing. Lewis Hudgins, the great-great-grandfather who was our common ancestor, was an honored citizen. James Winn, his counterpart on another limb of the family tree, was murdered in 1855 in a fight after a poker game. Do these miscellaneous forebears have in common any shared moral orientation, a family conscience? When I asked Deane this question, she responded: "I don't think there is a single family conscience. I prefer to think of different translations of family values."

Lewis Hudgins (1797–1866), Dolly's grandfather, was an enterprising merchant, shipbuilder, farmer, and leading citizen of Mathews County. He built 15 percent of the vessels constructed in Mathews County between 1825 and 1855 and helped make it a center of shipbuilding and prosperity. During the Civil War he was a blockade-runner, ferrying provisions past Northern forces into the backwaters and creeks of the Chesapeake Bay and then transferring these goods to wagons going to Richmond to supply the Confederate government. Hudgins was "a thorn in the side of the Union," according to a local historian who spoke to us, but the Yankees were unable to prove that he was the mastermind who organized smuggling operations. Another story attributed the survival of his home to a Masonic symbol on his fireplace mantel. The Union Commander sent to burn Hudgins' house saw the emblem and would not destroy a fellow Mason's home. The Yankees burned Hudgins's boats, freed his slaves, and destroyed his crops, including his seed corn, so that he could not replant in 1864. Lewis Hudgins, along with his second wife and his children, survived the Civil War, but financially he was ruined. He died the next year at the age of sixty-nine, exhausted by the struggles and losses of the war.

With a group of his descendants, I visited the original Hudgins home at Fitchetts Wharf, his main landing and trading station. Three Confederate reenactors dressed in authentic Civil War uniforms came to the porch and fired a twenty-one-gun salute in honor of Hudgins. I engaged one of them in conversation about the life of Civil War soldiers, discussing bayonets, wounds, medical conditions, and the range of rifles at that time. He displayed fierce pride in the South's fighting ability. He brought up the issue of race, anticipating what a Northern spectator might be thinking about. He asserted that large numbers of African Americans fought in Southern regiments. Unlike the Union troops, Black soldiers in the Confederate army were integrated into the same units as Whites. It is therefore impossible to know exactly how many of them there were. He argued vociferously that thousands of African Americans fought willingly for the South. When contemporary African Americans question his assertions, he said, he pulls out articles written by Black scholars that prove his claims. This Confederate reenactor was primed to argue with critics of the South. Among the thousands of people who participate in staged performances of Civil War battles, as well as countless amateur and professional historians, there must be many like him who are acting out inner dramas of defensiveness and pride about their ancestors. A sense of loyalty to kin may be as important as latent racism in explaining resistance to the removal of Confederate monuments and other efforts to rewrite the history of the Civil War.

Growing up in Minnesota, I viewed the Confederate flag as a symbol of racism nearly as blatant and offensive as a white-sheeted Klansman or a burning cross. I saw it only on pickup trucks and large semitrailers driven by people I called rednecks. I always thought that the Civil War was first and foremost about whether slavery would survive in the United States. On this October weekend, fifteen years before Black Lives Matter, I listened to the Southern version of "the War Between the States." Deane had explained this to me as a boy, when I was interested in Civil War history, especially Confederate generals such as Robert E. Lee and Stonewall Jackson. Now I heard again that Southerners were committed first to their homeland rather than to the Confederacy or the institution of slavery. Hudgins loved Virginia above all, like Robert E. Lee, who turned down Lincoln's offer to lead the Union troops. I listened to descriptions of Southern bravery, generosity, and honor. Our ancestors were fighting for "states' rights," I was told, not the institution of slavery.

Will (as I'll call him), the second cousin who organized the reenactors' gun salute, asserted, "There is nothing to be ashamed of about the South, and a lot to be proud of. Lewis Hudgins was a brave and intelligent man who risked everything for what he believed in. He was the brains the Yankees suspected behind the blockade runners, but they never caught him." Will was a thoughtful, warm, and interesting person who I liked immediately. He is an archeologist who lives in the Tidewater region and travels widely to work on digs of many kinds. I sensed common values as well as kinship with Will, but I didn't see our great-great-grandfather the same way he did. I would have said that Hudgins risked his life to preserve a slaveholding society; Will asserted that Hudgins was defending his homeland against invaders.

Another fellow, originally from Michigan, married one of my Virginia cousins. I told him that I was interested in the Southern interpretation of the Civil War. "It's all crap," said this kinsman, who I'll call Fritz. "It's the same old story. The South shall rise again. In reality, the Civil War was all about money. They were fighting to defend a way of life based on slavery. That's all there is to it. The rest is rationalization."

Sometimes people from the North act as if they inherit a kind of moral superiority. They seem smug about living in the part of the country that most people would now say had the higher moral principle on its side. Fritz was too certain about his own values for my taste. He was also strikingly blind to a contemporary form of prejudice. Somehow 9/11 came up during our exchange, and it set him off: "I can't believe all this crap about respecting the rights of Arab prisoners. Did they respect *our* rights on 9/11?" I exited the discussion, not wanting to argue about this question at a family reunion. "You are losing your audience," someone joked to Fritz. "Goddamn Democrats," he muttered.

Fritz's cynical view of the South discounts high ideals and noble sentiments as moral posturing. This view is as simplistic as accepting all the high-minded rhetoric at face value. My Virginian cousins have a deep love of homeland, family, and history. At the reunion, they did the same thing that I do in this memoir: interpret how moral commitments and values motivated our ancestors' ambiguous actions. This Southern version of history—the War Between the States— appreciates the moral perspective that shaped our family. Yet the South's material interests were undeniable too, slavery was unspeakably cruel, and the way of life based on it was founded on hideous injustice. I struggled to recognize all this at once.

When I shared my musings with Deane, she responded: "The North and the South saw each other at their worst. The North saw the evils of the slave system. The South lost so much during the war, and then experienced the bitterness of corrupt carpetbaggers during Reconstruction. It is still an issue. When I saw those Confederate reenactors, I looked at their faces. I wondered if their ancestors had been members of the Ku Klux Klan."

Her Southern background deeply shaped my grandmother. By all accounts, Dolly had a deep love for Virginia and a gracious manner that reflected her generous nature and her culture's values. She could criticize certain things in the South. A cousin asserted that Dolly was "not really a Southerner" because she "married a Yankee," moved to Washington, DC, after her marriage in 1924, and was highly aware of the national struggle for Black civil rights well before the 1960s.

"But she was born and grew up in the South," I responded, "and it formed her character."

"That is true," said my cousin, "but Dolly would never use mean or derogatory language about Black people, and she was critical of siblings who took advantage of them, for example in financial dealings."

Dolly was traditional in her view of racial issues and, by today's standards, prejudiced. In a 1947 letter that my father wrote to his parents after visiting Deane's mother and stepfather in Florida, he said that although Dolly was kind and gracious, he would not invite her to dinner with a Black couple. Deane wrote in a journal that her mother "was paternalistic and thought colored people are like children who begged to stay with their good masters."

I want my grandmother to have been a good person. She was a Southerner, or more precisely a Virginian from the Tidewater region, and she was much else, too: a Christian, a poet, a daughter, wife, and mother. I imagine that Dolly would have said that she didn't like labels and tried to treat all people with respect and courtesy. I know her ideas about race were formed by her parents, church, education, and reading. I would like to think that she had encounters with African Americans that made her more aware of their humanity and dignity than most other White people of her time and context would have been. But I have no evidence, only scraps of information, hunches, and wishful thinking. Just like the Confederate reenactors, my desire to honor my ancestors is entangled with wanting to affirm their goodness. Fritz would surely say that I, too, am distorting the past, looking for mythical ancestors to believe in and idealize. If I want to find forebears who can serve as moral guides, can I ever really understand them?

In Virginia I heard from cousins about distant family members who had married people of other races. In an early draft of this memoir describing my visit to Mathews County, I wrote that some members of my family were slave owners and more recent generations have married an African American, a Hispanic American, and, in the 1920s, a Native Hawaiian. I presented my family as a microcosm of the racial changes in the United States. When I showed this version to Deane, she registered "a very large quibble" and asserted that my description was not accurate. In each case, she held, it was not a member of the family who married someone of another race. For instance, a man who married one of her cousins later divorced her and remarried an African American. In the case of the Native Hawaiian, a cousin's daughter had a child out of wedlock with this man, after which they lost touch with the family.

"But aren't they family, too? They were people who members of your family married or had children with. They were as much part of your family as my wife or Blair's husband, or for that matter Ian. Who is family, anyway?"

But Deane insisted that I had presented a misleading account of family history. "Too bad," I said, "I wish my family was more multicultural and interracial than it is." I was not hunting for scandal, but rather for evidence that my ancestors were open-minded by my standards. I wanted a certain kind of past.

Deane was bothered by my account of Fritz, the man from Michigan who said the Southern version of the War Between the States was "crap." She said that Fritz was not really part of the family. Again I challenged her: why isn't he as much a part of the family as Ian or anyone else who married into it? This time Deane conceded the point but asserted that Fritz was "a very odd person." She asserted that Dolly would have said, "I think he's a little bit common."

This term of moral vocabulary interests me. Does "common" indicate a class bias in that part of my family? Meg, my former wife, thought so, and asked if she, too, was common, an ordinary person, rather than part of an elite group based on bloodlines or aristocratic status. "Common" does not refer to economic status or social class, I argued, but to a standard of courtesy and manners that in Dolly's eyes reflects a moral sensibility. To say "crap" or to speak slightingly of others shows coarseness and insensitivity.

One set of dictionary meanings for "common" includes "falling below ordinary standards"; "second-rate"; "lacking refinement"; and "coarse." Historically, the standards that common people did not observe reflected class privileges and ideas of refinement. The people who judged individuals to be

Family Conscience

common hopelessly confused good manners and good morals. The term "common" in Dolly's moral vocabulary, like "honor," now sounds archaic and morally questionable in light of egalitarian ideals. But I think I know what Dolly meant. And I wonder: am I common myself when I describe Fritz or my grandfather? Would Dolly recognize me as a member of her family?

At the Virginia gathering, I was surprised to feel a bond with Southern relatives who honor their slaveholding ancestors, and to feel alienated from a Northern man who was judgmental about Southerners. The roles of race and class in my family's moral orientation continue to puzzle and intrigue me.

* * *

My grandfather's suicide affected his descendants in ways that are sometimes easy to see and in other ways hard to understand. In trying to interpret family history, I find gaps in memory, remembered stories that turn out to be false, and a confusing and fascinating mix of indisputable fact, speculation, and fictionalized reconstruction. My mother cannot answer the question: "Is there a bottle there or not?" I puzzle over where certain memories come from and what they mean. For instance, I remember my brother, David, telling me that he went to the C&O Canal in Washington, DC, the scene of Everett's suicide. There he cursed the memory of his grandfather, saying: "You destroyed my mother's life and my own." When I told Deane this story, she surprised me by responding, "Good for David." But when I asked David, he said it didn't happen. He went to my grandfather's grave in Arlington Cemetery but did not curse him. Where did this vignette about David at the canal come from? I surmise that it reflects my anger and harsh judgment of my grandfather, protectiveness of my mother, and some self-pity. The vivid details of the scene surprise me: David in tears, shaking his fist, speaking words he never said that express my own feelings. I could not articulate or even admit these powerful feelings but needed to project them onto my brother, imagining and vicariously experiencing his grief and rage.

When I look at Everett's life only as that of a person who will one day commit suicide, this surely distorts my perspective. The ending of his life dominates everything else; I scrutinize each incident or anecdote for details that will explain why he killed himself. I see every generous action as wasted goodness and every flaw as an indication of hidden fractures that will eventually crack apart his character. In notes for a church group presentation, my mother wrote that she did not tell me about her father's suicide until I was seventeen because she did "not want him [John] to think that my father did not love us, or that this event was the main thing about a grandfather whom he would have loved." Yet Everett's suicide has seemed to me the main way that his life influenced mine.

My mother described other facets of her father's character: his kindness and generosity, his sense of humor, and his love of literature. In a caption in a family photograph album, she mentioned these qualities: "Everett Deane Kern, 1896–1937, was a fifth generation Washingtonian. All his life he had great interest in national and international events. He read widely and was a wonderful conversationalist." Deane recorded in a letter to her children a precious memory: "Each Christmas Eve, at 11:00 p. m., he woke the family to come downstairs, drink cocoa, and listen to a superb radio reenactment of Dickens' *Christmas Carol* with Lionel Barrymore as Scrooge. Christmas Past, Christmas Present, and Christmas Future seemed very vivid. The children remembered this yearly ritual as one of the most deeply felt and happy events of their childhoods." I love this image of Everett's gathering the family to hear a story in which themes of conscience and repentance are so powerful, and in which Scrooge's stingy character is transformed. This is a grandfather with whom I can identify.

Everett influenced Deane's character in some good ways, as will be seen. Yet for me, the knowledge of how he died casts a shadow backwards on his entire life. The ripples caused by his descent into the water go in all directions, receding back to his earlier life and still reaching me on this far shore.

Chapter 2

"I think I shall call you Honor"

Deane thought a lot about how her parents shaped her conscience in constructive and in questionable ways. Especially significant were several incidents that taught her the meaning of honor and shame.

In a creative writing class in 1984, Deane wrote several short stories that focused on a significant place, object, or person. She gave her children copies of six of these stories. Three of them deal with her mother and three with her father. All the stories explore guilt, shame, and honor. One story describes an unforgettable, searing moment:

> My father did not live beyond my childhood. I do not remember his ever being angry with me until a day soon after my seventh birthday. It is Autumn, 1933, and he, my mother, little sister, and I are driving on a country road in Virginia. We are singing, and everything about us is green, scarlet, and gold. We lose the way, but ahead we can see a hill with a shack. I still remember as though in slow motion how we pull up beside a woman who has come down to look in a mailbox. When she is asked the way, she points slowly, with her arm outstretched. We start on. In the back seat I sit thinking a few moments about her face, which is broken-out, full of fiery red pimples with pus. I say something about it and laugh.
>
> Suddenly my father stops the car. Abruptly he turns, and his eyes look at me with an entirely new expression. Out of the complete stillness he says: "I want you never . . . ever again in your life . . . to judge a person by the way the person looks." I cannot move. I am fiery red. He is an exceptionally handsome man. I know he did not learn this from having been otherwise.

"I think I shall call you Honor"

The car starts down the road again. A long time later a cool breeze begins to come through the window.

Deane was a redhead. Her sensation of being fiery red as blood floods her face echoes the image of the pimples of the country woman at whom she laughed, and her feeling of internal ugliness mirrors the woman's disfigured visage. The seven-year-old girl would recover from her mortification: "A long time later a cool breeze begins to come through the window." As a mature woman, she would learn to cope with painful feelings growing out of her family's history. Yet the effects of experiences of shame were long-lasting and formative. In this experience of moral self-accusation, Deane internalized certain of her father's values. She admired his compassion and fairness and felt excruciating embarrassment for having failed to live up to his expectations. One person in my family sees Everett's confrontational challenge to his daughter as shaming her in a destructive, humiliating way. I disagree with this view. In any case, this moment seared into Deane's consciousness a moral conviction about not judging others by their appearance.

Another story describes how all through her childhood Deane admired her father's Annapolis class ring. The ring evokes memories of Everett working around their home and being a companionable, loving father. The light glints off it as he lifts a shovel to plant a pear tree, fills his favorite pipe with tobacco, makes eggnog, or works at his desk. "The ring was on his hand the morning I gave him the first carrot from my first garden, where it had been dug up several times to make sure it was growing. He put his hand on my shoulder, saying judicially: 'It's the very best carrot I ever ate.'" Deane's story ends this way:

> His letters were lively, observant, caring. He wrote eleven of them—one each week—the last summer of his life, when my mother had taken the three of us away from the city. One evening in the twelfth week my father put the Annapolis ring on his chest of drawers, together with a paper on which he wrote the words "No one is to blame for this but myself." Then he walked through Washington streets to the cool and quiet canal and ended his life.

The ring, symbol of a naval officer's honor, survived a dishonorable death. By leaving it on his bureau, Everett tried to save the best part of himself as he destroyed the rest. Deane affirmed that aspect of her father and kept it alive in memory.

Deane described how Everett's suicide altered her friendship with Margaret, the girl whose character Everett praised in his final letter to his daughter. Margaret had artistic interests and abilities, cared about beauty, and made pronouncements about what was "distinguished." Neither Deane nor Margaret spoke to each other of Everett's death:

> My childhood seemed to end in one day when my father unexpectedly took his life. My mother took the three of us away to live near her family, for one endlessly long, homesick year. In her letters, Margaret never once referred to what had happened, and I was too shy ever to mention it to her. Just once I wrote her a letter about it, knowing that she had admired my tall, kind father. Hot tears streamed down my cheeks as I tore it up in as many pieces as I could.

Deane saw Margaret on the far side of a wide playground on her first day back home in Washington and was unable to cross over to her. "I felt as though there were new and ugly things in my life. I did not feel at all distinguished." She fabricated excuses when Margaret invited her to play and walked home in "a morass of self-hatred." Forty-five years after this experience, Deane wrote: "I will never know whether she rejected me, or whether I rejected myself." Clearly, Deane did reject herself.

Like the story of her father's ring, an anecdote about Deane's mother explores the reverse side of shame: honor.

> Whenever I am in Washington and pass the corner where a little shop used to be, I remember a small cabinet with money in one of its drawers. It stood by our front door, to be handy for the fruit huckster and the bread-man.
>
> My best friend was given pennies to spend on candy during our school lunch-hour, but I never was. I yearned for the moment of choice before the case of tootsie-rolls, candies shaped like little watermelons, and "all-day suckers."
>
> I began taking coins from the little cabinet and going with my friend to spend them. I dreaded my mother's finding out what I was doing. I was amazed that several weeks went by without her noticing.
>
> One day she said quite casually, "I have always just loved the name 'Honor.' I think I will call you 'Honor.'"

Is Dolly's remark shaming? It is gentler than Everett's direct confrontation, leaving it to Deane to infer how her actions were honorable or not. Several people with whom I shared this story see Dolly's obliqueness as manipulative, making her daughter feel guilty and isolated. Deane was surprised that her mother did not notice the theft, as if she expected and wanted to be caught and confronted. In contrast to this view, I see Dolly's approach as gently respectful of Deane's increasing moral capacity. Instead of criticizing a moral fault, she set forth an ideal and linked it to Deane's identity. She left it to her daughter to judge herself, or not. Should Dolly have simply told her daughter that she had noticed that some coins were missing from the cabinet, and asked whether Deane took them? Perhaps not, with this particular child, if what was at stake was her daughter learning the meaning of honor.

Deane, about the time of her father's death, 1937.

We didn't talk about honor in my Minnesota hometown. This concept, with its deep roots in Virginia and the Southern culture that shaped Deane, is closely linked to conscience. When I asked what honor meant to her, Deane responded in a characteristic way, using a literary work as an analogy. She described two scenes in Harper Lee's novel *To Kill a Mockingbird*. One is when the Black maid Calpurnia reprimands Scout for rudeness about a dinner guest's manners: "Don't matter who they are, anybody sets foot in this house's yu' comp'ny, and don't you let me catch you remarkin' on their ways like you was so high and mighty! Yu' folks might be better'n the Cunninghams but it don't count for nothin' the way you're disgracin' 'em—if you can't act fit to eat at the table you can just set here and eat in the kitchen!" The other scene that Deane mentioned takes place at the end of the trial, when Scout's father, Atticus Finch, courageously fights for a falsely accused Black man, knowing that he will lose the case. As Atticus makes his lonely walk down the courthouse aisle, the Black townspeople stand up to show their regard and admiration for him. A minister tells Scout: "Miss Jean Louise, stand up. Your father's passin."[1] Both of these scenes depict a child learning to honor another person, a guest and a parent. To do this, Scout must act in a way that shows that she is herself a person of honor who has internalized certain standards. In these scenes, she still needs a little help. There is a painful side of these experiences, as what she learns is seared into memory.

The desire to be honorable in the eyes of others links how I view my own actions, how I see other people, and how others see me. Honor ties me into a web of moral expectation and performance, a community based on certain standards of character; it connects me to those I respect and love and requires that my outward appearance cohere with my inner character. When there is a discrepancy between my self-knowledge and a loved one's affirmation of me as honorable, I feel ashamed. If I don't, I'm shameless.

Deane's story about stealing as a violation of honor shows the complexity of family life as parents try to influence the formation of their child's conscience. Dolly wanted her daughter to develop her own values and not simply conform to imposed rules; she tried to respect Deane's freedom and developing moral autonomy. I think she was trying, not to make Deane feel guilty, but rather to nurture her desire to be an honorable person, a girl with a conscience and a commitment to act on her convictions. How does a parent respect a child's growing moral independence without being ambiguous, manipulative, or confusing to the child? Deane's stories explore the fine line between appropriate moral shame and destructive forms of shame that turn into psychological wounds. Through her writing, Deane was trying to sort out which values she truly chose, and which she'd acquired through family dynamics that were subtly coercive, if well intended. Deane's stories reveal a self-critical conscience remembering and evaluating its own origins.

Two of Deane's stories depict a painful moment when she recognizes that she has hurt her mother. When she tries to comfort her mother soon after Everett's death, she inadvertently causes more pain:

> My father dies suddenly and tragically when I am eleven. My childhood ends in one day.
>
> My parents' wedding anniversary is three weeks later. I have $3.20 saved up out of ten-cent allowances. One day after school I walk through a gold September haze to a florist. Three dollars of the money is counted out and placed on the counter.

---

1. Harper Lee, *To Kill a Mockingbird* (New York: Harper & Row, 1960), 27, 241.

"I think I shall call you Honor"

> On a small white card I write the words "With love always," and I sign my father's name.
>
> Saturday is the anniversary. Throughout the day I wait hopefully. At 5:30 there is finally the sound of the doorknocker. I do not remember the flowers being handed in the door. I do not remember seeing my mother unwrap the paper. But I will not—cannot—forget that she sits in a chair looking somehow smaller. The roses are in her lap and she is saying thank you. But I know that I have hurt her, not comforted her.

In trying to help, sometimes we hurt. It takes discernment to recognize this and not to flatter oneself that good intentions make every action good. Yet to be highly attuned to the ways in which even one's best intentions might hurt others can have a paralyzing effect on spontaneous expressions of love or generosity. To be extremely sensitive to other people's hurt feelings has complicated effects both on the person with this moral sensibility and on family members and loved ones. I think that a pattern of anxious watching for possible harm one may cause others is deeply rooted in my family's psychic life. I have often felt that I am "walking on eggshells," a phrase my mother used.

Deane's final story concerns a highly symbolic object, a walnut desk that she would later inherit.

> I love to watch my mother as she sits at her small walnut desk, she being rather small herself. The lines of the desk are classically simple, and the polished old wood gleams. Besides the drawers that can be seen, there is a secret drawer. On glassed-in shelves above the writing-area there are slender volumes of Shakespeare's plays and small books of classical and modern poetry. My mother knows large parts of them by heart.
>
> One of the little cubbyholes of the desk holds the personal letters she has received that month—soon to be answered with her special tenderness and humor. She is also a letter-saver. After she dies, her three children will find that every letter we have ever sent her has been kept.
>
> It is dusk and she asks me in her sweet Virginian voice: "Darlin', of all the things in this house, what means the most to you?" Her tone is surprisingly serious. I say: "I think . . . Your desk . . ." She asks my younger sister, who says softly, "You. You mean the most." I find myself hugging them both, and we all laugh shakily.
>
> When my mother dies in a car accident years later and her Will is read, I find that she has specified that her little walnut desk is to be mine. Sometimes when I look at it I remember her

Family Conscience

question. I believe that she loved both answers. In a way, I still wish I had been the one who answered "You."

Deane cherished that desk, which stood in the living room of her home until 2004, when she moved to an apartment and gave it to my sister Heather. The desk always seemed to me the most imposing and important piece of furniture in our house. For both Deane and me, it symbolizes our mothers and our shared appreciation of literature and personal correspondence. Deane, Dolly, and I are letter-savers, lovers of literature, and persons who sometimes feel great happiness at a desk.

Although she did not turn fiery red, this, too, was a painful but important moment, as the young girl grasped the significant difference between even the most valuable object and a person. Deane understood this moral principle already, or she would not have felt a pang of self-recrimination. Although she gave a straightforward and honest response to her mother's question, she felt as if she had failed to express her love. The situation is complicated by sibling rivalry, as her sister, Winn, gave an answer that clearly affirmed her love. Dolly knew that both her daughters loved her, and she did not judge Deane harshly for the response that directly answered her question. But for Deane, this incident precipitated the sting of conscience, a sudden internal stab triggered by an inadvertent action and only partially relieved by a hug and shaky laughter.

* * *

IN MARCH 2003, DEANE told me a story that she had not told anyone before. After her father died, she poured out her grief to the Episcopal minister who had spoken at her confirmation (April 25, 1937). She wrote about a dozen letters to him and he responded with concern and compassion. Deane confided to the minister that she planned to commit suicide on Christmas Day. She asked him to promise that he would not tell anyone about her secret plan. On Christmas Eve, at 11:00 p.m., the minister came to their home and told Dolly.

Deane's mother was devastated; she had not recognized the depth of Deane's despair. Dolly had not revealed to most people that her husband's drowning was a suicide. The family carefully avoided the facts about how he died. (It must have been a well-known secret since newspapers reported Everett's two suicide notes.) Deane said that by telling the minister, she had "trespassed against family folkways" and broken an unspoken rule. She felt terribly guilty for having hurt her mother. Many years later, in therapy in 1981, she realized that this transgression saved her life. "The worst thing I had ever done in my life" allowed the minister to intervene and prevent her suicide. Revealing the secret also helped her psychologically: "Telling saved my sanity because I got it out." Telling secrets makes public unseemly pain, shame, and brokenness. It feels dishonorable, as if henceforth other people will look down on one. Yet a basic survival instinct moves a person carrying a burden alone to reach out to others for help. Deane discovered that confession is morally ambiguous, a necessary transgression. What violated the family's moral code saved her life.

The next Christmas, Dolly gave her daughter a recording of Schubert's *Unfinished Symphony*. This was the first music that moved Deane to tears when, at eight years old, she heard it at a concert. Later, she saw the *Unfinished Symphony* as a metaphor for her father's life, whose goodness was not invalidated by its incompleteness. That Christmas sixteen months after Everett's suicide was a turning point, the first in a long series of small steps towards recovery from grief. Deane told me: "I began to think that the love in the family all those years would reappear."

After her father's death, my mother chose to be called by her middle name, Deane, the family name of her father's mother, instead of Catharine. When I asked her if this was because of a desire to identify with him, she responded: "I think that unconsciously, ever since I was born, I could remember the loving tone of voice in which my mother said the name 'Deane' when she called me 'Catharine Deane.' Also I felt as though part of my life had been left behind. I needed to be made anew. And the name helped with that. I identified with the Northern part of the family. It was one step in distancing myself from the Norfolk year, that Southern year. It was wonderful to grow up in Washington. And then that was snatched away. We felt alienated and lost in Norfolk, like outsiders. My mother's relatives had adored my father for years, but now they seldom mentioned him. They were inwardly angry that his family was left that way."

Deane wanted "to be made anew," as if what happened to Catharine happened to someone else.

* * *

THE MOMENT WHEN DEANE chose to reveal her father's suicide to each of her children is significant. I do not remember what I felt about that disclosure on the night before I left for college; I only recall sitting in the living room with a feeling of suspense and anticipation. The lamps in the living room cast pools of light. My mother disliked overhead lights. (That setting is a metaphor for this memoir: small patches of clarity amid much that remains obscure.) "It was so hard to tell you, John," Deane said in 2003.

"How did I react?"

Family Conscience

"You were amazed, moved, sad."

She told my oldest sister and brother as they were on their way to the airport to return to a boarding school in New England when they were fifteen and sixteen. Blair and David were deeply conflicted about leaving home. Deane saw a connection between urging her children to take full advantage of their opportunities and her father's "throwing his life away." Everett's early death informed one of the chief messages Deane transmitted to her children: the importance of using one's time wisely. She often described activities of which she disapproved as "not worthwhile" or "not a good use of your time." Her father had said: "We live only once."

As we discussed our family's sense of time, Deane quoted lines from Robert Browning's verse play *Pippa Passes*. These words are spoken by a young girl who lost her parents and works in a silk mill in Asolo, near Venice, on her only holiday of the year:

> Oh, Day, if I squander a wavelet of thee,
> A mite of my twelve hours' treasure,
> The least of thy gazes or glances,
> (Be they grants thou art bound to or gifts above measure)
> One of thy choices or one of thy chances,
> (Be they tasks God imposed thee or freaks at thy pleasure)
> —My Day, if I squander such labour or leisure,
> Then shame fall on Asolo, mischief on me![2]

Like Pippa's, my awareness of finite time is monitored by conscience. Thou shalt not waste a precious moment. Don't "squander" this fleeting interval. I constantly inquire as to whether activities are worthwhile and question my expenditure of time and energy. This orientation combined with my father's efficiency and work ethic so that conscience and consciousness of temporality are intertwined. "Teach us to count our days that we may gain a wise heart," says the psalmist (90:12 NRSV). Can a person so scrupulous about the use of time ever relax, simply enjoy the moment without counting its cost and weighing its value? How much do I miss when burdened by the task of constant evaluation? Whose timetable am I on? I cannot stop assessing the worth of every moment, measuring quantified blocks of time in terms of an elusive criterion of qualitative value. Like one sibling, I try to pack so many activities into a day that it becomes hectic and chaotic. Like another one, I hold back from commitments because I want to "protect my time." Some of this hoarding of time is inevitable, just life, and some of it is typical WASP drivenness. It also expresses a particular family's values. We

---

2. Robert Browning, "Pippa Passes," in *Robert Browning's Poetry*, selected and edited by James F. Loucks, A Norton Critical Edition (New York: Norton, 1979), 18.

spend so much time thinking about time and make it a moral issue: what a waste of time!

On certain occasions Deane gave herself fully to the moment. For her, *carpe diem* meant total engagement in conversation or reading. When I hesitated before reading a massive volume by Dostoevsky or Faulkner that she recommended, she said: "Live as if you would die tomorrow. Learn as if you would live forever." (This quote is by Gandhi.)

Deane told us about her father's death as we were leaving home because she feared it might be her last chance to do so. Goodbyes were traumatic for her; she struggled to hold back tears. I am sure that she was recalling other farewells that she did not know would be final. She lost her father, and then, just as suddenly, her mother died in an automobile collision in 1961. Deane, age thirty-five, had just decided to talk to Dolly about the past and to ask questions that had long troubled her. When she said goodbye to us as we left for school, Deane knew that her own death or that of one of her children would cut off any opportunity to tell us about our grandfather in the way that she wanted. She put off and postponed a painful subject and then grabbed what might be her last chance.

"Sometimes people pick odd moments for confession," she told me. "When I told David and Blair on the way to the airport, it had to be rushed. It was like when my friend told her mother that she had cancer as they drove to the hairdresser. It made it easier to be in a context where emotions had to be kept under control while a practical task demanded attention."

* * *

ALTHOUGH I DON'T REMEMBER my mother regularly looking somber or grief-stricken, I sometimes saw her sadness. A particular incident stands out. I must have been about six or eight years old. I do not recall where I was playing or what she told me. Preoccupied, I mumbled something in acknowledgment, but I did not really take in what she said to me. Memory begins a few minutes later when I run through the living room. She is seated on the couch, crying, with the mother's grief that terrifies a child. "Mom, what's wrong?" Struggling for control, she tells me that I had not paid attention to her words, had ignored them. I am shocked. I had no idea that a casual action such as a lapse of attention could have such a devastating effect on her. She tried to reassure me that it was not my fault.

At the time I dimly sensed, although I could not have put it in words, that my mother carried a heavy burden. The grief that my action triggered was caused by a deep melancholy or sorrow I did not understand. Somehow, confusedly, I felt both obscurely responsible for my mother's pain yet aware

Family Conscience

that her reaction to me came from within her. I did not want to trigger that grief, to make her sadness overflow in tears. Awareness of her vulnerability and determination to protect her were seared deep in my psyche. This scene, which echoes Deane's stories about how she accidentally hurt her mother, seems to me a defining moment in my sense of identity. For me both then and now it centers on my sensitivity to another's pain—especially to a woman's—and contributes to my own timidity about uninhibited self-expression. These characteristics are related to conscience and can be crippling. They influence certain choices I made in writing this memoir.

With Ian and Deane, 1951.

* * *

FOR MANY YEARS, DEANE struggled with depression and occasional thoughts of suicide. It is not unusual for the children of a suicidal parent to consider repeating the pattern. It is a way to join the lost parent. Deane would never inflict on her children the kind of pain she had suffered. Still, she knew that her depression affected her family, and this recognition contributed to the downward cycle. In Joanne Greenberg's *I Never Promised You a Rose Garden*, an adolescent girl suffering from mental illness wonders if she is toxic, poisoning everyone around her.[3] In 2004, Deane told me that at moments in the past she, too, had wondered whether she was toxic, since so much pain seemed to come to those she loved.

---

3. Joanne Greenberg, *I Never Promised You a Rose Garden: A Novel by Hannah Green* (New York: Holt, Rinehart & Winston, 1964).

"I think I shall call you Honor"

I told her that she was not toxic: "Mom, you are not a victim. You have confronted the pain in your past life and showed your family that it can be faced. I don't want to say that you have triumphed, but you haven't merely coped. You have shown courage and grace and self-transcendence. My writing about you is a story about these good qualities."

Tears came into her eyes; she said that no one had ever put into words that she was not toxic. I was struck by this way of expressing her relief and gratitude.

What does it mean to honor one's parents? For most of human history and in most cultures, including Christian ones, it has meant not revealing one's parents' vulnerability, not exposing them to shame. Today honoring one's parents can take other forms. I honor my mother by showing how she experienced shame, overcame its most destructive effects, and learned from it what is most important, what gives life.

"I think I shall call you Honor." I wonder whether she would say that to me now, and with what meanings. Would she feel shamed or honored by this version of her past?

* * *

ACCORDING TO A THERAPIST who knew me when I was ten, there is a connection between certain of my family's moral ideals and emotional disengagement. Bob was a therapist who in the early 1960s worked with my mother in the aftermath of Dolly's sudden death in an automobile accident. He also had several sessions with me and took me to activities with other boys. My parents were concerned about my tentativeness and lack of confidence, Deane told me later. In August 1975, just after my twenty-fourth birthday, I returned to Bob's office. My journal entry summarized my session with this psychologist:

> I talked to Bob this morning and had some important insights. First about my "tentativeness" in relationships, even at that early age (of 10 or 11). I seemed not to be able to commit myself to outright expressions of affection for others. As a result I seemed "namby-pamby" and other people couldn't understand what I was trying to do. I seemed passive and somewhat bland as in my efforts not to hurt anyone I was covering up even my best reactions to things. This ambiguity was due, thinks Bob, to my getting two messages from Mom on how much one should be committed to a relationship. On the one hand was natural love and affection and open expression of it. But on the other was Mom's indicating that too close a relationship can only bring pain. Mom's father's suicide was an incredibly traumatic event

which has haunted her all her life. She determined that none of her own kids would have to feel that grief at her death and she tried to maintain a certain distance and detachment. This made us somewhat ambivalent about how close it is possible to be to another. "Her death": according to Bob, Mom lived "from hour to hour" with the feeling of her imminent suicide. She felt enormous pressure to take her own life—or a fear of doing so—but in any case, a feeling that suicide was somehow *inevitable* for her. She concealed this from her kids and her husband and "her face was often like a mask." Bob saw himself as Mom's only outlet, her only confidante, and very much responsible for my becoming able to express myself better. I am dubious about this, as I only saw the guy a few times and can hardly believe he was Mom's only resource.

Five decades later, I still doubt Bob's self-congratulatory view of his role in Deane's and my own psychological health. I don't buy his theory that Deane wanted her children to be emotionally detached so that they would not experience the pain of losing a loved one. But Bob's comments help me understand the connection between moral scruples about hurting people and shutting down as I timidly withhold my deepest responses to life. This reflection on tentativeness still rings true: "I not only am afraid of expressing the negative parts of myself but am afraid even of asserting the positive things of which I feel proud. How crazy, to fear hurting anyone by being oneself." A misplaced sense of moral responsibility for others' feelings contributed to a kind of dishonesty, as I held back on expressing anger or even enthusiasm for whatever I was excited about. In my journal I vowed: "No more kid gloves, no more walking on eggshells!" As if I could change my character by a simple decision.

* * *

MY MOTHER GAVE ME the Protestant religion of the book. Not only the Good Book, but works of literature by Shakespeare, Dostoevsky, Faulkner, and others, especially huge tragic novels about families. Like her mother, like her son, Deane was a person for whom literature and personal experience constantly illuminate and influence each other. She identified strongly with Quentin Compson in Faulkner's *Absalom, Absalom!*, who imagined the morning before Gettysburg when the South was still undefeated. He keeps repeating: "It hasn't happened yet." Deane compared this to the way she thought about the time before her father's death and how her life could have been different. Quentin Compson could not reconcile a glorious, idealized past and the hideous reality of slavery. He is a Southerner whose conscience recognizes the evils of racism. Unlike his roommate Shreve, a Canadian who simply denounces the South and its antiquated code of honor, Quentin has an insider's knowledge and love of his homeland at its best. He sees its postwar ordeal not simply as deserved punishment, but as a tragic waste of goodness. Burdened by these contradictions, Quentin commits suicide. Faulkner's fictional character, with his sympathetic imagination of his ancestors, his efforts to reconcile moral judgment and historical understanding, his displacement to the North, and his struggle not to be overwhelmed by the tragic history he inherits, is a strikingly apt figure for Deane's own identity as she sought to come to terms with her father's legacy. The novel ends with Shreve asking Quentin why he hates the South. "'I don't hate it,' Quentin said, quickly, at once, immediately; '*I don't hate it,*' he said. I don't hate it he thought, panting in the cold air, the iron New England dark; *I don't. I don't! I don't hate it! I don't hate it.*"[4]

I was deeply moved by *Absalom, Absalom!* when I first read it in 1975. Only much later did I see that I was bowled over by this great work not only because of its literary quality and significant themes, but also because of its resonance with family history. I think my mother and I each repeated inwardly: "I don't hate him."

* * *

DEANE WAS A CLOSE reader and insightful editor. For many years I usually gave manuscript drafts of my scholarly writing to my parents for suggestions. Ian's comments focused on the major ideas, reflecting on what struck him as most interesting or significant. Deane's comments were what she called a "fine toothed comb," stylistic suggestions that might at first seem trivial, but showed great sensitivity to nuances of language. She would propose that I use "differing" instead of "different," or "the ways in which" rather than "how," or a synonym with a slightly different shade of meaning. Editing of this kind seems to be related on a deep psychic level to a scrupulous conscience, similarly requiring acute attention to detail and hypercritical doubt. Freud describes the superego as functioning like a censor as it searches for flaws and suppresses what is objectionable. But the superego represses unacceptable thoughts before they reach consciousness, while the ethical conscience, like a writer's self-criticism, aspires to clarity and control.

Dolly told Deane to "take care how you put things" in writing. One should always ask whether what one writes could appear on the front page of the *Washington Star*. This way of warning about careful use of language

---

4. William Faulkner, *Absalom, Absalom!* (New York: Random House, 1936), 378.

may reflect Dolly's unwanted experience of having Everett's death portrayed in the newspaper. My mother, too, was always keenly alert to the proper boundary between private knowledge and public statement, and attuned to the way in which a person finds out something. Deane found out about her father's suicide in an accidental and painful way. She knew that he drowned in a Washington canal but could not understand how, for Everett was a good swimmer. At the family gathering for his funeral, by chance she found the newspaper clipping describing the suicide.

Deane sometimes expressed her editing impulses by doctoring family photographs. When I was a child, she cropped the images of individuals in group photos when she considered the portrait uncomplimentary. She frequently disliked the way feet looked. She asked my former spouse, who is a photographer, to destroy certain negatives. Deane was very shy, even averse, to being photographed, and in group shots she hid behind others. She had a strong desire to pass on certain images of the past and not others. My version of family history, too, omits many aspects of the past. Whose facial expression have I cropped?

* * *

MY MOTHER TOLD ME that when she was young, she idealized her father and blamed her mother for not preventing Everett's death. She also felt that she herself was somehow responsible. Deane experienced depression for many years because of her burden of grief, anger, and unfocused guilt. As she grew older, she became more critical of her father: "When I was young, I worshipped the ground he walked on, to use southern parlance. My forgiveness and mercy went too far. I love him but now I'm not sure I like him. How could he not think of how his death would affect the four of us?" She became more forgiving of Dolly: "I have come to admire my mother, after resenting and blaming her for so many years for not having prevented the suicide. She was silent about the past because she wanted to protect us. She didn't want to tell us anything negative about him. She adored him in spite of his faults. But at the end of that summer of 1937, she still had doubts about his drinking. Now I can admire her for not wanting to be an enabler."

In December 1982, my mother wrote a letter responding to my brother David's questions about her father. The end of Deane's letter describes how sessions with a therapist, Lynn, helped her work through unresolved feelings about her parents:

> It was Lynn in Chapel Hill in 1981 who really helped me finish it up, and I have a sense of *peace* about it—both in relation to my father and to my mother. In the first place, Lynn helped

me to accept the fact that there are many unknowables; there are things neither I nor anyone will ever know with finality, and that is now all right. Then there were two breakthroughs toward the end of therapy, which utterly simple as they may sound were somewhat earthshaking for me. It hit me that since I was eleven, I had somehow carried around an imagined sense of my father's anger and depression (knowing they must have been involved). It was as though he didn't have a chance to live these out and finish up with them, but died because of them, and I must somehow carry them around for him. I found that I simply didn't need to do that anymore. Then I remembered for the first time in about 45 years, being in the back of our car on a cold day when I was 10 or 11, being driven home from a friend's house. My father stopped across from a wine store, saying he would be right back. With all the courage I could muster I said, "I wish you wouldn't. Daddy, I'm kind of worried about what's happening in our family." He turned around and looked at me seriously, then with the nicest smile. He said quietly, calling me by his nickname for me, "Well . . . Maybe you can help, Caki." That's all we said, but there was this little bit of joy. When we got home, I went upstairs and found my mother. She was in what we called the den, going through her "treasures" (mostly letters). I shyly told her something had happened, told her the whole thing, ending with what he said. She looked up. I can still see her beautiful eyes when she smiled, hugged me, and said "Maybe you can, Darlin.'" There was no "how?" Maybe it was just a "Love believeth . . . Love hopeth . . ." thing. Not till 1981 did I know that two of the nicest, gentlest answers any parents could have given their child had gotten buried and had wrought havoc because later I couldn't figure out what could have been done. I hope that this de-mystifies some of this. I am sorry our children were grown up before it was clearer to me.

My mother sent me a copy of this letter. In the margins she wrote a note linked to the sentence that refers to Everett's anger and depression: "John—I avoided using the word guilt here. It would have said it as well or better perhaps."

One breakthrough was Deane's new sense that she did not have to carry any longer her father's unfinished business, his anger, depression, and guilt. The second breakthrough is her recognition of how a specific incident had settled a burden of responsibility on her shoulders. The motif of inadvertent hurt appears again when "two of the nicest, gentlest answers any parent could have given their child" were misinterpreted when Deane took their words of encouragement as a duty to save the family. "Maybe you can help," said each parent, but it was not clear to Deane how to do that. Her strong sense of responsibility produced misplaced guilt feelings that lasted decades. Moreover, brooding about what she ought to do was at odds with her father's advice in his last letters to be cheerful and "never worry about things you can't help."

Conscience can be overly sensitive, too eager to take on blame for what could not have been helped or hindered. If we are each our brother's keeper, and our mother's and our children's, how do we understand both our responsibilities to those we love and the limits of responsibility? Deane suggests that one's ambiguous responsibility for another person may call for religious faith. She interprets her mother's words—"Maybe you can help, Darlin'"—in terms of "love believeth," an allusion to I Corinthians 13: "Love bears all things, believes all things, hopes all things, endures all things." Perhaps Deane meant that sometimes we can only understand our responsibility for another person when we trust God and go on loving that person even when we cannot do anything specific to help. If so, she only came to understand this much later. There is something brave, good, and honorable about this eleven-year-old girl's determination to do anything she could to save her family, yet it brought her a great deal of suffering.

CHAPTER 3

Not Passing by on the Other Side

Deane's adult moral concerns expressed thoughtful deliberation, imagination, and Christian commitments. At Duke University, she quit a sorority because she did not like the system of blackballing potential members. She majored in sociology in college, inspired by a liberal professor who believed that it was possible to address social issues such as civil rights and to plan a better society. After graduation, she organized work camps for the American Friends Service Committee in Philadelphia. As a student at Chicago Theological Seminary, she was a counselor for a project in which students found low-paying factory jobs and studied the problems of industrial workers.

My father told me: "If you asked me about Deane's conscience, the first thing I would say is that she was critical of the values she grew up with in the South, especially racial attitudes." She was already concerned about racial justice when she went to Duke. She criticized the way that cousins in her Virginia family made fun of "the help" and their pronunciation. Deane's upbringing merged the Southern worldview of her mother's kinfolk with the Kern family's deep roots—six generations—in Washington, D C, and, further back, New England and Pennsylvania. When I asked Deane about the sources of her views about race, she singled out her father's mother, also named Catharine, who had a Black maid, called Mammy, who worked for the family for forty years. This Kern grandmother was "paternalistic in the best sense": considerate, warm, and gentle with servants. Similarly, Deane's mother was kind and had a sense of humor that servants appreciated, but she did not recognize the legislative and civil rights issues that would erupt decades later. Deane contrasted this with Ian's mother, Dorothy, who was liberal and progressive in her political views, but formal, reserved, and rarely humorous. To contemporary ears, Deane's view of her mother will sound antiquated and insensitive to structural racism and the condescension that accompanies paternalism. My mother wanted her children see the goodness of certain things about the South, above all Gam's character and gracious manner.

Mammy made a deep impression on Deane. In the journal she kept during the 1984 intensive journaling workshop, Deane addressed her grandmother's servant:

> Mammy, you knew so much. But you could keep your counsel. You saw the human weaknesses in people, the fears, the successes, and you could love people and hope they would be at their best. You did not worry too much that in part of their minds they would condescend. Some other part of your life lived in the Black neighborhoods. I would love to see you hold out your arms to us again, see your smile, sniff the cleanest, starchiest white apron and cap in the whole world. I knew your forgiveness that part of our family was Southern. When my father died, you knew reasons too deep for words. And you put your arms around my mother and she could accept that gratefully. Imagine! Patience. Serving. Doing things nicely. Ritual. Accepting the family's appreciation with appreciation. You *endured*. You were bigger than the kitchen part of the house. I think "The Lord have mercy" was real to you. You could detect "acting" or deceit. You wanted people to be "a little kinder to each other" (Dickens). If someone gave you not-just-the-needed present, you never showed it. *You* were kind. And I think you understood better than anyone the terrible danger in "my child grown crooked up without my wall," because you discerned fragmentation in me. Perhaps you said, "Wait awhile," but took care to watch.
>
> Thank you for the dignity. Thank you for the kept-counsel, and the hope that people would grow out of their faults. Thank you for the immaculate against the brown skin. Thank you for the sorrow and the pity. Thank you that when *your* heart was heavy, and no one fully realized the capacities of that heart, you survived the wounds.
>
> I am 60. There has been a sickness of depression in my own experience and in the family. Somehow help me, that life may give me your goodness and purity of intention as redemptive. "Help me to accept the things I cannot change, to change the things I can, and the wisdom to know the difference." Thank

you, too, that because of you I was more able to hear Martin Luther King.

Some readers will see this as a typical White projection of the need for forgiveness. It is a cliché of many books and films: the long-suffering Black servant who loves the White master or employer in spite of the sins of racial oppression. For me, this passage of Deane's, written only for herself, rings true as a grateful acknowledgment of generosity received, an attempt to imagine what lay beneath the surface of Mammy's role in the family, and a strong identification with a moral exemplar who, enduring suffering, was able still to love. Deane admired Martin Luther King Jr. because, among other qualities, he expressed and articulated so well values she first encountered in Mammy's care.

I recall vividly my mother's immediate reaction to learning of the assassination of John F. Kennedy: "Thank God that it was not a Black person who shot him."

* * *

Ian and Deane at their wedding, 1947.

DURING THE SUMMER OF 1948, six months after their wedding, Deane went with her new husband to Germany to take part in a postwar reconstruction program. She was twenty-two years old and enrolled at Chicago Theological Seminary when she and Ian were asked by the Congregational Church Service Committee to serve as counselors for a group of Dutch, German, and American students in Münster and Hamburg. The work camp volunteers removed rubble so that the cathedral and university could be rebuilt. In devastated cities, they witnessed German homelessness, poverty, and anguish. In 2004, Ian transcribed his and Deane's diaries from the work camp in a sixty-page document for their family that later I revised and published.[1] They recorded their thoughts late at night after exhausting days when they were emotionally overcome by their experiences. Deane's diary entries reveal her conscience deeply engaged in reflection about the ethical and religious meaning of what she witnessed.

Ian and Deane on boat returning from Germany, 1948.

The work camp was important not only for the physical tasks accomplished, but because it provided an opportunity for reconciliation between wartime enemies. Americans worked with German students, one of whom was a former SS officer, and with Dutch students whose relatives or friends had been imprisoned or sent to concentration camps during the Nazi occupation of Holland. The Dutch and the Americans tried to comprehend how Hitler came to power, how much the Germans knew about the concentration camps, and how Germany could best face its guilt and responsibility for the war and move into a different future. It was a challenge for the Americans not to simply condemn the Germans. The example of the Dutch was crucial and compelling, for although they had been bombed and badly mistreated by the Germans, they came to Germany to help with reconstruction and to attempt reconciliation. Deane was struck by one Dutch student's

---

1. John D. Barbour and Joachim Reppmann, eds., *Toiling with the Defeated: American Diaries from the Ruins of World War II; Deane and Ian Barbour in Hamburg and Münster, 1948* (Northfield, MN: Stoltenberg Institute, 2016), printed and distributed by LuLu.com and available on Amazon.com.

comment that their presence in the work camps was "not to teach, for the Germans were considered the most educated people in the world. Just to have *contact*. The Germans must learn to educate themselves through the contact." Deane understood that the challenge for the German people was not only to rebuild their country, but also to find a way out of isolation, guilt, and shame.

For the victims of the Nazis, what would make forgiveness possible? Deane analyzed the conditions and the mystery of such a breakthrough:

> There is on the part of the Dutch the underlying question, almost with racking tears, "Why did you do it?"—sometimes swallowed for a few minutes and asked more creatively. God bless them. They are so much to be admired. Yet I hear admiration for the Germans, too, who want desperately to think things out and to have things spoken: want it consciously, yet subconsciously cannot bear to look at past horror and moral weakness. But this is not a camp of accusation, nor is it a camp of martyred "forgetting and forgiving." This is hard to explain. It is not a matter of forgetting, for that is impossible and unrealistic. For one thing it is not fair to the Germans, for it would be a failure to value truth, to look at and learn from history. Yet it is a group experience of quiet forgiving, in a more mature way each day. It is amazing how it comes, and I cannot possibly describe it. It comes from laughter, it comes from the terrifically hard work at the hospital, it comes from laborious, sincere conversations out on the green or in the tents, lasting far into the night. It comes from things being "said right out," and from individuals making mistakes and coming to like each other. It comes from believing in Ilse's integrity, for instance: in believing that she too loathed what we outside, looking in, were loathing; from understanding, though not agreeing with, the silence she and other Germans kept, that they might live; from seeing her untiring work in camp these days, sometimes doing other peoples' work. It makes one wish that one's own character might be nearly as lovely if one were carrying, too, the load of guilt she had in her heart.

Deane linked forgiveness to sharing a common life, honesty about the past, and recognition that there is finally a mystery about forgiveness, an amazing giftlike quality that cannot be controlled, earned, or completely understood. In an experimental and intuitive way, the volunteers at the German work camps were seeking healing with goals and methods similar in certain ways to later formal procedures such as South Africa's court-like

Truth and Reconciliation Commission. The shared Christian commitments of the participants in the work camps made possible certain bonds and experiences that would probably not have been possible with a more diverse group of people.

Deane discerned the deeper meaning of Nazism as not simply evil, but tragedy: a terrible corruption of what was good about the German people. This was the land that produced Luther, Bach, and Goethe. Deane was reading Rilke that summer, and later admired the novels of Thomas Mann. In Hamburg, she listened to Beethoven's Ninth Symphony and gazed at the faces of the audience:

> The hall overflowing. We stand and hear the concert free. Rapt attention of all, the notes weaving into that incomparable pattern. I think of a deaf Beethoven writing this. Out of Germany came this too, as surely as did the insanity of war-madness and the hatred of the Jews . . . Finally the chorus, "All men will be brothers," and we are filled with the solemnity of it, and the experience is perhaps one of the mountain tops of one's whole life. Then thunderous applause . . . and the people filing quietly out. I wish someone could paint their faces: "Faces of Hamburg Citizens, July 1948, after listening to Beethoven's Ninth Symphony."

Those faces showed silent, sober reflection on beauty in a context of devastation, defeat, and horror. Deane loved the brooding faces in the art of German artist Kathe Kollwitz. My parents owned several of her prints, and Deane gave me a book of Kollwitz's etchings and lithographs. On the dust jacket of my book *The Conscience of the Autobiographer* I used Kollwitz's 1934 self-portrait, with its haunting black pools for eyes and a finger across her brow as she holds her head.

Deane was deeply moved by the way the Germans struggled to come to terms with their guilt about the past and their responsibility for the future. Conscience did not permit her to view this as an exclusively German problem. She saw the Nazi period as a stark reminder of truths about the human condition. She listened as German friends explained the difficulty of protesting against Hitler, especially for those with families, and she compared it to her country's aversion to confronting racial injustice, especially the lynching of African Americans. German students said that when Hitler was appeased at Munich, it seemed as if other countries approved or were unwilling to take a stand against him. The 1936 Olympic games showed the world's tacit acceptance of the Nazis. Without excusing Germany from its guilt for the evils of Nazism, Deane asserted that other countries must acknowledge their own faults, discern the potential for goodness in the

Not Passing by on the Other Side

German people, and recognize that the destinies of all nations are tied together.

Sometimes it is difficult to know how to respond when one sees an injustice. Deane recorded an incident at the American embassy in Hamburg when she "passed by on the other side," alluding to those individuals in the parable of the good Samaritan (Luke 10:25–37) who did not help a person in need:

> I go to the American consulate with Heite and Kurt. The picture of George Washington on the wall, which had never meant much before, brings suddenly and overwhelmingly close the knowledge of how precious are the best things for which the U. S. stands, including freedom of speech and of religion and the concept of "liberty and justice for all." Into my head comes the melody of America the Beautiful: "beautiful for pilgrims' feet . . . for mountains' majesty." This was shattered utterly for the moment by the American accent of the well-dressed, brusque receptionist replying to a thin German lady who is fighting to hold back the tears as she asks for some sort of extension. She is refused. "But you told me I am sure that if I did (such and such) I might come back. The British Office just sent me over to you." Then the secretary, in an icy, curt voice I cannot forget: "You TOLD me that." Not a kind word as the woman leaves. Yet the secretary is then sweet, helpful to me; my American passport makes things easy. Kurt, the German, one-quarter Jewish, says: "Of course they are like that to the Germans. That's all we expect. And we Germans have been like that to others, we know." Yet the curtness, the flagrant discourtesy, distresses, frightens, and makes an American feel sick and ashamed. And yet, and yet . . . I "passed by on the other side" at that moment as surely as I ever did. I said nothing to the lady in gray with the white face, the cultured voice, the anguish in her eyes (was this somehow tied up with someone she loves as much as I love Ian?)—nor even a word of suggestion of what I thought to the suave, beautifully-dressed receptionist who sits in the Consulate Office in Hamburg.

Like her German friends, Deane struggled with her own complicity and responsibility for her nation's actions. She discerned the ramifications of massive historical conflict in ordinary interactions and felt responsible for a stranger.

That summer in the German work camp was an unforgettable and formative experience. Deane felt at once an urgent sense of calling and uncertainty about how to fulfill it. "And still we are seeing darkly," she confessed, believing that the significance of this experience would become clearer in the future. Towards the end of the work camp, she described a moment of utter exhaustion, gnawing hunger, and longing for religious understanding. She had taken the wrong train with her German friend Ilse:

> The experience of too few calories for needed energy . . . the experience of really thinking that if no one were around, if Ilse were just not so brave, one would eat grass and leaves . . . of utter weariness while knowing that all around one are people inestimably more weary . . . of trying not to faint for it would take so much of someone else's energy to help you. The feel of the cool metal of the railing beneath one's hand. All of this experience that is unforgettable may in some unknown way be a gift to my life. Somehow out of it one must formulate for oneself a message, a plan, meaningful when this is a part of past experience. My need of God and a vision of things beyond myself, a greater understanding of the meaning of "spiritual values," is deep and urgent.

In the German work camp, Deane discerned both tragic suffering and the possibility of reconciliation. She built on what she had learned in her family of origin about guilt, responsibility, and the potential for forgiveness and hope. Her conscience was enriched, complicated, and extended in new ways. Even when she did not know exactly what she should do, she determined not to "pass by on the other side." Sometimes the resolution to hold in memory a crucial incident like this, keeping it alive for an unknown future, is the best one can do. It is not enough, but it is essential, and enough for the moment.

Their participation in the work camps had long-term effects on Ian and Deane. In a Christmas letter of 1948, they described their return from Germany to the United States, where they recognized unmet religious needs: "We saw how much our lives are controlled by material values rather than 'the things of the spirit'; how dollars and 'saving time' occupy our minds more than love of God and neighbor." For the rest of their lives, they were keenly interested in Germany, especially its literature, film, and Rolf Hochhuth's play *The Deputy*. Deane often recommended to me works that dealt with the dilemmas of "bystanders," those who were disturbed or appalled by Nazi deeds but afraid to protest, often because of concern for family members. Their encounters in Germany shaped my parents' view of events in the United States, including struggles against racism and the Vietnam War. The German work camp experience helped them understand the need not only to end injustice, but to heal the resulting wounds. They sought ways to confront and work through guilt and shame about the past and to find a constructive response and reconciliation.

* * *

IN KALAMAZOO, MICHIGAN, IN the 1950s, Deane worked with displaced Latvians. She arranged choir engagements, one of the few ways in which they could help support themselves immediately upon arriving in America. Deane had liberal political convictions about civil rights and the Vietnam War and supported many local projects of the church she and Ian joined in Northfield, Minnesota, a congregation of the United Church of Christ (UCC). In the 1960s, she was involved in the Human Relations Council at the local high school, a group that urged the inclusion of Black history in the curriculum and supported the A Better Chance program that sponsored Black students from out of town who enrolled in Northfield High School. A group called Concerned Parents opposed these efforts.

Deane was more inclined to express her ethical concerns in personal relationships than in political action. She befriended women and children in difficult circumstances. The phone often rang in our home on Winona Street, and my mother would interrupt what she was doing to talk to someone in a crisis. She was a wounded healer whose empathy for suffering was balm for those who sought her out. After she died, countless people told me how she comforted them at a difficult moment.

Deane believed strongly in the potential impact of summer camping experiences. In the summer of 1939, at the low point of her life, family friends gave her a scholarship to go to a camp in the Shenandoah Valley. She told me in 2003: "It really changed my life. It was the first time I was ever out in nature all by myself. I used to walk along a forest path or to the rocks and river, or be among a group who would climb at five o'clock in the morning to the top of a mountain. The Shenandoah Mountains became so important to me. There were songs we sang at camp that put into words the aspirations for one's life. One song in particular, 'The Ash Grove,' meant so much to me. I would walk along under those trees on the forest path, and think, 'The Ash Grove is calling me.' I knew what that meant for the first time. It was an introduction to nature that would bring Wordsworth's 'Tintern Abbey' to life for me. And living by a rushing river was so exciting." Deane went to camp for several summers and as a teenager was a counselor in Virginia and western Pennsylvania. She made sure that all her children went to summer camp, and I was a counselor for three summers in Minnesota and Maine.

Family Conscience

She developed a particular loyalty to a Lutheran canoe camp near the Canadian border where I worked one summer. Wilderness Canoe Base changed the lives of several troubled adolescents whom she knew. Deane helped the local community center arrange camp scholarships, persuaded doubtful parents or children that the experience would be at once safe and exciting, contributed money to pay for scholarships, and helped families organize and equip their children. During the 1970s, when she was worried about her own children, it was therapeutic to realize that there were children with greater problems from broken and desperate families whose lives could be bettered.

At a church synod meeting in 2007, I greeted a former minister of my local congregation. Out of the blue, she told me that when her daughter was a teenager, she had had a hard time being teased in school. Deane and Ian paid for this girl to go to a camp for two summers, and it made a huge difference to her feeling of self-worth.

"Thank you, I'm so glad you told me this," I responded as we said goodbye. "My parents never said anything about it."

"Of course not," said the minister. "I knew that they wouldn't have."

* * *

THE PURITANS FASCINATED DEANE. As a girl, she read certain books about them "over and over," such as Mary Wells Smith's *The Young Puritans of Old Hadley* and *The Boy Captive of Old Deerfield*. Her Reed, Wells, and Deane ancestors had deep roots in New England, and one of them, Samuel Cooke, signed the Mayflower Compact. This Puritan heritage is one point of overlap between my mother's and my father's families. Both branches had ancestors in Deerfield, Massachusetts. One Dickinson forebear had the name Consider, which seems wonderfully appropriate for someone with a Puritan conscience. Consider: stop and deliberate, weigh your act's motivations and consequences, think carefully before you decide.

Jewish tradition also has a form of hyperconscious scrupulosity that can be either profound or neurotic. But Jews laugh at themselves more readily than Puritans and their Protestant descendants. Perhaps this memoir is like a Woody Allen movie without the humor.

Puritan roots help explain certain characteristics of my family's collective conscience, for better and for worse. We are constantly engaged in moral assessment but feel guilty about judging each other. The Puritans shaped our moral compass, introspective gaze, and sense of responsibility for each other. Deane recognized this in a twelve-step group in 1983, when she sought to understand how our family had influenced one of her children who was struggling with chemical dependency: "Some of my favorite childhood books were historical novels on Puritan life. Puritans felt responsible for each other's consciences. I realize that this fostered a didactic, teaching relation to the consciences of others, rather than sticking to the job of 'owning' my own. Though some teaching is essential in bringing up young children, I let that slow down my acceptance that I am responsible only for my own decisions." Deane was trying to understand the limits of her responsibility for an adult child and to accept that person's decisions even when she thought they were mistakes. She realized that chemical dependency is a disease that can be treated and that "no one is to blame." The Puritans' strong sense of responsibility for each other illuminates a pattern in my family history when we can't discern where one person's conscience leaves off and another's begins. As if there is something larger and more powerful than any one of us: a family conscience.

Another legacy of our Puritan forebears is anxiety about pride, a scruple based on ideals of modesty and humility. Constant vigilance about suppressing pride makes a person fearful and self-centered. One form of Puritan scrupulosity viewed any good feelings about oneself as suspect. Because they stressed a Christian's absolute dependence on God's grace, strict Calvinists emphasized the inevitable unworthiness and sinfulness of even the best human intentions and actions. If you start feeling too good about yourself, watch out! This reflex seems to me deeply ambiguous: at times neurotic, yet related to the capacity for self-critical wisdom epitomized by Reinhold Niebuhr.

Deane could also laugh about the inevitability of pride. With an amused smile, she several times quoted this phrase from Abigail Adams: "Down, vanity!" She caught herself being proud of something, tried to disavow that attitude, and found this whole pattern of self-monitoring absurd, because pride is unavoidable and true humility elusive. Augustine and Ben Franklin pointed out the irony of a person becoming proud of their lack of pride. Mock humility is a recurring form of humor in my family. We are caught up in a habitual process of scrupulous self-criticism, yet sometimes we recognize that there are more important issues to worry about.

In December 2004, I asked Deane and Ian whether and how they think of our family as influenced by the Puritans. Deane immediately brought up Arthur Miller's play *The Crucible*: "That Salem scene seems so vivid to me: girls wanting to be righteous but having their righteousness skewed by judgmentalism." She asserted that there is much to admire about the Puritans, although "many things about them, such as their idealism, have been ridiculed." She preferred the term "pilgrim," adding that she loved the line in "America the Beautiful" about "pilgrims' feet that see beyond the years." Pilgrims had an ultimate loyalty and a final destination that put everything finite and temporal in a larger context. Ian reflected that one negative aspect of Puritanism has been the American assurance that our country is a beacon on a hill, a moral example for the entire world to follow: "The way George W. Bush led the United States into war with Iraq shows what happens when you have absolute confidence that you are right and have a mission in the world to spread your ideals, if necessary by force." Puritan ideals contribute to American self-righteousness and arrogance yet can also inspire prophetic criticism of self-interest inflated to idolatrous proportions. The Puritan heritage is profoundly ambiguous in the histories of America and of my family.

* * *

SOME OF MY MOST intimate and powerful experiences with my mother involved discussions of literature, which trigger pleasurable memories of her reading to me when I was a child. I know from reading to my sons how mesmerizing this can be: how still the little body, how wide the eyes, how alert the eager mind transported to a different world. And then deep sleep, as the child slips into an imagined world and the aloneness of dreams with the assurance and security of the parent's love.

Deane and I shared an extraordinary final episode of reading aloud during Christmas vacation of my senior year in college. I had had all my wisdom teeth extracted and was in a great deal of pain as stabs penetrated the sedative medication. I lay half delirious on the couch in the living room with my eyes closed, fading in and out of consciousness. Deane offered to read to me. I loved *Moby Dick* but didn't know Melville's other works. Somehow, we settled on one of his short pieces. Sitting beside me in a rocker in the living room, Deane read me "Bartleby the Scrivener" in one long incantatory spell. Bright sun reflected into the house off snowbanks, and then, as dusk fell, she read on by lamplight. We were transfixed by Melville's wonderful story of the alternately empathetic and exasperated Wall Street lawyer who cannot help his remote, enigmatic scribe. My eyes closed as I lost myself in the story and in my mother's voice, at once so soft, gentle, and intensely concentrated on each word, each exact shade of meaning. I floated above my body and my pain, and then there was only her voice and the tale. We were again mother and child as we had been for bedtime stories before she tucked me in for sleep. For the last time I enjoyed this maternal connection, even as we shared an adult appreciation of Melville's use of language and poignant characterization.

Not Passing by on the Other Side

Deane came to the last lines. After Bartleby has died, the narrator receives a report that the scrivener had been a clerk in the Dead Letter Office in Washington, DC, until he lost his job during a change of administrations. The lawyer sees potential significance in this rumor:

> Dead letters! Does it not sound like dead men? Conceive a man by nature and misfortune prone to a pallid hopelessness, can any business seem more fitted to heighten it than that of continually handling these dead letters, and assorting them for the flames? For by the cartload they are annually burned. Sometimes from out the folded paper the pale clerk takes a ring—the finger it was meant for, perhaps, molders in the grave; a banknote sent in swiftest charity—he whom it would relieve, nor eats nor hungers any more; pardon for those who died despairing; hope for those who died unhoping; good tidings for those who died stifled by unrelieved calamities. On errands of life, these letters speed to death.
> Ah, Bartleby! Ah, humanity![2]

As she read the final words, Deane broke down in tears. I think that Melville's story resonated with her on many levels as a parable of all the ways in which good will, compassion, and love sometimes fail to reach another person. "Bartleby" surely evoked her feelings about her father and her wish that she could somehow have saved him from despair. The suggestion that Bartleby had earlier been trapped in a dead-end job in a Washington bureaucracy again makes me wonder about the nature of Everett's work in the 1930s and how much it contributed to his depression.

This scene of communion over Melville's haunting story is linked in my associations to the time three years earlier when Deane told me how her father died. We were alone then, too, in the living room at dusk. That was a moment of entrance into adulthood, an initiation into the knowledge of suffering and loss. This time, our shared engagement with "Bartleby" was at once a reversion to childhood and a movement beyond the fall into a new possibility, another way of being. For in those final words—"Ah, Bartleby! Ah, humanity!"—I see in condensed form the suggestion that a personal experience of loss may be transformed into compassion for others in all their unreachable pain and mystery. Sometimes that hope is what it means to not pass by on the other side, even when one has not been able to relieve another's suffering. Ah, Everett, Deane, all of us.

---

2. Herman Melville, "Bartleby, the Scrivener," in Melville, *Billy Budd, Sailor and Other Stories*, with an introduction by Frederick Busch, Penguin Classics (New York: Penguin, 1986), 46.

Family Conscience

* * *

THE PURITANS WERE DEDICATED to self-improvement. They were always working on themselves, refining character, as they did other things. For a writing workshop, my mother described her struggle with housekeeping:

> It is not the matter of tidiness that I keep mulling over, as the years go on; I like keeping things in order. It's the problem of cleaning. The list keeps lengthening of my efforts to outwit housework, or even to try to "schedule" it.
>
> One system is to clean every single aspect of just one room. I've also tried doing floors only—everything below the ankles, so to speak, throughout the house. Sometimes I try a criterion: "washable" or "dustable" or "mopable," and do nothing while cleaning but what comes under one of those categories. Or I'll do nothing but the "scrubables," no matter what needs to be scrubbed, from spots on the kitchen cabinets to an obscure corner under a radiator. If I see something else to be done, I treat it as some kind of temptation, and don't let myself out of the legalism . . .
>
> I have focused all cleaning into the hours before 9 a.m.; I've also relegated it to the two hours after dinner. I have decided to "improve" just five items, no matter what the size, in any one room and let it go at that. I've imagined I was leaving for England and had ten minutes to spend in each room of the house (really produces acceleration). I've spent one *whole* day a week, every ten to fourteen days, on housecleaning and not done any of it in between.
>
> I've tried doing the kitchen and bathrooms only, hoping their gleam would bestow a radiance on the rest of the house. Of the four floors in our house (including the basement), I've tried doing "one floor thoroughly" at a time, alternating days of the week. I've tried thinking very deeply about every single thing I did. I have also tried *not* thinking about it. I've tried writing letters in my head, though I keep getting distracted by what I'm doing and writing about cleaning. I've tried isolating a problem or decision and told myself I must keep cleaning until it is solved.
>
> To repeat: neatness is not a problem. But anyone knowing all this would think: "Either your house is awfully clean or awfully dirty." Neither is true.
>
> I've tried thinking which few square yards would mean the most to a particular person in the family and going after that. I've tried comparing the nooks and crannies in each of the

rooms in all the houses we've rented when away on leave to the nooks and crannies in the rooms in our house, and enjoyed doing ours far more. I've tried doing housework every day; every other day; only on weekends; only on weekdays. I've told myself it is interesting. I've told myself it is boring but character-building. I've also made myself do extra jobs if I broke my diet.

The strange thing—the good news—is, Every single one of these systems works. The trouble—the bad news—is: none is a cure-all. They have to be alternated and remembered/invented anew. But what will come back to me always are some of the lines from a little poem by Anne Glendenning that I found in my mother's desk on the day of her funeral:

To those who dust chairs where love sits . . .
Shine windows for love to see clearly
Both in and out,
Polish floors for dear returning feet—
To those who clatter heavy skillets,
Stir busy crocks…
And stand, dripping, over boiling jellies,
Set pans of rolls to rise—
To those who bathe sweet eager bodies,
Burnish hair to bright enchantment,
Scrub teeth for the best smiles of all—
You are high priestesses,
Lighting inner sanctuary candles,
Fastidiously tending cathedrals of love.

As Deane took care of her husband, four children, dogs, and home, she tried these strategies not only to keep on top of the endless chores, but also to work on her own character. She turned unending physical labor into a moral and spiritual challenge. She calls her various systems "legalism" and distraction a "temptation." But no method provides a permanent solution and, like a New England Puritan daily examining her conscience, she must constantly find fault, inspiration, and renewal.

The gender inequities of my family in the 1950s and 1960s now seem to me disturbing, though Deane did not see things that way. There were so many more interesting and meaningful things that she would have loved doing, especially reading, study, deep conversation, and prayer. Knowing her keen intellect and hunger for ideas, my heart goes out to my mother, and I wish I had done more to help her. As I recall, I didn't even make my bed every day, much less launder my clothes, wash dishes, or clean bathrooms.

Family Conscience

Deane's meditation on housekeeping reflects scruples about the wise use of time and about caring too much for possessions or appearances ("tidiness"). She prefaces her essay with a quote by Thoreau: "I had three pieces of limestone on my desk, but I was terrified to find that they required to be dusted daily, when the furniture of my mind was all undusted still and ... [so] ... I threw them out of the window in disgust."[3] At the end of the essay, she moves from housekeeping's effect on her own character to the work as an expression of love for her family. It is a familiar pattern for her: a piece of literature elicits a moral reorientation. After the long ordeal of frustrated self-improvement, Glendenning's verses tell her that finally "it's not about you," but your loved ones. Like a Puritan's memorized biblical passage, psalm, or prayer, the poem reminds her what is most important.

* * *

BEING A PARENT RAISES many questions of conscience. One of the most challenging is how to honor a child's decision when it conflicts with one's own values. There are clear answers when a small child endangers herself or as one's adult child makes choices that are properly her own. But when a child is an adolescent or young adult, there are ambiguous situations that are experienced as a dilemma. Deane wrestled with how to nurture the conscience of each of her children without being controlling, shaming, or manipulative.

In 1982, Deane wrote a powerful account of a difficult decision she faced when a son wanted to destroy some papers dear to her.

A Choice

> Our younger son is very angry at himself and at me. He is about twenty. He suddenly demands the whereabouts of his childhood essays and school papers.
>
> They are in folders in a locked trunk—along with similar folders for our other three children. This trunk is what I always hoped I could rescue first if the house caught on fire. I think: I can pretend to have lost the key. Instead, I act as though I just do not know quite where it is, and walk around in a bemused fashion. With great industry I look through the contents of a box in which I know that it cannot possibly be.
>
> Finally I "remember" where it might be. I go down the narrow basement steps as though going through a one-way tunnel. From the trunk I lift the folders of everything he has written in

---

3. Henry David Thoreau, *Walden; and, Resistance to Civil Government*, edited by William Rossi, 2nd ed., A Norton Critical Edition (New York; Norton, 1992), 24.

school. As though the flames I may have feared *are* behind me, I long to run out of the house and save these things—or even a few of them, such as the blue essay books from our year in England.

Later I hear him upstairs, leafing through the pages. Twice he laughs aloud. I hope that a memory of old and happy times will change something for him. Two hours later I realize he is no longer in the house. I do not know what he has done with the papers.

On the morning that the trash will be collected I open what I think is an empty outdoor trash can. There on the bottom lie all the papers, with the familiar, steadily-more-mature handwriting. Against the soiled can I see an accurate drawing of a little porpoise; it adorns an eight-year-old's story of the fun of swimming through the sea with his wise and loyal companion. Also looking back, I remember his definition of a family, written in third grade: "A family is when people have seen each other at their worst and at their best. And everyone remembers the same living room." I recall, too, his note to his little sister the year we lived in England: "For your birthday, I promise not to laugh when you are crying. If I do it, I will pay you 2 shillings and 10 pence. Happy Birthday!"

I hear the trash-disposal truck coming down our street. I want to reach in and gather everything up. If I lock it all in the trunk again, my son will not find out. But I remember how the idea of being "honorable" was talked about in my family of origin.

I close the lid on what is so far, so very far, from being "trash" in any sense. But I know that it represents *his* childhood and growing up, *his* own mind and being, and that he will remember from it what he needs or wants.

To whom did the paper record of that childhood belong? Deane had preserved these things, and they were as much hers as her son's. If I found my son's papers in the trash I would retrieve and hide them, saving them for a future day when he might appreciate them.

Deane wanted to honor both her son's past identity and the new self he was creating as an adult. Given how much she valued those childhood papers, allowing her son to destroy them was an act of great renunciation. She did the honorable thing and followed her conscience. By allowing her son to symbolically destroy his former identity, she affirmed the independent person he was trying to become, a person with values and a conscience different than hers.

Family Conscience

* * *

THE PROCESS OF INTERVIEWING my mother involved a lot of emotional ambivalence and moral uncertainty for me. It was hard for her to speak of the past, and she was reluctant to have this kind of attention given to her words. "I think I've said 'I' too many times," she said after one conversation. After another interview: "I'm afraid I've done too much talking." She did not like the spotlight. Several times, Deane admonished herself with a smile: "Down, Vanity!"

How I would use her words was unclear to both of us. She saw how important this project was to me and wanted to help. However difficult it was to talk about past suffering, she knew it can be liberating to remember, acknowledge, and move on. Still, we were both uneasy. In June 2003, I asked her whether she would be comfortable if I tape-recorded an interview. She said: "Well, I wouldn't be uncomfortable, but . . ." Although she didn't finish the sentence, her reluctance was obvious. Yet I turned on the tape recorder, she did not object, and we talked for ninety minutes. My spouse and siblings remarked on the awkwardness, irony, and possible insensitivity of my pushing my mother to disclose painful matters, given her strong need for privacy and boundaries.

As I wrote my interpretation of the family, I wondered and worried about whether to show early drafts to my mother. I wanted her response but did not want to hurt her. I sought openness, honesty, and dialogue—but, impossibly, without pain. I suppose, too, that I wanted her approval, her blessing. "Don't be such a mama's boy, just write what you need to write," my brother encouraged me at one point. My story is my version of the truth and does not depend on confirmation. Yet I seek a larger truth than simply my own perspective: the insights, challenges, and accuracy that can come through dialogue.

Part of my motivation for this writing project may be an attempt to overcome emotional distance from my mother during my childhood years. I sometimes sensed that she was brooding about the past and not wholly present. An oldest child displaced by younger siblings, I wanted her undivided attention. I can't blame her; I created much of the emotional distance. I didn't want to cause her pain and was afraid of raw feelings beneath the surface. To become myself, I had to detach, separate, and find my own way. When I pushed my mother to talk about the past, I was trying to bridge the emotional gap I created and expressing an insatiable child's demand for attention and love. Perhaps writing this book is an attempt to create a happy ending from ambiguous memories and an imagined intimacy with my mother and other loved ones.

Not Passing by on the Other Side

I do what she did, what all my ancestors have done: brood about family history. I am not sure whether going over the past frees me from its coercive power or perpetuates its hold. Every generation seems to the next one to be stuck in the past, unable to move on. I hope this journey takes me not only into the past, but into a future more freely chosen, even as I realize how much my choices are shaped by family history.

* * *

In 2011, Deane's health and strength began to diminish as she suffered pulmonary fibrosis. Her lungs slowly filled with scar tissue, she labored to breathe, and she was increasingly dependent on an oxygen tank. It became difficult to talk. During this time, Ian was completely devoted to taking care of her. She died in hospice care on December 23 with the family gathered around her and Bach's music playing.

During her final months, Deane was very deliberate and intentional about how she expended her limited time and strength. She passed on carefully chosen possessions with an explanation of the gift. She had last conversations with her closest friends. She wrote final letters in which she gave the recipient a parting message of appreciation, gratitude, and blessing. To Charlotte Smith, her closest friend, who had lost much of her hearing, Deane expressed her sorrow that they could not speak their last words:

> I know that in certain ways we are each experiencing a time of endings in our lives that God alone can sanctify to our use. And yet to be unable to *speak* of it together is torturous. I am balanced precariously, knowing that this period in life is a sort of now-or-never time. I long to think about and talk about it with my dear Charlotte, but that is not to be. Yet there is the voice from long-ago children's games that says "Ready; set; go" or "On your mark, get ready" because of the lung diagnosis. Perhaps at this moment you are feeling something similar. . . . This is just to tell you that you are being held in God's loving presence these days, though you know this already. Please do not feel that you must answer this odd outpouring, because the living and loving and being of all your years has been the answer, dear friend.

To more than one friend, Deane ended her farewell: "Please don't answer this; I already have the answer!"

To the end, she practiced certain spiritual disciplines with great intensity. A question in her healthcare directive asked when life would be no longer worth living. Deane's response: "Memory loss. Being kept alive if it is evident that I am unable to affirm meaning in 'Thou shalt love God with all thy heart and mind and soul and strength' and 'Thou shalt (try to) love thy neighbor as thyself.'" At Thanksgiving, our last family gathering, Deane sat with us for dinner at dusk, her favorite time for holiday meals. Clearly exhausted, she told the family that she must sleep. She quoted those biblical passages. With a smile she asserted, "I have fought the good fight" and, with characteristic grace and resolution, she left our company to lie down.

We received many tributes to Deane from people whose lives she had not simply touched, but deeply influenced. These cards offered insights into her character and stories of her reaching out to people in need rather than passing by on the other side. Several people said that because Deane believed in their goodness, they tried to live up to her expectations. One friend wrote: "By seeing the people that she loved as better than we are, Deane made us aspire to *be* those better selves." Mary Lewis Grow described the skillful way in which Deane integrated discriminating truthfulness with compassion:

> Many years ago, a young person, long gone from our congregation and our community, got up to play a clarinet solo during the church service. It was one of those performances that we imagine in our worst nightmares: every note emerged as a squeak, and the longer it went on, the more painful it became—less because of the discordant sounds than because of the congregation's anguish and embarrassment for the young person herself. All of us wished that she could have spared herself the discomfort of finishing her performance and would just end it quickly by saying that she was having a bad day and sitting down. But she played until the end of her piece.
>
> After the service was over, no one approached the young woman because no one could think of anything to say. It was like a collective averting of eyes away from a bad accident. The young woman, in her early teens, stood alone near the front of the church. But suddenly I saw Deane walking purposefully towards the young teenager. I followed close behind, curious to see what she could possibly find to say.
>
> "I admire your courage in being able to perform in public," Deane said. "It's such a hard thing to do, isn't it?" And soon a cluster of other people had joined the conversation—not to tell the young woman that she had played beautifully, because she hadn't, but to talk about how hard it had been when they were in school to give those awful oral reports or to perform in dance recitals. Deane's kindness led, I'm sure, to the young woman's being able to go home with her pride intact, and Deane modeled for the rest of us a *truthful* affirmation.

Not Passing by on the Other Side

My mother was unusually shy about any sort of public performance and knew how much that teenaged musician needed affirmation. In the background of this story is Deane's own childhood experience of playing violin at a concert. Her father inexplicably walked out just as she began her piece. Deane was deeply wounded and wondered if he was ashamed of her. Intentionally or not, he abandoned her at this moment, as he did in the way he died.

Another person writing a letter of condolence said that Deane practiced acceptance not by glossing the truth, but by finding a way to be at once truthful and hopeful. Over and over, those who knew her used the word "gracious" to speak of her combination of sensitivity, kindness, and what one person called "moral fiber." She was "like a grow light you wanted to be near."

* * *

FOR THE EULOGY AT my mother's memorial service in January 2012, I told a story about her. This incident, which took place at a critical moment in my transition from adolescence into adulthood, epitomizes her character, conscience, and continuing presence in my life. The work of mourning includes internalizing the admired qualities of the person one has lost. The eulogy that follows affirms what I most esteem and love about my mother.

> *When I was sixteen, something happened to me that was a defining moment in my life and a significant religious experience. My family was living in Cambridge, England, in 1967. On Christmas Eve, we went to a beautiful worship service in the ancient chapel of King's College. I was deeply moved by the choir singing by candlelight.*
>
> *After the service was over, the rest of my family drove home with my father while my mother and I walked home. It was only about five o'clock in the afternoon but already it was completely dark and very foggy. When we were about halfway home, a man suddenly appeared out of the gloom. He was old and bedraggled-looking, unshaven, dirty, and ragged. He stopped us and asked, "Hey mate, how 'bout a shilling for Christmas?" My mother didn't say anything, and I knew she was leaving this up to me. I had some money with me, but without really thinking about it I shook my head and said I didn't have any. I felt embarrassed and moved on quickly. As we moved away, he said kindly: "Well, Merry Christmas to you anyway, mate."*

Family Conscience

I felt torn up and burning inside as I walked on in silence with my mother. I told her I don't know how to react when someone asks me for money. Wouldn't he have just bought himself a pint of beer with it? Deane saw that I felt guilty and asked if we should go back to look for the man and give him something. Still I didn't want to go back. I said we would never find him.

Then Deane told me a story. There is an old legend that on Christmas Eve, Christ returns to the earth and walks around in disguise, and people have the opportunity to welcome him. Suddenly I was overcome with despair and disgust at myself. After having been to the most beautiful worship service of my life, I rejected the first person who asked me for something. There was no way to know how much or little that man needed a shilling, but I had avoided even talking to him.

I remembered that as I left him, he said: "Merry Christmas to you anyway, mate." Then I experienced a feeling that I can only call grace. It seemed to me that he understood my hard-heartedness but could accept it and even forgive me. How could I deserve that? I felt at the same time completely worthless and that, having been forgiven, I could start my life over again. As I walked home, I felt strong, full of potential, and connected to the world. The wet pavement and the cold city glowed and shimmered. I felt tremendously aware of the beauty of everything around me while still seeing ugliness. In myself, too, I recognized ugliness and sin and also goodness and capacity to love. The meaning of the words "forgiveness" and "grace" in the Christian tradition became significant in a new way.

The memory of this incident continued to reverberate in my life. At some point I realized that the legend of Christ's return to earth was loosely based on a particular biblical passage: the account of the great judgment in Mathew 25:31–46. When the Son of Man comes in his glory to judge the nations, the righteous ask him: "Lord, when was it that we saw you hungry or thirsty or a stranger or naked or in prison, and did not take care of you?" Jesus responds: "Truly I tell you, just as you did not do it to one of the least of these, you did not do it to me" (Matt 25:45 NRSV).

Matthew's story of the Great Judgment expresses the insight that the face of the neighbor in need is the face of Christ, and that suffering is one way in which God calls to us. This invitation comes to us anew every day in spite of our repeated failures to respond as we know we should.

Not Passing by on the Other Side

If I hadn't been with Deane that evening, I would probably have walked on and thought no more about the meaning of this Christmas Eve encounter. But her response to this incident is characteristic of her in two ways. First, it shows the way in which her responses to her experience and the people she was with were deeply connected with her knowledge and love of literature, including the Bible. My mother told me a story that reframed my understanding and altered my perception of myself. Deane had an unusual capacity to be present to people in all kinds of personal difficulty, and one of the forms that this took was her insight into how a literary or biblical passage might illuminate their experience. Many of us discovered books that have shaped us because of Deane. In my case it was Crime and Punishment and Absalom, Absalom! For Meg it was Kristin Lavransdatter and Precious Bane. She changed the way we understood ourselves by introducing us to stories about others. That evening in Cambridge, when Deane told me the legend of Christ's return, she planted a seed that would bear fruit much later—including today.

The incident on Christmas Eve reveals something else about Deane's character. She combined two qualities that don't always go together. She was a person with a very strong conscience who often had the effect on others of stimulating or forming their conscience. Yet at the same time, she had an extraordinary way of being open to and accepting of others, especially in their moments of weakness, meanness, or self-doubt. Without telling me or even knowing the right thing to do in that situation, she stirred my conscience, made me think, and helped me to understand confused feelings of guilt and shame. Deane showed me light in the darkness. I realized that guilt need not be the final word; I can begin once more, start over. This sense of renewal is a form of grace. Some of you here today may have had a similar experience with Deane, when by offering you a biblical verse, a literary passage, or her understanding and acceptance, she brought light to your darkness. You knew you were not alone.

Chapter 4

A Scot and a Dragon-Saint

My paternal grandfather, George Brown Barbour, begins his "Memories of Three Continents" (1968) with the French saying "*Qui s'excuse s'accuse*": one who defends himself reveals his guilt. George teasingly apologizes, not for revealing disturbing family history, but for "becoming a gossip" and boring us with ancient reminiscences. He does not disclose painful secrets, self-doubt, or ambivalent relationships. This memoir was intended for his grandchildren, but he knew others might read it. He suggests that "there should be an appendix for lemon-pips, grape-seeds, and other discards such as paragraphs that would better remain family possessions, like ghosts and skeletons." No shocking revelations will "hustle those still living" to their graves. In this jokingly apologetic way, George hints that much has been omitted, suggests the limits of truthfulness in autobiographical writing, and advises skepticism of those who excuse themselves. Now, as a grandfather writing a memoir, I see what he means.

While my mother's family history was shrouded in mystery, my father's family presents a different challenge: too much information. My Barbour ancestors were busy scribblers and hoarders of many forms of life writing. George wrote *Free*, a biography of his youngest son, who died in 1953 at thfe age of twenty-six. *In China When . . .* (1975) is my grandparents' memoir about the decade they spent in China, where Ian and his two brothers were born. In addition to George's "Memories of Three Continents," I have several boxes of his letters, World War I diaries, and collections of sketches and scholarly publications from his career as a geologist. *In the Field with Teilhard de Chardin* recounts his research, expeditions, and discovery of

A Scot and a Dragon-Saint

Peking Man with the great French paleontologist.[1] Other genres include a collection of Christmas letters, "The Barbour Yule Log, 1932–1975," and an unfinished biography that George wrote about his father-in-law, Robert Latou Dickinson. I have two boxes of tape recordings of memorial services, reminiscences, Christmas greetings, and oral letters. For their golden wedding anniversary in November 1997, Ian and Deane put together an album of photographs of five generations, from my great-grandparents through my sons' teenaged years. Ian updated the album several times; it ends with the birth of Ian's great-grandson, Edgar, in 2012. For a Festschrift presented to him in honor of his eightieth birthday in 2003, Ian composed an intellectual autobiography, "A Personal Odyssey."

In this chapter I use snippets of this huge documentary record to interpret the often-painful ways I experienced my grandparents as a child and young man. In the next chapter, I turn to letters written by George and Dorothy before I was born, which illuminate how their moral concerns developed. Some of George and Dorothy's values I embrace, some I reject, and some I continue to wonder about, weighing their flaws and virtues on my own peculiar scale.

* * *

MY FATHER'S PARENTS WERE the children of distinguished physicians in Edinburgh and Brooklyn who met through their common medical expertise in gynecology. My grandmother's father, Robert Latou Dickinson (1861–1950), has a mythic status in the family and is the source of my middle name. RLD, as family members called him, was for forty years a surgeon, gynecologist, and obstetrician at Brooklyn Hospital. He wrote several books on human sexuality, particularly female, and played a crucial role in the movements for birth control and sexual education. Dickinson was the pivotal figure in the American medical establishment's acceptance of birth control, which had been advocated only by radical feminists and women's organizations. As sex researcher, publisher, and advocate of more enlightened and liberal attitudes to sex, he provided crucial medical evidence and support for Margaret Sanger's work in Planned Parenthood. A historian of the birth control movement describes RLD as Sanger's "most astute critic, sometime rival, and finally, comrade-in-arms." Among Dickinson's many books and pamphlets are *A Thousand Marriages*, *Human Sex Anatomy*, and *The Single Woman: A Medical Study in Sex Education*.[2] His sculptures de-

---

1. George B. Barbour, *In the Field with Teilhard de Chardin* (New York: Herder & Herder, 1965).
2. Robert Latou Dickinson and Lura Beam, *A Thousand Marriages: A Medical*

picting pelvic structure and the cycle of fetal growth and birth were viewed at the 1939 World's Fair by more than two million people in what James Reed calls "probably the most successful single effort at sex education ever staged." Dickinson was "the mediator through whom organized medicine made its peace with the birth control movement" and the most influential researcher on sex before Alfred Kinsey, who admired and built on his work.[3]

Robert Dickinson's professional work seems to me related to conscience in two ways. First, although his expertise as a gynecologist was in anatomy and the physical aspects of sex, he was keenly interested in the influence of moral values and religious attitudes. Much of his research was based on women who came to his medical practice because of problems that were not only physical. Dickinson discussed how Victorian attitudes and guilt about sexual desires made it difficult for both men and women to accept and understand each other's physical and emotional needs. He thought that most sexual "maladjustments" could be prevented or remedied by education. Second, Dickinson was a courageous reformer motivated by moral convictions about the physician's role and women's rights. He was not a radical social critic but a liberal Christian whose sense of vocation shaped an enlarged conception of the physician's role in caring for his patients. Early in his career he fought the use of the corset and advocated bicycling for women. He was the first doctor to illustrate sexual positions and the American authority on female response during masturbation. Dickinson's research was repeatedly attacked by the American Medical Association, the Catholic hierarchy and conservative Protestants, opponents of women's rights, and other groups. But he prevailed, ever cheerful and energetic. According to Reed, "an abundance of self-confidence, optimism, and public spirit were necessary in order to brave public ridicule, loss of social position, and the indifference of the masses to force recognition of problems the general public preferred to ignore."[4] Dickinson believed that sexual expression was an end in itself, not simply a means of procreation, and he thought that a happy sexual relationship was essential in a marriage.

Study of Sex Adjustment, Medical Aspects of Human Fertility (Baltimore: Williams & Wilkins, 1931); Robert Latou Dickinson, *Human Sex Anatomy*, Medical Aspects of Human Fertility (Baltimore: Williams & Wilkins, 1933); Robert Latou Dickinson and Lura Beam, *The Single Woman: A Medical Study in Sex Education*, Medical Aspects of Human Fertility (Baltimore: Williams & Wilkins, 1934).

3. James Reed, *The Birth Control Movement and American Society* (Princeton: Princeton University Press, 1978), 143, 186, 182.

4. Reed, *The Birth Control Movement and American Society*, 147.

RLD was also an outstanding artist; his sketches illustrate *The New York Walk Book* and several textbooks of medical education.[5] He was idealistic, contagiously enthusiastic, vibrant, and good-humored, and he made a lasting impression on many people. According to the biographical portrait of him by George Barbour, on a weekend visit to a friend's country house, RLD "felled trees, sketched the view of the pond, taught the maid to swim, cut woodland trails, and uprooted poison ivy."[6] In his late eighties he still enjoyed doing a back flip off a diving board. A tape recording of his reminiscences, full of chuckles and jokes, conveys a warm, expansive personality.

When RLD saw something beautiful his usual response was: "Glory to God." He wrote wonderful prayers, such as one that asks the "Vacation-Giver" for "the secrets of rest and re-creation." Another prayer uses mountain climbing as a metaphor for spiritual and moral life:

> O Thou who flingest cloud shadows over lonely blue summits and fertile green valleys, thy prodigality amazes us. The vast wild uplands that are parks of thy planting; the steeps patterned in loveliness—and sky glory over all. Ever Thou lurest us aloft. Give us to "live as on a mountain": with wide outlook. May we go forward and upward, on difficult or dizzy ways, with eye fixed on the path, step by quiet step, until, in time, we gain that sinew and endurance that delight in toil and hardship . . . So do we crave a training for our other selves, that, though daunted, we gain, by plodding on, that swing of habit, and that joy in overcoming that our good bodies teach us. And, as after the long day of strenuous endeavor we are overtaken with utter physical content in every fiber of our being, may that other high enterprise bring us this very perfection of peace of mind and of saturation of soul with the clear high air of thy spirit. Thus pray we, Mountain lovers, O Mountain God. Amen.

RLD affirmed the classic Protestant virtues of hard work, self-overcoming, and deliberate character formation in a joyful, exuberant way not always characteristic of my tribe.

In a letter to his wife in August 1899, Dickinson quotes a remark about conscience that Mark Twain made: "A conscience is like a child. If you let it have everything it wants, it becomes spoiled and intrudes on all your amusements and most of your griefs. Treat your conscience as you treat anything else when it is rebellious—spank it, be severe with it and you will secure a

---

5. Raymond H. Torrey, *New York Walk Book*, with drawings by Robert Latou Dickinson, new and rev. ed. (New York: Dodd, Mead, 1934).

6. George B. Barbour, "R.L.D.: The Life of Robert Latou Dickinson," unpublished manuscript, 1.

good conscience, that is to say a properly trained one. I have reduced mine to order. I haven't heard from it for some time. Perhaps it is best when it is dead." RLD comments on Twain's statement: "A man can say that with grace only when he is old and has done a great task to repay his creditors." Dickinson agreed with Twain that conscience should not constantly nag and destroy life's pleasures. But, he suggests, to dismiss conscience without a lifetime of serious moral effort and service to others would be a sign of irresponsibility, not grace.

The oldest of RLD's two daughters, Dorothy (1892–1980), grew up in Brooklyn and went to Packer Junior College, Teachers' College of Columbia University, and Union Theological Seminary, where she earned a master's degree in religious education, "perhaps" the first ever awarded a woman (as my uncle Hugh's obituary of her cautiously ventured). She was one of the first women on the faculty of Hartford Theological Seminary. In 1920 she married George Brown Barbour (1890–1977), whom she had met in 1911 when he visited her family in New York. George and Dorothy spent the next decade in China, where their three sons were born: Hugh (1921–2021), Ian (1923–2013), and Robert (1926–1953), who adopted his middle name, Freeland, or "Free." After several years in England, in 1937 George accepted a position as professor of geology and dean of the College of Arts and Sciences at the University of Cincinnati, retiring in 1960.

* * *

MY EARLIEST MEMORIES OF my grandparents were when they came to visit and when we visited their home in Cincinnati. We all felt the heavy weight of Dorothy's judgments. Hugh's obituary of his mother says of her work in China that "her first concern was always character training, by experience, drama, and life situations, rather than ideas and information." Because of her character-forming project, Dorothy was a dominating and judgmental person. When it came to her need to correct others, she was incorrigible; she couldn't help herself. She made her grandchildren nervous, as if we had to perform for her. Deane told me that her mother, Gam, "rejoiced in your being." Dorothy, in contrast, "wanted you to be as good as possible." She never ceased trying to improve us, which made us feel that we were never good enough. We called her Grandmier, after my childish mispronunciation. My brother joked that her nickname should be spelled Grandmire, as in "to sink or stick in the mud." We resented her, tried to like her, and were dutifully submissive.

A Scot and a Dragon-Saint

Dorothy in her prime, perhaps 1950s.

Our achievements and interests inevitably seemed to fall short of some unobtainable standard. In high school, I was enthusiastic about the sport of wrestling, which I told her I chose partly because I liked the individual, one-on-one competition and couldn't as easily let down the team. In response, Dorothy praised the value of team sports. In the 1970s, when I had long hair, she assured me that Jesus had had short hair! She asked my wife whether we liked to go out to dinner in Chicago restaurants. When Meg answered cheerfully that we enjoy this, Dorothy responded: "George and I would always rather sit by the fire and open a can of soup than go to a fancy restaurant." End of conversation. Many such interactions ended in an awkward pause and changing the subject. If I had been more argumentative, self-confident, or assertive, I would have seized the opportunity to push to a deeper level of engagement with her, openly disagreeing or defining myself in contrast with her. She must have thought my evasive niceness boringly bland. Dorothy loved a vigorous debate, and now I wish I had risen to the challenge. I resented her heavy-handed pressure and cowardly withdrew. How petty of me still to nurse these grievances! That must be one reason I am still mad at her: I don't like the person I was around her, polite but false.

Many of my negative feelings about my grandmother are filtered through my sympathy for my mother. Dorothy meddled in others' child-raising, freely giving unsolicited advice and criticizing the parenting of Hugh, Ian, and their wives. In the first month after I was born, she wanted my mother to let me cry until the scheduled feeding time. Ironically,

Family Conscience

Dorothy often criticized the Chinese pattern of a dominating mother-in-law. In China, she said, a bride became the virtual slave of her husband's mother. Dorothy, too, had suffered from being dominated by her Scottish in-laws. She expressed bitterness when George's parents intervened in her family life and insisted on their way of doing things. Dorothy did not learn from her own experience of conflict with meddling in-laws or from what she observed in China; she repeated the same pattern.

Hugh's wife, my aunt Sirkka, told me in January 2006 that there was "a complete disconnect between Dorothy's high expectations and her own practice." A persistent trait came out in Dorothy's relationship to the Chinese, her Bible classes, and her family: "She didn't know her boundaries. She cut people down when they didn't meet her expectations; she sliced them to pieces." Deane was especially disturbed by Dorothy's inaccurate quotes and misstatements of fact, which sometimes amounted to lying: "The thing that drove me wild about Dorothy was misquotation. Sometimes she would attribute things to my children that they had not said. I felt like I would explode. Then there were times when I read what she had underlined in books of devotion and prayer and I felt guilty for being exasperated with her." My mother was caught between feeling oppressed by Dorothy's role in our family and feeling an intuition of shared spiritual kinship with her. She admired Dorothy's high ideals, aspirations, and religious devotion. Deane was deeply moved to discover this quotation that Dorothy wrote in her Bible: "A miracle is when God breaks through our despair, and something comes to us of God's power and presence." My mother told me: "I would rather have this quotation than all her silver and embroidery."

Deane said that Dorothy was at once a dragon and a saint. Although Dorothy's actions could be infuriating, it was hard to judge her because of her frequent warnings about the danger of judgmentalism. Deane was helped by a Quaker insight that if a person wounds a lot of people, she must herself have been deeply wounded. But what were Dorothy's wounds?

A story she wrote in 1958 hints at pain underlying one of her adult obsessions: the value of all things Scottish. "Mollie and Mac" was a thinly disguised account of a married couple visiting the husband's family in Scotland. The American wife is treated coldly and disdainfully by her mother-in-law, for instance when she awkwardly attempts to eat using the British method of holding silverware. Dorothy gave this story to her sons, saying: "Don't take this too seriously. I wrote it at a low moment when I was feeling sorry for myself." I wish I could reread this story, which Ian destroyed in 2005. It showed a vulnerable, wounded side of Dorothy. If I understood her other wounds, it might make me more sympathetic and forgiving. I remain appalled by her blindness to the ways she hurt others as she imposed on them her schemes of moral improvement.

* * *

OUR FAMILY WAS SITTING around the fire at 106 Winona Street one evening during a Christmas visit. Deane asked Grandfather what he remembered about his childhood. After a thoughtful silence, he said: "We used to get our feet wet when out tramping. We didn't complain." That's all this reticent Scot said. I am certain that he thought his grandchildren frightfully spoiled and wanted us to toughen up, both physically and emotionally. He grew up in a formal household on Edinburgh's Charlotte Square, where the children were cared for by servants and a governess and always on best behavior with their parents. I think the influence of his own upbringing, with its calculated indifference to children's fussiness, blocked spontaneous impulses of affection.

George as dean.

One of the very few times in my life that I saw my father angry was when he defended my brother David against George's reproach. The whole family was leaving our house in the car except for David, who had to stay home with a babysitter. He was crying, very upset at being left behind. As the car pulled away from the curb, my grandfather, sitting in the back seat with me, muttered that David was spoiled to make such a fuss. Ian slammed on the brakes, turned around in his seat, struck his father on the leg, and said fiercely: "He is not spoiled." I was amazed and proud of him. Ian immediately apologized for the blow but defended David's understandable emotional outburst. When Ian struck his father, he must have expressed anger that he had felt as a boy.

Males in the Barbour family have repeated a pattern as they criticize their own performance as fathers and compare themselves with previous generations. Ian told me that George spent very little time with his children. He did have warm memories of a summer when he was sixteen and assisted his father on a geological expedition in Colorado. In 1989, while sorting family papers, Ian found a letter George wrote to his father-in-law, RLD, in 1926. It conveys George's implicit criticism of his parents' remoteness, his unspoken affection for his father, and his sense of his own limitations as a father. Writing to his own children, Ian quotes a poignant passage of George's letter:

> To my own father I don't suppose I've ever written an affectionate paragraph in my life and still less has he to me, and yet in our letters both ways, and still more in unwritten actions, we are conscious of all kinds of shades of feeling of great depth that another reading our letters would never detect in their pages. And to a Scot it is worse than pulling teeth to mend his ways in this matter... Anyhow, we'll see whether Ian and Hugh cannot learn from the sad failure of their male parent in time to make better sons-in-law.

Ian says that this letter makes him sad and compares four generations of child-raising, including his grandchildren (Graham, Alex, and Reed):

> I think Dad did partially outgrow the Scots reserve which he inherited, and perhaps I have in turn moved a bit further, at least in recent years—though I think with me it has been more a matter of preoccupation with other things. Each of you is more in touch with your emotions and more able to express them than I have been. There is also quite a contrast in the amount of time which successive generations of parents have spent with their children. Except for vacations, my Barbour grandparents only saw their children for a short time in the living room after a governess had given them supper in the nursery upstairs. My father (and especially my mother) did a bit better than that. Deane was much more involved with you than I was. But Graham, Alex, and Reed are fortunate to see a lot more of both their parents than any previous generation in my family.

A Scot and a Dragon-Saint

Behind Ian's remarks I sense a young boy longing for his father to be more affectionate and attentive. Sometimes I have felt the same way about my father, though not often. Exactly like Ian, I wish that I had been more present to my sons, more patient, sympathetic, and insightful. I perpetuate the pattern of rueful reflection on fatherhood, acknowledging failures yet defensively claiming that although I was terribly busy, I was more involved in parenting than my father. The *mea culpas* of George, Ian, and I criticize our fathers, confess our failures as parents, and exculpate ourselves. *Qui s'excuse s'accuse.*

* * *

ONE MYSTERY ABOUT DOROTHY is why she turned out so differently than her father, Robert Dickinson. Perhaps it was the influence of her mother, Sarah Truslow, who my father said was a reserved and "perhaps moralistic" person. Sometimes traits skip a generation; maybe Ian is more like cheerful RLD and I resemble overscrupulous, fussy Dorothy. Conscience is not inherited like hair or eye color, but resembles musical or athletic potential or a sense of humor: a tendency or capacity that can find many expressions and take various forms. Dorothy may be more like RLD than is apparent, focusing on her family the reforming zeal that RLD put into his professional work. Whatever the explanation, Dorothy was a highly judgmental person who tried to mold the character of the people she loved, often in manipulative ways.

She was shaped by certain educational and idealistic movements of her era. In a 2005 letter responding to an early draft of this book, Hugh described some of these influences:

> You have tried to show the "double-bind" Dorothy put on people by pushing them to follow their own consciences and decide for themselves, and at the same time always trying to base her own conscience on reality, not rules, hoping everyone else could be brought to see the same reality. Some of this reflected her training at Columbia University Teachers College in the "project method" which taught children to solve their own problems rather than learn answers. But it also reflected the "Oxford Group" movement (later miscalled Moral Rearmament). They taught members to act on four principles: absolute honesty or truth; absolute love or kindness, absolute unselfishness, and (I forget the fourth; perhaps non-injury). They practiced a daily hour or half-hour of "Quiet Time," for reflection and/or prayer, which made people like Dorothy very "inner-directed." I suspect this is why I became a Quaker. Dorothy also learned from

Family Conscience

her school friend Lois Wilson, wife of Bill Wilson of the AA, the "twelve steps," which Bill learned from the Oxford Group and which could be applied to all personal shortcomings. She was usually alert to self-deception in herself and other people. She tried to teach me never to say something about another person until I had said it to his or her face.

The genealogy of Dorothy's solitary introspection and examination of conscience extends back through AA, the Oxford Group and Moral Re-Armament, and New England Puritans to early Christian spiritual practices. These groups are historical links between my family's Protestant roots and our contemporary semisecularized moral orientation. The Oxford Group was founded by Frank Buchman, an American Lutheran minister who was at Hartford Seminary when Dorothy taught there. Buchman promoted the missionary movement in China, and I think his influence was one of the reasons Dorothy and George pursued that work. Later Dorothy joined Moral Re-Armament, an international movement that Buchman founded in 1938 to seek peace and political reconciliation through personal moral conversion. The Oxford Group also influenced Dorothy via the twelve-step program of Alcoholics Anonymous. Lois Wilson, the wife of founder "Bill W," was one of Dorothy's closest friends. Bill and Lois lived on Clinton Street in Brooklyn, two doors from Dorothy's childhood home.

The Oxford Group, Moral Rearmament, and Alcoholics Anonymous shaped Dorothy's outlook in their common emphasis on scrupulous self-examination, moral reform, and inspiring others through personal example. These movements, like the Barbour family conscience, had Christian roots but broadened the message to apply more generally, for instance making room for "God as you understand Him," as the AA program puts it. They all asserted that to change the world, one must first change oneself, and the motivation to do this comes from a searching "moral inventory" of one's life during a daily "quiet time."

I encountered this historical pattern—Protestant moral fervor shaping what became secular institutions and perspectives—at Mount Hermon School in Massachusetts, where I graduated from high school in 1969. The school was founded by evangelist Dwight L. Moody. We sang a stirring hymn with words by William Blake, vowing to build the new Jerusalem with our Bow of burning gold, arrows of desire, and Chariot of fire. Mount Hermon required chapel attendance and a mandatory work program and had a greater commitment to economic and racial diversity than most New England private schools. The religious influence was waning, and chapel and the work program ended soon after I left the school. Still, I absorbed a certain kind of moral idealism. When I chose the quotation that would appear in my high school yearbook, I selected this one by "Channing": "The great hope of society is individual character." I had never heard of William Ellery Channing, a nineteenth-century Unitarian preacher, but I liked this line under another boy's photo in a previous yearbook. It greatly appealed to my latent idealism, so similar to Dorothy's, but without explicit Christian grounding.

I've learned the limitations of this optimistic hope. Reinhold Niebuhr scathingly criticized Frank Buchman's philosophy, especially his effort to convert politicians, powerful industrialists, and Nazi leaders:

> Now we can see how unbelievably naïve this movement is in its efforts to save the world. If it would content itself with preaching repentance to drunkards and adulterers one might be willing to respect it as a religious revival method which knows how to confront the sinner with God. But when it runs to Geneva, the seat of the League of Nations, or to Prince Starhemberg or Hitler, or to any seat of power, always with the idea that it is on the verge of saving the world by bringing the people who control the world under God-control, it is difficult to restrain the contempt which one feels for this dangerous childishness.[7]

My choice of a yearbook quote now strikes me as wishful thinking. I wanted to make the world better by being a good guy, through individual virtue rather than the demanding work of political advocacy and social reform. Dorothy, in contrast, was actively engaged in certain political causes, especially pacifist ones. Yet even there, her greatest passion and hope was for conversions that change moral character.

* * *

DOROTHY THOUGHT THAT ANGER should be contained and suppressed because it is unloving and not the Christian way. George was less didactic about this, but his stoical Scottish ideals and Calvinist context also emphasized strict self-control. A revealing story in George's biography of Freeland illustrates the family's attitude to the expression of emotion and even sharp pain:

> At the excellent Lotspeich School in Cincinnati, as in kindergarten in China, Freeland found himself among strangers. But he learned early to "consume his own smoke." Having been

---

7. Reinhold Niebuhr, *Christianity and Power Politics* (New York: Scribner, 1948), 160–61.

Family Conscience

forbidden to use his coaster-wagon on a steep drive beside his home, he received little sympathy when he came back crying after an upset. He soon quieted, but next morning his mother noticed that he wasn't using one arm. An X-ray showed that it was broken. "Didn't that hurt?" "Yes, a lot. But you told me I must learn not to make a fuss."[8]

That is a horrifying image: a child on fire trying to swallow "his own smoke." Ian thought that the source of this metaphor was Dorothy. While George seems proud of his son's toughness, for me this story is a disturbing illustration of how my grandparents could deny unacceptable emotions. My father expressed joy, enthusiasm, and affection, and in his later years he cried when deeply moved. He rarely showed sadness, anger, envy, or any emotion that might indicate weakness of character. If he ever felt those emotions, he didn't "make a fuss."

* * *

I MUST HAVE BEEN about eight. While my parents were out of town for a night, my grandparents were staying with the children. I had to get up to pee, perhaps more than once. Awakened, Grandmother sprang into action. She told me firmly that this was quite enough disruption; I should not need to go to the bathroom again. I got back into bed and immediately began worrying that I would have to go again. But Grandmier said I can't! I became desperate. What to do? After lying in bed for what seemed like most of the night and was likely half an hour, I stealthily closed my bedroom door and urinated in my metal trash can. The sound of my pee on the side of the metal container was thunderous, deafening. If she woke up, I would be mortified. Then the house was still. It was a beautiful waste container: on the outside was a gorgeous map of the world, with the oceans a jaunty shade of blue. Dorothy just wanted to improve my self-control, I'm sure, but I've never forgiven her for disciplining me in this way. My trash can was never the same. It began to rust on the inside.

* * *

ANOTHER DOROTHY REMINDS ME of my grandmother. In George Eliot's *Middlemarch*, the idealistic and stubborn heroine, Dorothea Brooke, wants to change her society and longs for intellectual challenges and a religious mission. Her more practical sister, Celia, tells her: "You always see what nobody else sees; it is impossible to satisfy you; yet you never see what is quite plain. That's your way, Dodo."[9] Although Dorothea makes many mistakes,

---

8. George B. Barbour, *"Free"* (Assen, Netherlands: Royal VanGorcum, 1954), 6.
9. George Eliot, *Middlemarch*, Penguin Classics (London, Penguin, 1994), 36.

her heart is in the right place and her unhappiness and lack of success are due not only to her naivete and obstinacy but also to her society's limitations, especially its constrictive roles for women. I have read *Middlemarch* about eight times and am always fascinated by and engaged with Dorothea's character, partly because my grandmother had a similarly complicated mixture of earnestness, arrogance, narrow vision, and high-minded aspiration.

A letter from Dorothy to George in 1936 reveals her combination of blindness and insight. She tells her husband about am astute remark made by Ian, then thirteen. Dorothy had reprimanded Hugh for "grousing." According to Dorothy, Ian said: "You didn't lose your temper and you were right, but you didn't give him the feeling that you saw his point of view." She goes on: "Just what you [George] said the other day. And yet they love us and with what cause." To her credit, Dorothy recognizes and admits her fault in this situation. She was often right, morally speaking, but there were other dimensions of a situation that she didn't notice, and she sometimes lacked imagination and empathy with other people's perspectives.

* * *

IN CHINA MY GRANDFATHER'S spirit visited me. In December 2001, I was on an overnight train between Taiwan and Beijing with my wife, two sons, and twenty-seven students from St. Olaf College. During the night I had the only dream of my grandfather that I remembered and wrote down. In the dream I am a grown man and he is very old and much smaller. He slumps forward and weeps as I hold and comfort him. No words pass between us, but I feel close to him, intimate for the first and only time. Waking up, I wondered why I had this dream. Although I hadn't been thinking of Grandfather the previous day, the journey through China seemed significant for understanding my family. On George's geology expeditions, he traveled thousands of miles by "virtually every mode of travel—river steamer, sampan, aeroplane, horse- and donkey-back, rickshaw, sedan chair, truck, bus, model-T Ford, Peking cart, even coolie-back," as he put it in a letter. When I dreamed of my grandfather, I think the train was passing over some spot where he had camped or prayed or formed a resolution.

I never understood or felt close to George, who was silent and reserved in family gatherings, especially after a series of strokes slowed him down. In the dream I felt strong affection for him and expressed it in a hug rather than words. I don't know what grief or pain he suffered, and I didn't feel sorry for him when he was alive. Once, when I was in church with him, I was surprised to see him weeping silently as we sang a hymn; I wish I knew which one it was. Forty years later, his reticence and tears found their way into my dream on the Chinese train.

Family Conscience

George describes in *In China When . . .* how he could not put into words his feelings of awe at a Japanese place of worship: "I find myself often moved inexplicably by things and haven't the power to find words for it. In fact, I find myself most helped by the experience if I am not obliged to betray it, even at times to myself. So much vanishes like the fairies when you become self-conscious about it."[10] This professor, scholar, and university dean did not trust the power of words to convey the deepest things, such as elusive spiritual intuitions. I feel similarly about explaining my train-rocked dream/vision of my grandfather and that moment of empathy with him.

* * *

FAMILY HISTORY WAS ONE of Dorothy's favorite topics. She praised her in-laws, the Barbour family, even more than the Dickinsons. One strand of Barbour ancestry could be traced back through the Stewart royal line to Robert the Bruce, King of Scotland. "Just think," I told Blair, "Since I am the oldest, I would have been a king!" I think the lesson Dorothy intended was *noblesse oblige*: children of illustrious ancestry have a responsibility to others. But this message got mixed up with what seemed to me bragging, and I bristled when she spoke of the Barbour clan. In a letter to me after George's death in 1977, Ian said, regarding pride in the Barbour family: "GBB could combine it with humility and sensitivity, but DDB has always been insecure enough in it that she labors to preserve it." Feeling anxious about her acceptability to her in-laws, Dorothy tried to be more Scottish than the Scots. At a Christmas gathering in the 1970s, Meg's mother, Peggy, wore a plaid skirt. Dorothy asked her if she knew what clan's tartan she was wearing. She said that in Scotland if a person were caught wearing a tartan when she was not a member of the clan, it would have been torn away from her. Peggy had the grace to respond with wide-eyed surprise and curious interest, but she must have wondered whether Dorothy was about to expose her before all eyes for her crime against Scottish clan rules.

What did it mean to be Scottish? Anything more than bagpipes, shortbread, kilts, and a charming accent? There had to be some deeper meaning. Why did old people feel this superstitious reverence for the past, for the ways of their ancestors? I puzzled over this feeling of belonging to a place, a particular chunk of land: Edinburgh, where George grew up, or Fincastle, where Barbour cousins still live today. I was supposed to cherish this heritage, but I didn't know why. My sense of obligation to Scottish roots felt like

---

10. George B. Barbour, *In China When . . .* (Cincinnati: University of Cincinnati Publications, 1975), 158.

an onerous duty. Like a nagging conscience, where ghosts live on, demanding pious loyalty. If I don't serve them, there will be trouble.

I went to the University of Aberdeen for my junior year in college. During that entire year I didn't visit my many Scottish cousins, except for Robin Barbour's family, who lived right in Aberdeen. I didn't go to Fincastle and Bonskeid, the ancient family home in Perthshire. I wanted to claim a Scottish inheritance, but I had to find it in my own way. I played rugby and hiked in the Cairngorm Mountains and the Isle of Skye. I bolted down abominable Scottish food and learned to relish curry. I got my feet wet and didn't complain, following George's example. The place entered into me and I love it, especially the people, Celtic music, and hiking in glens and mountains. I've led several walking tours of Scotland's Highlands and islands for St Olaf College alumni programs.

How did this land and culture influence my conscience? Perhaps my stinginess goes back to Scottish traditions of thrift and stewardship. My work ethic, constant self-scrutiny, or obsessiveness may bear the imprint of Calvinist ancestors. Scotland's influence may be so deep and pervasive that I can't see it distinctly. Responding to my question, an Italian or Jew might roll their eyes or laugh at my blindness to what is obvious to them.

* * *

ONE OF THE WAYS that Dorothy burdened her daughters-in-law and grandchildren was through her intense concern that we appreciate the gifts she gave us, especially family heirlooms. My mother's letters to Dorothy are full of gushing praise of toys and books given to grandchildren, and for financial and other gifts to Ian and Deane. Thank-you letters to Grandmier were very important as I grew up. Yet my sense of obligation and my resentments got in the way of spontaneous appreciation. She was generous, but I was not grateful.

Dorothy passed on material objects to us with ritual solemnity. She gave heirlooms from the Scottish clan and art objects acquired in China, always with a careful explanation, usually in writing, of the piece's origin. Several times she presented her young grandchildren with a present that mystified us: tiny white packets of sugar, salt, and pepper that came with airplane meals. We held the fragile packages carefully, trying not to giggle. I associate this scene with her telling us that in China her children only had one orange a year, received in their stockings on Christmas morning. I felt slightly guilty enjoying a banana for breakfast on an unhallowed day. Later I would laugh with my siblings and mother, amused at the way Grandmier could wring a lesson from any occasion. What may have been a whimsical gesture felt like a heavy but ridiculous sermon.

Family Conscience

Many years later, after George's funeral, Dorothy distributed his clothes. I was given a formal three-piece suit, very dark and dignified. Dorothy warned me sternly that this was not a suit to be worn on any ordinary occasion. I assured her that I would take good care of it. But her anxiety was not alleviated. She tried to think of a suitable occasion on which I could wear George's suit, and finally advised me: "This suit would best be worn when you are addressing the university Senate." I smiled politely. When I went back to my lowly position as a part-time lecturer at the University of Chicago, I wore the jacket several times without a tie or the vest or pants. It felt odd, teaching in this somber and unstylish coat worn over casual clothes. My long arms poked far out of the sleeves. The suit was an inheritance I tried to make my own, but it didn't fit. I don't remember giving it away, but now it's gone. Maybe moths ate into it as it hung in the closet.

* * *

IN DOROTHY'S LETTERS TO me, two ethical concerns stand out: her view of conscientious objection and her hope that I will feel a sense of responsibility to carry on family traditions. She supported my application to be a conscientious objector during the Vietnam War and tried to influence my ethical stance. Her liberal Protestant zeal and missionary idealism had some qualities in common with the 1960s peace and civil rights movements. Yet Dorothy worried about whether my generation was sufficiently grounded in Christian values. In July 1969, she wrote that she hoped that my father "hasn't been too modest or too nondirective to tell you some of his thinking." Dorothy was not only against the Vietnam War, but all war. "And I'm *for* what is incompatible with war." She was for the way of Jesus, "the only way that works." Rather than simply protesting, Christians should make a constructive difference in the world. In March 1970, she asserted her belief "in working for alternatives when things are wrong rather than against the wrong." She wanted to be assured not only that my conscience told me what to do about the issue of military service in the Vietnam War, but especially that my conscience was formed by Christian faith: "Yes, 'my conscience, my choice,' but a conscience whose values are those of Jesus." Dorothy was saying that conscience is not simply a matter of individual choice, for it should testify to a truth outside itself. Conscience should not just reflect one's values but be accountable to a standard that comes from God. I share her aspiration, but usually not her certainty and confidence about knowing God's will.

Dorothy set a burden on my conscience: she wanted me to carry on family traditions and to care about my inheritance. In 1971, she and George went through large collections of letters, papers, and photographs as they prepared to move from their home into a retirement community. She sent me some documents, including two nineteenth-century photographs of a gentleman named John Barbour, one of several Scots who bore that name. More than material things, she wanted to bequeath to me a moral tradition. While I was living in Scotland, she wrote: "Youth tends to discard the past and age to cling to it. But neither is good enough. It is bad to continue the past but sound progress demands knowledge of what one is building with and on. I'm glad you are seeing there some of the magnificent past which is yours to carry forward and make even better."

When the bulk of family letters and pictures went to Hugh's house, Dorothy wrote to tell me that these things belong as much to my family as to Hugh's. "And I very much hope that as the oldest grandson and as having some interest in 'roots' you will have some of all this under your roof as soon as you have a roof—perhaps all of it, since only you and Free carry on the name of the Charlotte Square [Edinburgh] part of the family." (She was wrong about this, for all five of her granddaughters continue to bear the name Barbour.) Now, five decades later, I have a roof but no desire or room to store the forty or so boxes of family records that Hugh saved. One of his daughters stores these archives and slowly sorts through documents. How much of this stuff will be passed on to her children and mine? How many mementos and documents of family history will they inherit? My children are interested in their grandparents, but I don't expect them to keep boxes of letters by their great-grandparents or George's publications in geological journals. Yet how sad I feel as I begin to sort these things and throw some of them in the trash.

Do those who bear the family name have a special obligation to preserve family history? (What would Dorothy make of my sons' hyphenated name?) No one believes any longer in the rules of primogeniture: the special responsibility of the eldest son to carry on family values, once connected to the right to inherit property. Whatever moral burden I carry is shared equally with Dorothy's other six grandchildren. How much of my grandparents' stuff, or my parents' things or my own, should I pass on to later generations? What values shape the winnowing process that must take place if we are not to become museum curators overwhelmed with the detritus of our ancestors? Sorting these old documents seems a metaphor for what must be done for inherited moral traditions and values.

For a long time, I avoided learning about my family's history and dodged opportunities to know Dorothy better. Now I regret this. In her letters, Grandmother repeatedly requested that I come down from Oberlin College to Cincinnati for a visit. She begged me to stay for a weekend and

Family Conscience

have "a real talk." I never went. Some ephemeral social engagement with my peers was always more enticing, week after week. I couldn't face Dorothy the dragon-saint, with her demanding personality, unapologetic forthrightness, and moral challenges.

What would she make of this writing project? Would she recognize it as an expression of family conscience, see it as an indictment of the family, or think it much ado about nothing in comparison with more significant ethical issues? In a game of Charades one Christmas, George selected for Dorothy to act out the Shakespearean phrase "much ado about nothing." I think this was a sly reference to some passing anxiety of the day, and I'm sure he meant his teasing as a gentle ribbing. It may convey a deeper truth, too. Perhaps all our bother and fuss about family—hers and mine—is what the Scots call kerfuffle. Sometimes the fretting of conscience is busy distraction from something we don't want to face.

* * *

IT IS EASIER TO appreciate her now. The sharp edges of her character, convictions, and moral passions add something important to the live-and-let-live ethos I am part of. At her funeral, several people said something like this remark I noted in my journal after that event: "She got you to do things you never thought you would do, but that needed to be done." Dorothy reminds me of several earnest people I have known on church and college committees, conscientious and hardworking souls who do thankless essential work.

I tried to love Grandmier, but an undeniable feeling of resentment got in the way. I disliked her obsession with the family and her judgmental nature. Yet here I am, carrying on her legacy in those two ways. As I trace the roots of my family's values, I see in Dorothy certain traits that shaped my character and conscience. Like her, I want the next generation to build on the past; I hope my sons are thoughtful as they sift and sort through family traditions and values. That I dislike Dorothy's judgmental nature reflects ambivalence about my own conscience. Like her, I often assess others and myself in ethical terms even when another kind of response—emotional, aesthetic, humorous, or spiritual—might be more appropriate. I have an uneasy conscience about having an overdeveloped, fussy conscience! Scruples about being overscrupulous! I wish my middle name would bring me the qualities of RLD (or, more helpful for a writer, of Emily Dickinson). But Dorothy Dickinson, my shadow self, flawed agent of virtue, is deep in my bones, always wanting to extract from life experience a lesson that will improve moral character, and always judging. As much as my mother's father, Everett, Dorothy is a dangerous ancestor who leaves an ambiguous legacy.

Chapter 5

Finding Them in the Archives

As I read through several large archives of letters and documents during the past several years, I came to a new perspective on George and Dorothy. These two individuals, who seemed to me so reserved, stiff, and moralistic, appear very different in their early correspondence. Their written record helps me understand their individual personalities and the larger historical forces and cultural influences that shaped their and my own versions of the family conscience.

In addition to books by George and Dorothy, unpublished memoirs, and the various genres mentioned at the start of the previous chapter, they wrote thousands of letters and documents now in archives. In the Yale Divinity School Library's Day Missions collection, the largest archive of missionary records in the world, Barbour correspondence fills seven boxes and requires three and a half linear feet of shelf space. At the Imperial War Museum in London, I explored George's World War I diaries, letters, and photographs. The University of Cincinnati archives store the records and correspondence related to George's work as professor and dean of the College from 1937 to 1960, thirty-eight boxes taking twenty-two linear feet to shelve. This cache houses a surprising amount of personal material, beginning with a letter from an aunt taking care of George as an infant, which refers to her charge as "His Majesty Bimbo"! And there are still other collections I didn't consult, such as records of George's geological work at the Smithsonian Institution, the University of Wisconsin, and the Leakey Foundation, and his correspondence with Teilhard de Chardin, copies of which were donated to several universities. I don't know how my grandparents had time to do anything else but write.

Family Conscience

I won't describe all the twists and turns of their lives, fascinating as they are, but only how their correspondence reveals aspects of the family conscience as I understand it. I focus on four topics: George's World War I experience, the couple's long epistolary courtship, their shared search for vocation, and their decade in China.

When the First World War erupted, George was studying several fields of science at St. John's College at Cambridge University. In a letter to his father on August 22, 1914, George expresses uncertainty about what to do, given his ethical doubts:

> It is hard to see how much one needs to justify the war to oneself: I am not called on to fight and don't think that is merely a veiled form of moral cowardice: but I shall be ready to do ambulance or clerical work if needed, otherwise I shall go back to work in October unless things are too unsettled for all ordinary work to go on. One feels it is criminal that so many people are giving up their ordinary work for the more exciting occupations of war; especially is this true in the case of the doctors and nurses . . . so that there are only two residents left in the Glasgow Western infirmary. The excitement of it makes them lose all sense of proportion . . . I don't see that one is called on to justify war: it is bound to be unchristian to fight thus and Christ never hinted at war as being necessary to gain anything at any time.

Although George sees the German attack on Belgium as wrong, he "would like to see the German point of view of the war before condemning this apparently unprovoked attack." I think his cautiousness about judging the Germans reflects sympathy for the nation in which he had spent his sixteenth year, in Marburg studying languages and playing the organ. Unlike most of his friends, George did not enroll in the military. Unable to justify the war, but feeling the call of duty, in September he joined the Friends Ambulance Unit, which was sent in November to the Ypres front in Belgium.

There George drove his own Renault automobile, retrofitted with strong springs and a cavass top to function as an ambulance. His war diaries are a harrowing account of his service, sometimes driving at night without lights over muddy and cratered roads as shells exploded a few seconds ahead of or behind the vehicle's route. He was often exhausted: "You can't really go to bed with 900 wounded untended at the station, and all need dressing." Terrifying detonations launched by "Big Bertha" artillery made sleep impossible. In May 1915, he described a predictable pattern of bombardment: "one hour's vision of hell, undilute, and always on Sunday afternoon." He tended gruesomely maimed and dying soldiers. In April,

George witnessed the horrific results of the first poison gas attack: "The moral effect on the asphyxiated soldiers is extraordinary. Altogether it's most damnable . . Oh God, if it has to come, blast the devils off the earth in the quickest way possible." He participated in frantic investigations of the gas's unknown chemical composition, which turned out to be a form of chlorine. In August 1915, George volunteered to help the Italians, who had joined as Britain's ally and were short of ambulances. For the next two years he served as Quartermaster of the First British Ambulance Corps in Italy. In one busy two-day period he carried 652 patients, driving winding mountain roads from 6:00 a.m. until ten thirty at night "through continuous bombardment." An outbreak of cholera added to the miseries of the wounded, many of whom died on the way to hospital.

In 1917, George decided to leave his noncombatant role and enlist in the military as an artillery officer. This is an unusual change of views about the morality of war; usually exposure to the horrors of the modern battlefield moves men in the opposite direction. Half a century later, in "Memories of Three Continents," George reconstructs his decision: "Letters from home spoke of the death of cousins and the majority of the students I had known in my Cambridge days. I felt it my duty to face the kind of things Ian Bartholomew and Robert Whyte had been meeting to protect the homeland we loved. I wrote my family that, though it would hurt them, I would not continue to live a sheltered life but would go back to London to enlist."[1] A sheltered life!

George in officer's uniform, 1917.

1. George B. Barbour, "Memories of Three Continents," unpublished manuscript, 62–63.

Family Conscience

George's mother was a pacifist, as was Dorothy, and I sense underlying tensions in his correspondence with them about the morality of war. He had been thinking about this issue for some time; in November 1914 he wrote to his father about the contrast between his work in the ambulance corps—"much needed, with greater hardship, more exciting and interesting"—and a "more direct helping of one's country" by military service. Even though he admired the Friends' (Quakers') international outlook, he asserted that "though in one sense all men are brothers, patriotism is a real and distinct thing . . . It is everyone's duty to take their share of the beastliness. But perhaps ideals aren't any good in the army!" Having witnessed first-hand the war's brutal conditions, he was skeptical of high-minded moral rhetoric and arguments either for or against it.

George went back to England in July 1917 to join an artillery regiment and eventually became a lieutenant. He spent the next year training for this new role and arrived at the Italian front a week before the armistice was signed in November 1918. His letters express frustration that his long preparation was never put to use. Yet he was also relieved. In his memoir, he says: "I never pulled the lanyard to fire a gun that killed a single human being."

George was traumatized by the war and afterwards went through a period of "shell shock" or posttraumatic stress, according to Hugh, who also asserted that George suffered from survivor guilt. A quarter of his university class died, including his best friend, and many others were severely wounded. In a 2007 letter, Hugh said that his father "seemed to Dorothy to be emotionally drained and depressed" compared to the man she had known before the war.

George's relationship with Dorothy deepened during the war as their friendship turned into epistolary courtship and love. The letters between them reveal a growing bond as they challenge each other, express affection, and discuss crucial moral concerns and George's uncertainty about a future vocation. The couple had spent hardly any time together; they met in August 1911, when as a graduation present George's father gave him a trip around the world. He was twenty, Dorothy eighteen. They looked forward to meeting in Scotland in August 1914, when Dorothy was in Switzerland with her family, but when war broke out, the plan fell through. Correspondence alone sustained their relationship for eight years. Their letters increase in frequency, candor, and intimacy and reveal a growing bond based on their discovery of shared values and commitments that would shape their lives.

As they earnestly debated religious and moral ideals, the couple came to trust and admire each other. Early in the war, in January 1915, Dorothy thanks George for sharing his convictions: "Sometimes I suspect it's 'small talk' that needs apology." George should not be ashamed of how he spent the four years since they met, nor "lament decisions conscientiously made, even if later knowledge shows them mistaken." Coming to a similar understanding of conscience—including its difficulties—was a crucial aspect of their growing bond. Even as Dorothy reassures George that he can take comfort because he tried to do the right thing, she confesses her own unhappiness, "being a person prone to be very miserable because of the capacity to see just sixty seconds too late the thing I should have said or left unsaid—or done." To help deal with regret, Dorothy has "worked out a theory" that by thinking about the past she will learn from experience. Yet she also aspires to "leave the past with God" and turn to the present: "Christ's 'Go, and sin no more' implied a new beginning." As she struggles with guilt and remorse, she hopes that in time she will understand her actions differently and be able to forgive herself in light of "what even a perfect person could have done under certain circumstances. But meantime, even afterwards, it's no joke, is it?" Regret, guilt, and remorse were painful ordeals for Dorothy and George, and each felt that the other understood and sympathized.

Dorothy not only examines her conscience and theorizes about it, but questions how much she should do these things, and to what end. Then she apologizes for "sermonizing." She resolves to "be less serious minded" but signs off as "incorrigibly serious." In a postscript, she confesses that she has had "too much experience on the subject of losing one's self respect, to be less than serious when the subject comes up." With her back-and-forth shifts between earnestness and a lighter mood, Dorothy tests whether George understands her struggle to be a good Christian and self-inflicted ordeals of conscience. She admits to her brooding and self-tormenting introspection and then displays brisk, chipper self-confidence. Much later, in a 1934 letter, Dorothy described something she admired about her husband: his concern for others showed "a mind at leisure from itself." George didn't agonize or get distracted from the needs of others by questions about his own virtue or integrity. I see in Dorothy's ruminations my own tendency to subject the operations of conscience to withering scrutiny and to veer off into theories about conscience. I empathize with her desire to find someone who understands all this and loves her, nonetheless.

George's relationship to Dorothy sustained him during four-and-a-half years of military service. At moments when he despaired, it kept him going. In December 1915, writing from the Italian front, he recalls his visit to her family's cottage on Long Island as "a single prolonged day of sunshine." He confesses his doubts about the purposes of the war and his own sense of inadequacy. A striking difference between these two is Dorothy's steady and certain conviction that she is following God's will. In contrast,

Family Conscience

George writes in February 1917 that he doesn't consciously seek to do God's will:

> I feel in a way as if I must be a most awful hypocrite to be able to give you the impression that I am animated by high ideals and that I accept God's guidance in the complete way that you are able to: I didn't seek God's guidance enough at any point and wasn't clearly conscious that I was doing His will. To be abominably frank to you D2 [one of George's nicknames for her], I feel as if I had just gone the pleasantest way, although at no point have I felt that I was acting wrongly; so it is really no credit to me that I am doing this job, but I seem fairly well fit for it . . . Although I feel now it is God's will, it isn't thanks to my own power that I am doing it, but the trust of my friends is a heartening thing and I am glad you wrote.

George expresses confidence that God is guiding his life despite his limitations, as if he were being "used." He had an Augustinian sense that God is providentially involved both in individual lives and the overall course of history, working through humans' limited agency, knowledge, and goodness. But he was much more cautious than Dorothy about claiming to know, at a moment of decision, that he was doing God's will. In October 1918 he tells Dorothy: "I'm glad you think as you do about the war. I wish my spirit were as noble and that duty was as clear."

Much later, George expressed in a humorous way his detached perspective on Dorothy's certainty that she was doing God's will. In their 1954 Christmas letter, he described Dorothy's work on committees of the World Council of Churches. There was a discussion of the idea that every person's job offers opportunities to make clear to others what Jesus taught in The Sermon on the Mount. George comments: "Quoth Dorothy with due solemnity, 'Every minute and every cent belong to God. When one takes a vacation or buys a hat, it must be because one believes it is what He wants done.' Said a friend after the meeting: 'My dear, I think God wants you to buy a new hat.' On the way home, Dorothy did!" I think George mentioned this incident with fond amusement and loving tolerance, but it suggests the absurdity of believing that everything one does is what God wants—and the temptation to self-deception inherent in this belief.

In contrast to Dorothy, George was skeptical that God was guiding the Allied war effort. As the war drew to its close, his disillusionment and exhaustion are evident, even in carefully composed trans-Atlantic correspondence that might be shared. He writes to Dorothy's mother, Sarah Truslow Dickinson (whom he addressed as "Aunt Sarah," as if a family member), "I wish I could live up to the view Dorothy has of this war... But sometimes at close quarters it [the ideal] doesn't lead to a course of action that tallies with the particular facts. It would be hypocrite's clothing for one who has not the character or life to support it." Sometimes the Christian admonition to love one's enemies just isn't possible: "It is hard to tell a man he has no right to curse his enemies when he has just lost four of his best friends and two relatives within six hours. This war has sides of it that come as near hell as anything one ever wants to see."

Dorothy's fervent faith and ethical integrity were a large part of her appeal to George. He formulates a striking image of her in a letter of May 1919, when, now candid about his love, he describes her using an image from a devastated cathedral in Belgium: "Your white-hot purity (not cold and snow-like), your fine sensitiveness and your dauntless courage stood revealed standing clear of the dross, like a white marble statue that stood untouched in the centre of the debris of Ypres Cathedral." Her moral confidence and idealism inspired him through the war and its aftermath when he lost faith in everything else. She became the center, or rather the central symbol, of his religious faith: "To a real man it is given as a reward, to worship his ideal." This reverence for a female icon of purity and goodness in a darkening and brutal world resembles many European and American idealizations of a woman, for instance Kurtz's view of his "Intended" in Joseph Conrad's *Heart of Darkness*. For Dorothy, too, loving a future spouse was inextricably bound up with religious faith. Writing to her parents in July 1919, she says: "I love him most for his deep Christlikeness—in prayer, conscientiousness, and the observant helpfulness we've come to call Georgian."

As the end of the conflict neared, even before they became formally engaged, they began to discuss the future together. They collaborated to discern a satisfying vocation for George to pursue. George was completely uncertain about his future when, at age twenty-eight, the war ended. He felt inadequate and ashamed that he had failed his comrades, as he confessed in December 1918:

> The truth is that the war has tried me and found me wanting; it's rather a bitter story of compromise and you will not understand how anyone could think along such lines and still hope to be a Christian. It's an awful thing to say, but much of the thankfulness one would have felt at the Declaration of Peace at an earlier date is obscured by the feeling of degradation at having failed to see one's duty in time, and at present I feel as if I shall feel ashamed until the day I die at not having arrived in time to do my share.

Family Conscience

He lacked self-confidence, ambition, and a sense of purpose. Discussion of what he might do to satisfy his longing for a meaningful vocation is the central topic in the letters of late 1918 and 1919, foreshadowing one of the main preoccupations of family conscience as I have known it. To Dorothy's inquiry about his plans, he appeals: "I have none. I wish I did. If you can help—." He cannot rest without knowing what to do with the rest of his life: "I want to go somewhere wild and smoke a pipe for months on end. And yet I know I would be vilely dissatisfied. My mind will never know real peace until I've found my work."

In response, Dorothy encourages him to become a teacher. Or he might get involved in land development in Canada or Australia or find a form of service in China. "I'm glad you're not a lawyer! Or a banker!" George was reluctant to go back to graduate school in one of the sciences. After only introductory work in three different sciences during his two years at Cambridge, by this time five weary years past, he would have to start over. He would finish at thirty-four or thirty-five and be competing against men a decade younger with longer training. Geology appealed to him, but there were few teaching opportunities. Although he could get a scholarship funded by an oil company, he balked: "You wouldn't want me to take up oil, would you?" He ponders a bleak and depressing future: "Now has come this old war and one is landed with a variety of interests and no specialist knowledge or qualification."

At a loss for what to do, George received a life-changing letter: "Just as I was casting around for what work I should lay my hand to and just when there was little or nothing on the horizon a letter came from John R. Mott inviting me to the US for six months to a year to do YMCA work either in the schools, colleges, or at New York headquarters." Mott was a prominent evangelist and the leader of the YMCA and the World Christian Student Federation; he won the Nobel Peace Prize in 1946. He inspired countless idealistic young people to become missionaries. This was the vocational choice made by many of the brightest, most energetic, and adventurous young people at this time, like the Peace Corps several decades later. In 1900 Mott wrote *The Evangelization of the World in This Generation*, which the 1910 World Missionary Conference in Edinburgh adopted as its slogan and goal. George may have attended this conference in his home city; he would certainly have known much about it, for his father was active in endeavors to support Christian missions.

During the summer of 1919, George and Dorothy decided to become missionaries in China. Their understanding of mission work was not evangelization; what they wanted most was to teach. Their falling in love and marriage coincided with the resolution of George's vocational crisis—and

Dorothy's. Discussing her future, she says she is "back on my old hobby horse: religious education in its broadest sense, as the answer to most problems." Dorothy had a strong background in the newly emerging field of Religious Education. She earned a master's degree in this field at Union Theological Seminary and completed all but one course credit for her PhD at Columbia. She had been a religious-education director at an Episcopal church in Rochester, New York, and according to Hugh was fired when conservatives objected to her emphasis on the Social Gospel. She was one of the first women on the faculty of Hartford Theological Seminary. Her sister, Jean, was already planning to become a missionary and teacher in China and would arrive in Beijing a few months before George and Dorothy.

In April 1919, George crossed the Atlantic to work for the YMCA. He and Dorothy must have immediately fallen into each other's arms (or something more decorous), because their letters suddenly become openly affectionate. George used a charming collection of greetings in his letters: Baby Mine, Dearest Heart, Childie Darling. (Later, writing to her in China when he was traveling: Woman of My Heart, Dearest Lassie, Lover so Dear, Delight of my Dreaming, and more.) George enrolled in courses at Columbia, where he eventually earned his PhD, based on fieldwork in China. George's family memoir depicts a dramatic moment of recognition while they were both visiting family friends in New Jersey: "It must have been a night in July that a terrific thunderstorm right overhead made sleep out of the question and we came down to the living room in wrappers. I was trying to offset the noise with a Brahms Intermezzo on the piano, when we saw in a particularly brilliant flash that we two were meant for each other; a physicist might have said that two spirits fused." A few of the letters in the Cincinnati archive lack an envelope or identifying address and are hastily scrawled. I think these furtive avowals of love were passed under doors while they were visiting friends, such as at the time of this incident. They wrote letters "for public consumption" to be shared with family members and added postscripts meant only for each other. George's cheerful agreement to this plan suggests quite a discrepancy between the public version and what he acknowledges to her alone: "P. S. All right! I shall keep the Postscripts for news not for general publication—and straightway cancel all the rubbish in the main part of the letter."

Family Conscience

Dorothy.

Dorothy's scruples and relentless analysis apparently made some forms of intimacy difficult for her. She wrote to her Aunt Emma that she was worried about her responses to George: "I sat on all my feelings for years, but now I find myself unable to get up from the sitting." Aunt Emma reassured her niece, encouraged her to allow more intimacy, and said other feelings would come in time. When Dorothy was alarmed by some of his letters, George advises: "Do not analyze so much. Overconscientiousness destroys the spontaneity of the Christian life, which should be its peculiar hallmark." They express in guarded ways sexual longing and frustration and try to reconcile passion with the propriety expected of their social class. Dorothy says to her mother that although "I'm in imminent danger of being swept off my feet, there's no question of me being a proper engaged girl." She had been "positive I would never love because I knew Father" and could not settle for second best. Now she is relieved: "Somehow I admire Father more than ever!"

How intensely they idealized and revered each other! Dorothy told her mother: "Love of God and love of George have gotten hopelessly mixed up. I've given up trying to disentangle them, since each grows into the other." Their supremely high estimation of each other's goodness made them each feel unworthy and afraid that they would fail to live up to expectations. George's high standard also inspired Dorothy: "Since I'm not all the wise things you think, the only honest thing would be to try and to pray desperately to become them, for I'd hate to have you change your mind." An unusual undated note with no place indicated (so I surmise they were staying in the same place): "George, dear, how can you think such things about me? —But please don't stop." This quasi-religious idealization of one's spouse is a very lofty standard for a marriage; it sets a high bar that to their descendants seems unattainable or unrealistic. Yet I also admire their example and that of my parents. Having had several long-distance relationships that involved a lot of letter-writing or emailing, I've learned how projection and idealization can complicate one's knowledge of a partner. But for George and Dorothy, a long epistolary courtship laid the foundation for a lifetime of love and commitment.

George and Dorothy were typical products of their upper-middle-class, liberal Protestant, and well-educated background. What's most intriguing to me in relation to family conscience is how shared moral scruples and concerns drew them together and shaped their lives during the trials of prolonged separation, war, courtship, and vocational uncertainty and decision.

* * *

SOON AFTER THEIR WEDDING on May 15, 1920, George and Dorothy departed for China. Arriving in Peking in January 1921, they took up their work at Yenching University, George as professor of geology and Dorothy as professor of religious education. They were affiliated with the London Missionary Society (LMS). The 1920s were the high-water mark of missionary outreach to China. In 1926, there were 8,325 missionaries serving there, representing a wide range of theological beliefs, practical skills, and knowledge about China.[2]

George's application to the LMS reveals his progressive understanding of what it means to be a missionary: not preaching, but service. In accord with the Social Gospel movement in American Protestantism, the Barbours understood the Kingdom of God not as a prediction of what would happen at the end of time, but rather as a call to make a better world through social reforms and demanding personal ethics. George believed "that the standards of the Kingdom of God are applicable on earth, as demonstrated by Christ, and that the aim of all His followers should be to make human society governed by these standards; that one of the main methods of accomplishing this will always be by the principle of sacrifice, and that sacrifice through love will attain results which are not produced in any other

---

2. Lian Xi, *The Conversion of Missionaries: Liberalism in American Protestant Missions in China, 1907–1932* (Allison Park: Pennsylvania State University Press, 1997), 165.

way." He explains his choice of China as the field of mission work in terms of his "intermittently growing interest and desire partly fostered by family connections for two generations with missionaries in many lands, especially China, becoming more specific after visiting missionaries in Shanghai, Peking, and Manchuria in 1911, and increased by the realization during the war that the only hope for humanity in the future lies in the practical application in everyday life of the principles and spirit of Christ. At this point in history the place where the most far-reaching results are to be expected is where a nation is waking up to self-consciousness." Answering a question about what he saw as desirable qualities in missionaries, George ended his list: "Realization in good time when he has become dispensable." In other words, a missionary's job is to work himself out of a job as the native Chinese church becomes self-sufficient. It was a bittersweet moment for many liberal Protestant missionaries when, sometimes after many decades in China, they turned over their work to Chinese colleagues or were forced out of their positions.

George's application mentions family connections with missionaries in China. His grandfather, George Freeland Barbour, a Scottish businessman, started a Presbyterian mission in Fukien and in 1855 wrote a book about the Chinese missionary movement. He linked his call to mission work in China with the West's promotion of the opium trade there: European nations should ban this horribly destructive and lucrative business and as restitution send faithful Christians to preach the gospel. My great-great-grandfather saw the hand of Providence in China's current situation: "The opium iniquity has melted the nation, that it may be cast into a new mold; and thus the opium trade is proving at once the destruction and the salvation of China."[3] In the mid-nineteenth century there was little interest in salvaging aspects of Chinese culture or forming a version of Christianity suited to China. Instead, that culture's destruction was necessary for the triumph of the gospel as Europeans understood it.

Missionaries are often seen as imperialists, racists, and narrow-minded bigots who want to impose Western codes of morality and conservative Christianity on native peoples. For example, Barbara Kingsolver's popular novel *The Poisonwood Bible* portrays missionaries in the Belgian Congo as arrogant, hypocritical, and dismissive of the cultures and insights of the people they want to convert.[4] For all his well-meaning and high-minded purposes, George Freeland Barbour's book epitomizes such an attitude.

3. George F. Barbour, *China and the Missions at Amoy: With Notice of the Opium Trade*, 2nd ed. (Edinburgh: Kennedy, 1855), 78.

4. Barbara Kingsolver, *The Poisonwood Bible: A Novel* (New York: HarperFlamingo, 1998).

Finding Them in the Archives

Fundamentalist and fervently evangelical missionaries continue to believe today that as the apocalyptic end of the world draws near, all that matters is rapid conversions to Christianity. Yet there are other understandings of mission work. By the twentieth century, another group of missionaries was better educated, inspired by the Social Gospel, and willing to work for the long-term betterment of other societies by building institutions and introducing new practices. They also hoped by the force of personal example to show how Christian faith can be the foundation of a life of service and generosity. These progressive and liberal Protestants expressed their understanding of mission work not by direct evangelization but indirectly, in the way they practiced medicine, taught, and worked for social reforms such as in China the education of women, forms of democratic government, modern agriculture, and the suppression of foot-binding and the opium trade. Liberal missionaries were more open to other traditions and saw Buddhism, Islam, Confucian teachings, and other "world religions" as offering important spiritual insights, although they usually considered them to be early stages of a progressive spiritual development that must culminate in Christianity. Indigenous traditions, such as Taoism in China, were seen as primitive, superstitious, and unworthy of respect.

David Hollinger argues that the significance of the missionary movement was not only its effects on the places that Westerners served, but also how living in a foreign culture affected missionaries, their children, and American society.[5] He describes how three "mish kids" raised in China inherited the Protestant zeal to make the world better and translated this impulse into secular causes. This was the pattern for novelist Pearl Buck, publisher Henry Luce, and the influential writer John Hersey. Like these figures, the Barbours brought home from China a cosmopolitan outlook, a desire to reform society, and a critical view of American arrogance. In contrast to secularized veterans of missionary experience, George and Dorothy believed that Christian faith is the best basis for a more just society and a world community.

Their desire to teach at Yenching University expressed my grandparents' fervent belief in education and their hope to help Chinese young people determine which aspects of Western culture should be adopted and which ones rejected. George's letter to President Leighton Stuart explained why he wanted to join the faculty:

> The more I see of China, the more I am convinced that the hope of developing a public opinion, a feeling of responsibility to

---

5. David A. Hollinger, *Protestants Abroad: How Missionaries Tried to Change the World but Changed America* (Princeton: Princeton University Press, 2017).

> the community and a change of the essentially selfish outlook of so many of the people is sufficient to free the country from the many forms of bondage in which she is held and yet not emancipate her only to fall victim to each new idea or form of self-seeking that the Western world offers . . . The teachings of Christ, working and applied consciously and unconsciously to the problems of the country are going to be the only thing that can save the country from a very terrible catastrophe. It is too late to do anything with the older generation except in a few individual instances . . . We feel that to be at Yenching is to be at the right place in the world at this moment.

George asserts that the West offers as many temptations and vices as it does positive influences. For him, the most significant contrast is not between the West and China, but between self-seeking and concern for others, a choice faced in every culture.

Yenching University was a small yet remarkable institution that for several decades had a major formative influence upon many future Chinese leaders.[6] It was an experiment formed by a merger of four Christian colleges from 1915 to 1920 and led by John Leighton Stuart, a former seminary teacher who would later become the American ambassador to China. The university had a liberal arts college and schools of religion, law, and medicine. Its organization and practices reflected Western ideals, including the integration of humanistic learning and scientific training, education for women, bicultural dialogue, and the possibility but not requirement of academic study of religion. Instruction was in both English and Mandarin. The goal of the university was to prepare the future leaders of China, whether they were Christian or not. Yenching's motto— "Freedom through truth for service"—expressed its ideal of a harmony of intellectual freedom, Christian faith, and active concern for others. In his autobiography, *Fifty Years in China*, Leighton Stuart describes his vision of Yenching: Christian in atmosphere and influence while free from "propaganda" and dedicated to seeking truth with the best academic methods. The university would

---

6. On Yenching University, see Dwight Woodbrige Edwards, *Yenching University* (New York: United Board for Christian Higher Education in Asia, 1959); Daniel H. Bays and Ellen Widmer, eds., *China's Christian Colleges: Cross-Cultural Connections, 1900–1950* (Stanford: Stanford University Press, 2009); Arthur Lewis Rosenbaum, ed., *New Perspectives on Yenching University, 1916–1952: A Liberal Education for a New China* (Leiden: Brill, 2015); and Philip West, *Yenching University and Sino-Western Relations 1916–1952*, Harvard East Asian Series 85 (Cambridge: Harvard University Press, 1976).

provide opportunities for faith to be expressed by individuals in "adventurous demonstrations of the Christian way of life."[7]

Yenching was criticized from many directions. For conservative Christians, it was not Christian enough because it did not focus on Bible studies. For nationalistic Chinese, it was too closely tied to a Western curriculum and model of education. Yenching's cosmopolitan and internationalist ideals were attacked when anti-Western views, and later the Japanese invasion, created a wave of nationalist fervor. The Christian counsel of nonviolence seemed to undermine China's need to defend itself. For the growing Communist movement, Yenching was an elitist institution out of touch with the pressing needs of the masses. Given China's immense problems, many critics thought education should concentrate on engineering, technology, agriculture, and practical skills that could be put to use immediately, rather than the luxury of liberal arts. Of what use is Romantic poetry to the suffering masses? Can China wait for gradual reforms administered by an educated urban elite, or does it demand the mobilization of China's rural population and a political revolution?

Similar criticisms of the liberal arts have long been leveled at the colleges where I studied and taught. Like Yenching, St. Olaf College is seen by the secular minded as too Christian and by more conservative Christians as not Christian enough. It is a challenge to maintain an identity committed at once to free intellectual inquiry and to the conviction that Christian ideas and beliefs should have a central place. As happened to Yenching, liberal Christian educational institutions are prone to a loss of distinctive religious identity over time, as happened at Carleton, where my father taught, and Oberlin, where I went to college. As I learn about Yenching's mission and history, I resonate with the idealism that inspired my grandparents to want to teach there. At the same time, I see in that context how optimistic liberal Protestant endeavors often dissolve. Generosity in serving others and loss of specifically Christian character often seem to go together. I've come to doubt—or, more hopefully, be self-critical about—the sustainability of one of my family's bedrock values: liberal education linked to progressive Protestantism focused on social justice.

George and Dorothy were in China from 1921 to 1931, including a year when George was "loaned" to Pei Yang University in Tientsin and the family's two-year leave in New York. The China Records Project at the Yale Divinity School Library archives hundreds of letters that George and Dorothy wrote to their families and to each other during this period. When they

---

7. John Leighton Stuart, *Fifty Years in China: The Memoirs of John Leighton Stuart, Missionary and Ambassador* (New York; Random House, 1954), 66.

were separated (one-third of the time they were in China), they wrote to each other every day. A selection of these letters was published in 1975 as *In China When* . . . .[8] Although George is listed as the author, Dorothy did most of the editing and commentary on the letters, as well as writing half of them. This book and their unpublished correspondence present a vivid picture of their daily lives during a crucial period of Chinese history. It is an amazing story of adventure and close calls, featuring antiforeigner riots, an attempted poisoning by a disgruntled servant, innumerable incidents of life-threatening disease, dust storms and floods, battles between warlords, bandits endangering George's geology expeditions, Japanese snipers and bombing raids, and George narrowly escaping the disastrous collapse of a Japanese dock during an earthquake.

As liberal Protestants, George and Dorothy believed in the universal significance of the Christian gospel and hoped to share their faith more by example than by explicit instruction. "Being a missionary consisted in caring about people's problems and working with them to find a better way," wrote Dorothy. Far from being agents of imperialism and Christian triumphalism, they were remarkably appreciative of Chinese cultural values, sympathetic to Chinese anger at the West, and modest about their role in China. Six months after they arrived in China, Dorothy describes her uncertainty: "It is so hard to decide about this paradoxical land. We wanted to wait until we knew our own minds. We do not know yet what we think of China." In 1926, five years into their stay, George addressed a meeting of missionaries in Tienstsin with remarkable tentativeness, even agnosticism, about the basic meaning of their work:

> It is too easy to adopt without revision the standards that hold good in the West. Without stopping to verify whether they are really suited to the mind and psychology of the East, we tend to apply them as criteria here and then wonder why the effect produced is so slight and why so many years of work seem to go for so little. We are not even sure, judging from what has been said recently, just what the Christian Experience of a Chinese convert may involve or what the most natural steps of progress in this experience ought to be . . . I myself am not yet certain what "to be a Christian" ought to mean to a freshman student. How far should this be different from what it should mean to a boy leaving Middle School? Or from that to the same student a year after he leaves us to take up his lifework? Must we expect it

---

8. George B. Barbour, *In China When* . . . (Cincinnati: University of Cincinnati Publications, 1975).

to be different from the Christianity of the farmer or the merchant whom this same student goes out to serve as pastor?

He concluded by recommending humility to his fellow London Missionary Society colleagues:

> We foreigners come to learn, rather than to give advice. Often the most we can do is to live our daily life beside them, letting them realize that if there is anything we can do, we are waiting to do it. It is not our business to find answers to the problems of China. They must do it. Our business is the setting up, by example and organization, of an atmosphere and surroundings in which they can work out these experiments themselves—wherever possible arranging so that their first experiments are liable of success, thus leading to repetition.[9]

Although there is a hint of manipulation in that behind-the-scenes "arranging," George strongly affirms Chinese efforts at autonomy. He and Dorothy searched for a culturally sensitive understanding of Christian missionary work to replace the older approach, a single Western model applicable everywhere.

They could afford to hire servants, but it was a once-a-year treat to have an orange. "Chickens and servants are dirt cheap, but butter, glass windows, and running water are out of sight. We can afford all the luxuries but none of the essentials." One of the main challenges—both economic and ethical—was dealing with theft by servants. Dorothy wept after she fired the "boy" who persisted in stealing even after several serious talks. (I imagine him squirming while she lectures!) The guard at the gatehouse removed stamps from envelopes she had mailed and destroyed the letters. A terrifying incident took place after a servant was caught going out the door with coal and George's keys. This man returned to poison my grandparents and kill Hugh by leaving a leaking gas stove under his bed. Luckily, the attempted murder was discovered in time, and the food he had poisoned immediately nauseated Dorothy and George. Dorothy was frustrated by the recurring pattern of dishonesty and sometimes uncertain how best to address it.

I am surprised by my grandparents' sensitivity to Chinese moral values and, most of the time, their nonjudgmental attitude: "It is important to realize the true greatness of the Chinese people. Those of us who have lived there came to 'identify' to an extraordinary degree. As we grew to love

---

9. George B. Barbour, "The Position of a Student in a Christian University in China Today," unpublished paper, 1926.

Family Conscience

them, we learned not to *blame* them for behavior which by *their* standards was right, while still strongly criticizing some of those standards and trying to offer better ones." They understood the cultural relativity of values without being moral relativists. It was not imperialism, Orientalism, or religious exclusivism to make forthright judgments about what they considered moral evils, such as the opium trade and the subjection of women to lives of drudgery. It seems to me highly ironic that critics who see missionaries as conscious or unwitting agents of imperialism do not also condemn all the other "imports" from Western culture: science, democracy, the nation-state, Marxism, gender equality, and new forms of education.

George and Dorothy appreciated the important role in Chinese culture of "face," the respect of others that is tied to self-respect. Dorothy recalls her care not to shame a dishonest servant:

> We were slowly learning to improve a servant's behavior without either the permissiveness of Arline Stuart, or the scolding tone of a friend, which made the servant lose face, and so feel the need to retaliate. Dorothy left on her bureau a thimble decorated with coral. Next day it was beside the mirror. The next, it was gone. She looked carefully on the floor, then said to the "No. 1," "Look on the floor and see if the thimble has fallen behind the bureau." A few minutes later he brought it to her: "Yes, it was on the floor." She smiled. Both understood. Had she accused him she would have lost a good servant. Had she done nothing she would have lost a succession of other belongings—and encouraged theft.

In this incident, Dorothy skillfully negotiated with servants by honoring the cultural value of saving face, and she is confident about her approach. But often such situations are not only difficult to understand, but ethically problematic. "Face" in China corresponds in certain ways to the value of honor in my mother's Southern ethos and to every family's concern with its public image and "what people think." Outward appearances may or may not correspond to the underlying reality of an individual or family. Knowing how to deal with these discrepancies in one's own life poses one kind of challenge for conscience; learning how to deal with other people's discrepancies calls for a different sort of wisdom and is especially challenging in a foreign culture. In China, the concern with face often conflicted with the value of truthfulness and with Christian emphasis on humility. Dorothy contrasts saving face with "facing reality."

In situations where face and honor were at stake, George and Dorothy learned to balance strict veracity with prudence. Dorothy visited a Chinese professor to apologize when her sister offended him by asserting that footbinding still existed in the villages. This was true, but the embarrassed Chinese professor left the table in protest. Dorothy concludes: "Tradition and face are more powerful than law or facts, and they will take generations to change." In "Memories of Three Continents," George said that in China one should "always leave a defeated man a ladder to climb back down so that he can escape the laughter of his friends and salvage his own pride."[10] Dorothy avoided trouble with the cook by refusing to discuss certain topics on a dust-storm day, "when under tension he might say something he would regret afterwards and feel his pride would not let him withdraw. We did not want to lose a good cook." Given how strong-willed, even adamant, Dorothy was about her values, I am struck by her adeptness in dealing with differing Chinese norms. Knowing her only in her old age, I had thought of her as rigid, dogmatic, and not particularly sensitive to the nuances and moral ambiguity of a situation.

At Yenching University, a continuing challenge was how to respond to student cheating. George wrote to a colleague about a student who was amazed that he was confronted for lying about cheating, because he was thereby dishonored. In this case, George decided, the right thing to do was not to observe Chinese ideas about face but to insist on the Western value of integrity: "one big thing the foreign schools are doing is breeding a conscience." Tact and prudence were necessary, but certain moral standards could not be compromised. George and Dorothy were remarkably agile in dealing with face in China. Perhaps their experience in China influenced their own version of face: their intense concern with how family history was told. With reference to Dorothy, my mother once put this cautiously: "Self-presentation was very important to her."

* * *

A DIFFERENT KIND OF moral dilemma grew out of a conflict within the family when in 1923 George's parents visited Beijing. Because of Hugh's many life-threatening illnesses, they insisted that the entire family return to Great Britain. And there was another agenda. Dorothy describes how for up to three hours at a stretch the Scottish Barbours criticized her "infinite selfishness in ruining George's career" by encouraging him to "bury himself" in China. Her in-laws rejected their missionary work as a "farce" because George and Dorothy did not press students to convert to Christianity. These deeply wounding remarks dismissed their most fundamental commitment. After much agony, a compromise was reached: Dorothy and George would

---

10. G. B. Barbour, "Memories of Three Continents," 76.

Family Conscience

remain in China while Hugh was sent with the Scottish Barbours to New York to be cared for by Dorothy's parents. Dorothy struggled to forgive her in-laws: "It's the old story of loving and admiring a person, but not all their acts or opinions." To her parents she wrote that if they did not send Hugh back, "it would really mean a complete family break." During this traumatic time, George's "hair went quite white during his parents' visit" (though the color apparently returned later, as photos show). The couple grieved for Hugh and plunged into their work to distract themselves.

In a letter to the Dickinsons, George explained how this conflict revealed different ways of parenting:

> My Father and Mother come of a tradition which has other ideals both on missionary matters and on bringing up children—it would be sheer hypocrisy to pretend these ideas were our own. The real issue is our belief in cuddling a child and expressing affection, whereas Dr. L and the parents are convinced that a child should be treated impersonally, "scientifically" and completely in accordance with the greater knowledge of the person in charge. Therefore, no affection should be shown and the parents should never enter the nursery or see the children except as requested by the nurse. We believe that hours of hard crying are not necessary, and that the alternative is not just giving in, but may be finding the cause of the tears or making the needed behavior easier.

It is hard to comprehend the calculated coldness of George's parents, which now seems like child abuse. George disagreed with his parents but was unable to stand up to them, especially when his father weighed in as a physician on Hugh's medical condition. Rather than live with their disapproval and anger, he submitted to their wishes. In "Memories of Three Continents" he says, "I have never known whether I was right or wrong in agreeing to let them leave, for it was very hard on both the baby and the mother to be separated."[11] This confession of uncertainty—the only doubt acknowledged in his memoir—hints at anger, regret, and residual guilt. George grew up in a culture where family solidarity and deference to elders were imperative, even when it meant acting against his better judgment and deepest affections.

Dorothy wrote several books about raising children in a Christian home, published in Shanghai in English and (with the help of a translator) in Chinese editions: *Desired Bible* (1926), *Christian Home Education*

---

11. G. B. Barbour, "Memories of Three Continents," 81.

Finding Them in the Archives

(1932), and *Principles in Child Training* (1932).[12] These books attempted to apply modern psychology and John Dewey's pragmatic philosophy to Christian education. The Yale archives contain several unpublished drafts of essays and stories about children. Dorothy discusses several times a particular question that preoccupied her: whether to pick up and carry a crying infant, which she asserts will lead to a demanding child and exhausted parents. Several anecdotes depict a power struggle with her youngest son, Bobby (Freeland), who became much happier when he accepted that his mother would not pick him up. Dorothy's stance in these stories contrasts with George's letter to RLD about their desire *not* to treat their own children in this strict way; I don't know what to make of this discrepancy.

Although Dorothy brought most of her ideas with her to Peking, her character-building mission took new forms as she raised her children and taught Religious Education in 1920s China. She wrote about specific challenges in teaching Chinese women about the Christian home. Crucially important is Confucius's teaching about obedience. For a woman, this means obeying her father, husband, and son. In China, love of children is exceptionally strong and "the mother's love of her son expresses itself in obedience to his every wish." For instance, a tiny old woman with bound feet carries on her back a boy as big as she. Dorothy calls the Church to reorient Chinese parents, "in order to use this love of children in ways that are more likely to train them in Christian character." Bible Women Training Schools can prepare teachers to show Chinese women that it is best to feed their children at regular hours instead of when the child demands it. A mother must have a plan or system rather than yielding to her child's demands. Children should be taught to dress themselves and play alone. China is leaving behind the teachings of Confucius, says Dorothy. "But parents still love their children, and they seek for ways to express that love in a more excellent way." I wonder how much her conception of that excellent way, which I experienced in the 1950s as rigid and cold, reflects her reaction against China's patriarchal culture. She set limits on a mother's need to respond to her child's demands. I think Dorothy's strict rules were motivated partly by a desire to free women from "unrelenting obedience to every wish."

---

12. *Desired Bible* was published as Dorothy Dickinson Barbour, *Making the Bible Desired* (Garden City, NY: Doubleday, 1928). In a letter to her parents, Dorothy explained the title of her book, which was written for teachers of religion in Christian schools and churches: "I've been giving the summer to showing people that giving up compulsory Bible classes—'Required Bible'—is not loss of Christianity, but a challenge to make lives and classes such that students will *choose* it." See also Dorothy Dickinson Barbour, *Christian Home Education* (Shanghai: Christian Literature Society, 1932).

Family Conscience

Another source of Dorothy's no-nonsense, tough-guy approach to child-raising was what she learned in dealing with servants in China. After she describes the challenges of responding to theft and threats in *In China When . . .*, she makes a surprising leap to her grandchildren: "We were coming to understand that, with servants or students, an apparently unruffled assurance 'works.' Years later, Dorothy overheard one grandchild say to another, 'There's no use crying, Grandmother doesn't scare.'"[13]

* * *

A RECURRING THEME OF *In China When . . .* and Dorothy's conversations in later years is the conflict between Communism and Christianity. She saw China's future hanging in the balance in a forced choice between these two commitments. Christians and Communists both want a more just society, she asserted, but Christians hope to achieve it with love, not hatred. She was delighted when a Chinese student told her: "Christianity really does what Communism promises."

Dorothy had a very negative encounter with Anna Louise Strong, an influential American journalist who advocated Communism. She arranged meetings with Yenching students for Strong, who claimed no longer to be a Communist. Students informed Dorothy that the meetings were Communist propaganda. Confronted by Dorothy, Strong justified lying as necessary to advance the Communist cause. Dorothy asked, "Do you think Communism would be good for China?" Strong replied: "I think Communism would be chaos for China. But chaos for China would be good for Communism." Strong misquoted students in order to advance Communist interests. Her deceptions epitomized the distortions of truth Dorothy criticized in Communism and other contexts: "Only Christians and scientists consider it necessary to make statements accord with facts—to tell the truth, and not simply 'the *truths*' in which they believe."

A central ethical question with which missionaries wrestled concerned extraterritoriality, that is, the right of Westerners in the treaty ports to be tried in their own courts rather than China's. This privileged status created bitter resentment, for in practice Europeans and Americans were seldom convicted of crimes against the Chinese. In the eyes of the Chinese, foreigners could do anything with impunity. In an unpublished reflection written in 1969, George explained the issue with a contemporary analogy. He compared the Shanghai incident of 1925 to a recent American crime: "A police sergeant, Everson, in the British Settlement at Shanghai ordered his men to fire into a crowd of unarmed Chinese marchers, mostly students, and eight

---

13. G. B. Barbour, *In China When . . .*, 21.

people were hit. This raised for us sharply the issue of extraterritoriality. Last year when Senator Robert Kennedy was killed should Sirhan have been tried by American or Arab law?" (Sirhan was a Jordanian citizen.)

A related issue was whether Westerners should seek protection from their legations during dangerous times, such as antiforeigner demonstrations that became violent in the 1920s. This was a serious concern at Yenching, especially after the incident in Shanghai. George thought that to rely on military protection was inconsistent with Christian trust in God. Yenching faculty refused to be protected by American Marines or British soldiers and let it be known that they were unarmed and not afraid. Dorothy told the legations that "we relied on the Chinese to protect us, and that if anything happened to us there were to be no reprisals."

Yenching University was a hotbed of student radicalism during the 1920s and '30s. Like Leighton Stuart, the Barbours were sympathetic to the goal of social reform, yet they criticized from a Christian perspective the Communists' materialism, violence, and hostility to religion. George opposed punishing students who were involved in protests and strikes and sought dialogue with them. Yenching students who were disturbed and uncertain during this upheaval wanted to hear George's perspective; he met secretly at night with them because they would have been attacked for talking with a foreigner. During anti-Western riots in 1925 and 1926, he calmed them. He tried to persuade students being told that they must "die for the country" that there were better ways to serve China's needs. Acknowledging the justice of Communist and nationalist outrage at Western imperialism, he tried to steer students toward peaceful and productive actions.

Letters Dorothy wrote to her parents in June 1925 reveal her apprehension of danger, her courage, and her sympathy for the Chinese:

> On the thirtieth there is to be a one-day strike—nothing is to be done for, or sold to, foreigners. Pi-chen, our "No. 1," spends his day reading wild literature and refuses to work. Passions are aflame and quite out of the hands of the moderate students. . . . We are seriously wondering whether we are going to see any of our possessions again. The shooting in Shanghai was a match thrown on tinder long smouldering. While it was fanned by Russian influence, this was only possible because there was so much real ground for resentment. Businesspeople have been chiefly at fault, because they have treated the Chinese the way whites at their worst have treated negroes, and this in their own land, and toward the proudest people on earth.

Family Conscience

While she cared for three small children during George's absence, Dorothy defied "old China hands" who, remembering the Boxer Rebellion, urged letting it be known that they were armed. Instead, she piled crockery against the door to warn them if someone broke in, and "again we awoke to broad daylight."

* * *

DOROTHY'S YOUNGER SISTER, JEAN, arrived in Peking in 1920, a few months before the Barbours, and stayed until 1927, including a year's furlough to raise funds for Yenching. Jean was probably the first professor of sociology in China and served as a missionary for the Congregational Mission Board. She spent a good deal of time with Dorothy's family, often taking care of her three nephews. These two sisters were very different in temperament. In a letter to her parents in 1921, Dorothy appreciates Jean's boundless energy: "A whirlwind comes shouting across the courtyard to envelope me with hugs and kisses and before there's a chance for 'O Girlie' it is gone. Her joy in life and exuberance about China and being a missionary know no abatement." Dorothy's competitive and critical side came out in sharp judgments about her sister: "Jean's unpopularity is due to her tactlessness." My family always relished Aunt Jean's generosity, warmth, easy manner, and light-heartedness, delightful qualities so different from our grandmother. Jean loved walking and swimming, coached basketball at Yenching, and was a happy, earthy person who took pleasure in many things. She enjoyed rambunctious children and worked in a day-care center well into her eighties.

Jean shared the same liberal Protestant faith as Dorothy, as expressed in a cache of letters shared with me by her daughter, Mary. Jean criticized the Evangelical and Catholic missionaries who focused on conversion, though she approved of their work when they tried to make living conditions better: "Their way of saving souls may be of some use in a future life, but it does not make much difference in this!" Jean had more encounters with China's native religions than Dorothy. She was appalled by the "Lama Devil Dance" in Peking's Tibetan Buddhist Temple: "How even the most abstract purpose of driving out evil could be inspiring from such actions was hard to see." She was moved by the dignity and beauty of a sacrifice to Confucius that focused on the gold-lettered tablet of his teachings: "China has so much to be proud of and to treasure in the ethics and teachings of Confucius, and while not willing to worship him even in the more formal Chinese way, we are exceedingly glad to encourage this rather than other forms, and to use so very much of what he taught." As progressive missionaries, both sisters approved of Chinese traditions in so far as their ethical teachings overlapped with Christian ones.

Although Jean shared her sister's commitment to the Social Gospel, cautious affirmation of aspects of Chinese religions, and confidence in the good effects of a Western liberal arts education, she expressed her moral sensibility and conscience very differently than Dorothy. While devoted to her work and students, she rarely emphasized self-sacrifice: "Some of you pitied me coming out to China, and a few spoke of a 'sacrifice,' but you didn't know what fun it is here, how utterly congenial, varied, appealing, and delightful the work is, and how beyond words worthwhile and lovable the Chinese are." She could cheerfully set her scruples aside on the right occasion: "I object to the principle of bargaining for goods, but it is rather fun on the whole."

In November 1921, Jean met a Scottish fellow student of Chinese language who had studied medicine under George's father in Edinburgh. Jean "much enjoyed a talk about the Barbours," mentioning only that they had "discussed conscience." That this is the sole topic that Jean noted in a conversation about her sister's in-laws is striking; how I wish she had said more.

Like her sister, Jean was certain that certain practices of Chinese society should be eliminated, such as foot-binding, opium, prostitution, and female infanticide. Partly because of her training as a sociologist, however, she had a better ability than Dorothy to observe and investigate Chinese culture. To learn about China's problems, she visited "frightful local shelters for the insane, child-killing factories . . . and a home for orphan girls (boys got adopted)." As a single woman pursuing her research, she visited rural areas and in 1924 spent two months in a remote village fifty miles south of Beijing, dodging battling warlords and bandits raiding the area. In a scholarly article, "Observations on the Social Life of a North China Village," Jean Dickinson was cautious about her conclusions: "In so vast a country any generalization might be true somehow, and no generalization would be true everywhere."[14] She spent many hours sitting on her host family's k'ang (heated platform) with three generations of women, chatting about village life and relationships while they all darned stockings. A letter home reveals how she earned the village's affection by throwing herself into every activity:

> I have had such a good time with my family today. In the intervals of teaching and since school I have been hanging round the threshing floor causing great amusement and winning my way

---

14. Jean Dickinson, "Observations on the Social Life of a North China Village," Publication of the Department of Sociology, Yenching University, Peking, Oct–Dec 1924, 1.

surely and swiftly into their hearts by sharing in every possible process. I have helped to turn the sorghum while the donkey ploughed round and round dragging the roller over the dried heads to break off the grains and their husks and swept up and raked up. I have watched the winnowing, the hired man filling the basket from which the old man flung the grain in a great arc so that the chaff blew into one pile while the grain fell in another. I have been husking corn and find it an excellent way to open up conversation. Shelling beans and suchlike brings one into close contact with them all . . . They are much impressed that I brought my "work" with me and knit in all interstices of other occupations . . . Third Mrs. Chang was tickled to pieces to learn to knit, this afternoon, and I expect to teach the family soon.

Her relish of these mundane details and joie de vivre is evident. Jean's desire to make the world a better place was combined with a wonderful capacity to appreciate things just as they are: to marvel, like her father, at "the glory of God" revealed in the world, including in its variety of social patterns. In this regard she is for me a better role model than Dorothy, with her intense but one-sided determination to improve society or individual character.

The Barbour family left China in November 1931 because of the undiagnosed illnesses ("Peking fever") of Hugh and Ian. They had a close call as they left that Dorothy describes to her parents: "Sleeping with Tientsin LMS friends, we pulled out our beds so that the Japanese sniper's bullets, coming through the window, hit the wall and fell harmless behind the bed. At an intersection each of us took a child and ran as soon as a sniper fired, George going back for Hugh who could be trusted to wait for him. The train travelled without lights and was the last for weeks." The Japanese were bombarding Shanghai when the family fled that city.

Two years later, after their leave in New York, growing unrest in China and the Japanese invasion made it impossible to get visas to return to China. In 1934, George went back alone for fieldwork. He worked again with Teilhard de Chardin, with whom he had collaborated earlier in the discovery and analysis of the hominid known as Peking Man. Their ambitious 1934 research project, funded by the Rockefeller Foundation, intended to link the Peking Man fossils with similar ones in Europe by a long traverse across Tibet. Chinese geologists argued to the Rockefeller Foundation that they should be in charge. Dorothy asserts in *In China When . . .* that the expedition was sabotaged: "'Even George, who saw in advance the probability that, after [Davidson] Black's death, Chinese members of the Survey would try to get Rockefeller funds for themselves, did not realize that one of them was trying to make both him and Teilhard fail in their research, and lose face and time all along the way. The man reported to the Rockefeller Trustees much inefficiency and dishonesty on Teilhard's part, being sure he could himself replace Teilhard if he could get rid of him and thus get the money he supposed Teilhard was getting."[15] The Trustees ended the expedition.

According to a substantial biography and assessment of George Barbour's geological research, his work in China was "classic, definitive, and seminal. This is truly the case for his work on the origins of loess, the structure of the Yangtse basin, and the relation of Chinghsing to the thrust of the Himalayan tectonic plate into China."[16] Yet his work is rarely cited. This was partly because he never supervised graduate students and also, I think, because since one of his chief goals was to support the emergence of Chinese scientists, he did not insist on getting credit.

"Memories of Three Continents" ends with George describing how in 1926 he determined the best site for the water tower at the new campus of Yenching University, near the Imperial Summer Palace. After a careful study of the entire area, he settled on the most auspicious location and predicted that water would be found 124 feet deep. After drilling 120 feet, the contractor had not found water and stopped. George offered to pay to go down another ten feet. Digging began again, and the next morning brought good news: "Overnight a free flow had developed . . . an artesian spring spouting twelve feet above the ground and yielding 16,000 gallons an hour, rising from the 122-foot level. So the University erected a striking cement pagoda in Chinese style, housing a tall water tank from which Yenching could be supplied to the end of time. I had to get official permission to copy a famous pagoda nearby."[17] Today the grounds of former Yenching University are the beautiful campus of Beijing University, with winding lanes and bridges that cross small lakes. In water-starved northern China, a lush, green garden surrounds this premier university.

In 2016 I visited the campus while I was teaching a short summer course at nearby Beijing Normal University. Several Chinese graduate students took me to Beijing University, nicknamed "Beida," and helped me find the house where the Barbour family lived. They took a photo of me with the pagoda-themed water tower in the background. On a whim, I wondered aloud if the archives of the university held any records about my grandparents. The students jumped at the chance to help me, and for

15. G. B. Barbour, *In China When* . . . , 236.

16. Roger Mark Selya, "George Brown Barbour: 1890–1977," *Geographers: Biobibliographical Studies* 23 (2004) 27 (full article, 14–34).

17. G. B. Barbour, *In China When* . . . , 82.

Family Conscience

an hour we pored over documents in Mandarin and English. They were delighted to learn how George dismantled and reassembled a car, and that he played the organ every week during worship. His exquisite ink drawings depicted the campus in its first days. They found an official account of the siting of the water tower and George offering to pay for more digging when funds ran out after ten days. The students were impressed that George was responsible for determining the proper locations of 4,997 village wells in Hubei province. On another day, they took me to visit the museum about the discovery of Peking Man at Zhoukoudian, where we saw photographs of George with Chinese and European scientists.

I was delighted and proud. The students said George was "a friend of China," and that if I was enjoying my time in Beijing, it was because of my grandfather's "good karma." In this land of utmost respect for lineage and ancestors, my students viewed me in a new way. Digging into the Yenching archives was an act of filial piety that they could understand. I was grateful for their appreciation of the contributions George and Dorothy made, and I got a taste of the kind of relationships with Chinese people that my grandparents developed, at once cautious, decorous, and warm.

* * *

IN CHINA WHEN . . . and "Memories of Three Continents" present my grandparents' curated versions of the past, and even their letters, of course, do not tell the whole story. Above all, George and Dorothy wanted to present lessons that would form character and conscience. They must have known that a later generation would draw from these documents only what it needed. What I need is grandparents known more fully and, with better understanding, loved more unreservedly. I'm grateful that they left these documents for me to find, and thankful to belatedly recognize and be reconciled to two fascinating individuals.

The crotchety, fussy, brittle elders who seemed so out of touch with my generation were once bold, energetic young adults who created careers and formed a family amid challenges I can scarcely comprehend. They wanted to make the world a better place and me a better person. At its best, the missionary impulse to reach out to people from other cultures by serving them and if possible meeting their needs expresses generosity and a cosmopolitan vision. This liberal Protestant impulse is quite different from narrower versions of Christianity and the chauvinistic American attitude that we should just take care of our own. Unlike evangelistic missionaries or my compatriots who want only to impose their own ways on the world, George and Dorothy tried to help Chinese people to work out their own solutions, for instance by creating their own forms of worship, forming a curriculum that integrated the best of Eastern and Western knowledge, disbanding Western institutions when the Chinese created their equivalents, and cooperating in efforts at social justice and material welfare such as educating women, ending prostitution and opium addiction, and digging wells. There is so much to admire in my grandparents' lives of generous service that I feel ashamed of the smallness of my own efforts to help others.

Their version of Christianity was usually self-critical and open to other truths. In Dorothy, though I think not in George, the missionary impulse was sometimes distorted so that it became self-righteous and bullying. Later generations adopted a more live-and-let-live attitude toward those with different interests and values, people from other cultures and religious traditions, and our own children. Liberal Protestant faith often turns into something else: either a social justice movement, or skepticism about intellectual orthodoxies, or exploration of spiritual truth expressed in other traditions. Although my grandparents' example did not inspire any family members to follow in their footsteps as missionaries, I see their influence in these other ways.

Is my conscience, too, a missionary one, feeling—perhaps overly so—responsible for others' lives? George and Dorothy wanted people to consider how we are each other's keeper. I am one kind of keeper as I preserve certain stories about them and assess their legacy. I sort through my moral inheritance, asking: what shall I keep? To understand this question as part of their legacy and to discern their humanity after many decades of estrangement are blessings I did not expect to find in their archives.

CHAPTER 6

Pros and Cons, Regrets and Grace

One of my oldest memories: my father sits in the living room in his rocking chair, underlining books. I wonder why he puts lines, always in pencil, under certain words. I try underlining my own books—before I can read! I carefully draw a wiggly line through the narrow white space between rows of text. Yes, I can do this. But I have a quandary. Going downstairs in my pajamas one evening, I ask him, "Dad, how do you know which words to put the lines under?" I don't recall his answer, but this question stays with me.

* * *

How much of my conscience is based on a conscious choice of moral values and how much is superego, originating in the desire to please my parents? To what degree are my ethical convictions the result of voluntary and deliberate reflection, and to what extent are they conditioned responses? These are not either-or alternatives: my family both indoctrinated me and influenced my limited but crucial capacity for moral freedom. In the acknowledgments of *The Conscience of the Autobiographer* (1992), I wrote: "My parents, Ian and Deane Barbour, read and commented on the entire manuscript and shaped my conception of its ideal reader. In addition to gifts of love beyond recall, their insights into conscience over the years have contributed substantially to the writing of this book, which is dedicated to them."[1] My parents mediated cultural traditions that shape how I deliberate, think for myself, and come to my own conclusions.

1. John D. Barbour, *The Conscience of the Autobiographer: Ethical and Religious Dimensions of Autobiography* (London: Macmillan; and New York: St. Martin's, 1992), ix.

Pros and Cons, Regrets and Grace

My father's character and choices reveal his own mixture of freedom and conditioning. He was born in Beijing in 1923. After the family left China in 1931, Ian went to schools in Pasadena, Cincinnati, and New York, to a Quaker boarding school in England for three years, and to high school at Deerfield Academy in Massachusetts. All this movement "did not facilitate long-term relationships," he told me in one of the tape-recorded interviews I did with him while working on the first version of this book in 2003. Yet he was a happy, well-adjusted boy according to Ian, his brother Hugh, and letters by George and Dorothy. I don't know much about his boyhood moral experiences, except that his earliest memory was of his brother being punished unfairly. He entered Swarthmore College in 1940. He graduated in 1943 in an accelerated program because of the war, first studying engineering, then switching to physics.

During World War II, Ian did alternative service as a conscientious objector. The Quaker boarding school in England, Friends meetings at Swarthmore, and a Quaker work camp one summer influenced his pacifist stance. He tried to join an overseas ambulance unit, the American Field Service, but was turned down because he was a British subject. From June 1943 to June 1946, he did Civilian Public Service (CPS), first with a forest crew in Oregon building access roads and fighting fires, and then caring for mental patients at Duke University Hospital in North Carolina. In CPS Ian lived and worked with other men who took a principled stand against a war that the vast majority of Americans supported. Despite this unpopular position, he had a supportive context for being a CO and encountered little prejudice. He was an absolute pacifist, not a "selective objector," as I tried to be during the Vietnam War. Later in his life, Ian was less certain about pacifism; he said that if ever a war was justified, it was the war against Hitler. In 1943 he did not know about the concentration camps. Although he did not regret the stand he took during the Second World War, Ian came to recognize the probable inefficacy of pacifism against an organized system such as the Third Reich. Still, he thought that some Christians should testify or witness by their actions that nonviolence is always a vital option, regardless of whether it changes others' minds.

In long letters to his parents and brothers, Ian described questions of conscience that preoccupied the "work campers." They understood pacifism variously from Quaker, Mennonite, Tolstoian, and other perspectives. Ian organized discussions of the meaning of pacifism and its broad implications for human society. He wanted to explore the goals and problems of pacifism, which he believed meant not only opposition to warfare, but a philosophy and way of life that could be applied in their own work camp community. He criticized "apathetic" COs who only wanted to get through their time of service. In contrast, Ian wanted to use the experience as "training for life," an exploration of possibilities for human cooperation. He was equally critical of other men who had an "extreme individualistic approach" to ethical decisions and were unable to work cooperatively or make any sacrifice for the sake of unity. Ian thought they succumbed to another danger: "If you get too much absorbed in conscience, it is easy to make conscience and convenience too closely allied in your thinking." Ian was usually reluctant to appeal to conscience and skeptical of those who saw it as a direct link to God, thereby insulating themselves from challenge or further thinking. He recounts an amusing anecdote about performing a skit that angered fundamentalists when he pretended to call up God on his private telephone line: 222-DIVINE! Yet like all the men there, Ian opposed the war for reasons of conscience, grounding his stance in fundamental religious and ethical convictions. Throughout his life, he was cautious or dubious about claims made in the name of conscience, especially when supposedly based on the will of God.

While working in CPS in Oregon, Ian made a difficult moral decision, which he told me was his first significant moral choice. In November 1943, Swarthmore College, short of teaching faculty, invited the twenty-year-old recent graduate to return to the college to help with physics instruction. Ian could have received a military deferment for this work because it was classified as a critical occupation during the war. It was a tempting offer, for it would have been intellectually interesting and directly related to the career in physics that Ian envisioned. It might do more real good in the world than he could contribute as part of a forest crew. But since some of the students were in the Navy, teaching would be at least an indirect contribution to the war effort.

As we discussed this dilemma in his office in the Carleton College chapel in 2003, Ian pulled out an old manila file labeled "Decisions 1943–55." It contained several documents related to his Selective Service classification, including letters to his parents and the local draft board explaining his decisions. Most interesting to me was Ian's list of considerations, pro and con, bearing on whether to accept the Swarthmore offer. There were six or eight good reasons to accept the job ("Reasons Why") and an equal number weighing against it ("Against Swarthmore"). Ian addressed whether taking the job would free someone else to participate in fighting, whether teaching physics had any military value, the pressure of family and friends to accept the offer, the legitimacy of career advancement, and whether staying in the Oregon crew "would be too much from a martyr motive." A crucial point was whether accepting a temporary reclassification to an occupation that would supposedly assist the war effort was inconsistent with his claim to be a CO. Ian thought that his local draft board would not later reinstate his status as a conscientious objector if he had compromised in this way. In December 1943, while he was on leave in San Francisco, he cabled the Chair of the Physics Department:

> REGRET EXCEEDINGLY HAVE TO TURN DOWN MOST ATTRACTIVE PROPOSITION BUT FEEL CANNOT TEACH OR REPLACE ANOTHER TO TEACH NAVY MEN OR ACCEPT RECLASSIFICATION AS ESSENTIAL TO WAR EFFORT STOP REGRET MY ACTION MUST INCONVENIENCE YOU BUT DO NOT SEE WAY CLEAR TO COMPROMISE STOP

In a letter to his parents explaining his decision, Ian said that he was not certain that he had done the right thing. But he thought that he probably did because only this choice could end his state of indecision without second thoughts:

> I had two pages of arguments for and only one against, so on the basis of weight the Pros had it. But one of the factors which finally helped me was the very fact that I couldn't make up my mind. Whether this is valid or not I don't know but I had a feeling that if I had gone this long without seeing it clear to accept, I probably never would, and would have a somewhat troubled conscience if I went ... I felt beforehand what has been the case, that I wouldn't necessarily be satisfied myself once I sent the telegram ... I'm still not sure I took the right move, but I think I did. I may never know. And I couldn't say exactly why I didn't take it.

When Ian's conscience did not endorse his actions unequivocally, he tried to avoid a bad conscience. He reasoned that his doubts about taking the physics job meant that it would be wrong. Ian's way out of this situation—of what ethicists call moral perplexity—admits uncertainty about ambiguity even as he takes resolute action.

This decision epitomizes Ian's logical, orderly weighing of rational reasons for and against two courses of action. This is the *modus operandi* of Ian's conscience at its most deliberate and articulate: informed by religious values and personal commitments, publicly open to challenge or argument, and above all carefully reasoned, as he searches for a decision that can be explained and justified. He always weighed the pros and cons of alternatives, subjecting his options to searching evaluation as he interpreted his beliefs, circumstances, goals, and the likely effects of his choices on other people. This kind of deliberation, the reasoning about a particular case that

Family Conscience

Christian tradition calls casuistry, is a crucial aspect of conscience. For those who want to follow a simple moral rule or see black-and-white alternatives, it is too difficult, subjective, and deliberative.

Conscience is at once logical and psychological: it is shaped by reasoned deliberation and by desires and fears that are sometimes unrecognized. In addition, moral decisions reflect values that are deeper than conscious choice, ultimate concerns that a person intuits or believes in. Conscience may deliberate and choose, and sometimes it also responds immediately, as if to an independent voice that calls from elsewhere. It relies on imagination, gut feelings, and inspiration as much as logic. After one lists all the reasons pro and con, one must finally weigh these considerations on a scale of one's basic values. Then making a moral choice isn't a calculus, but a commitment. Sometimes the shorter list of considerations wins over the longer list. At a certain point, Ian came to the limits of rational justification and had to say: "*this* is decisive for me." One can give reasons for a moral choice, but much more is involved than logic.

Ethical claims are sometimes viewed as nothing but masks for self-interest or disguises of a political group's ideology. I share Ian's commitment to seeking rational clarity, his ideal of hearing outside criticism of one's deliberations, and his hope that conscience can help one to discern wisely which among many conflicting values one wants most to affirm. Yet the nonrational dimensions of conscience are powerful, too. Ian's life story, like Deane's, like mine, reveals aspects of conscience that sometimes conflict with rational deliberation: unconscious psychological forces, the repetition of family dramas through the generations, and the involuntary suffering of regret or remorse.

* * *

AFTER THE WAR, IAN enrolled in a graduate program in physics at the University of Chicago. He conducted experiments on cosmic rays and was a teaching assistant for Enrico Fermi, who had presided over the project that culminated in the first sustained atomic reaction. Physics students were being recruited to work on the hydrogen bomb at Los Alamos. Ian deliberated about the ethics of scientific research and his vocational direction. He turned down several offers at major research universities (including Yale and Penn State) because he wanted to teach at a liberal arts college, and in 1949 accepted a position at Kalamazoo College in Michigan. After four years of teaching physics, Ian made a crucial decision that would change his intellectual direction and sense of vocation.

Pros and Cons, Regrets and Grace

He was increasingly interested in the relationships between science and religion. Having received a Ford Foundation fellowship to study for a year in another discipline, he enrolled in 1953 at Yale Divinity School to study theology and ethics with H. Richard Niebuhr, Roland Bainton, and others. He stayed for a second year and then faced a difficult decision that he describes in a 2004 autobiographical essay, "A Personal Odyssey": "I believed that a vocational choice should reflect a person's abilities, interests, and (in a religious context) response to God and human needs. I enjoyed physics and was familiar enough with it that I could teach and still have time for other activities. Moreover, I knew that scientists are respected in the academic world, and their voices carry some weight on educational, ethical, and religious issues. In addition, I shared the Reformation's conviction that any useful vocation can serve God and human need. But I increasingly felt that it would be more interesting and more significant to spend at least part of my time learning and teaching in religious studies."[2]

In our tape-recorded conversation, I asked Ian whether his choice of vocation was a matter of conscience. In response, he described a paper he wrote at Yale for H. Richard Niebuhr that deliberated about a crucial vocational choice he faced: "I was rereading that paper. It's funny that so many of the reasons really are reasons for not giving up a full-time physics job. The status of a scientist is higher on most campuses. I knew the material so well that I could teach it without a lot of extra preparation time. Deane and I had been leaders of a student Christian fellowship. I did quite a lot; there were numerous chances to express my religious concerns. Then there were many uncertainties. I guess I was listing in a perhaps overrationalistic way the different criteria for vocation, such as one's abilities. I knew I had abilities in physics. I didn't know whether I did in religious studies. I had some inkling I wanted to relate the two fields, but it was too early to tell. On the second criterion of Christian vocation, what contribution one was making to society, you would have a hard time saying that one was clearly better. I felt strongly the Reformation idea that any vocation can be a service to God."

I asked: "If the rational arguments were stronger for staying in physics, how much was your change of career a call of conscience? And how much was it because of intellectual curiosity and passion?"

"I think it was intellectual. I wanted to study and teach what I thought was most important. I can't say that I felt a clear call. I didn't have long periods of agonizing prayer expecting divine guidance. It wasn't conscience in the sense of clear right or wrong. But it was certainly more than rational

2. Ian G. Barbour, "A Personal Odyssey," in *Fifty Years in Science and Religion: Ian G. Barbour and His Legacy*, ed. Robert John Russell, Ashgate Religion and Science Series (Aldershot, UK: Ashgate, 2004), 19 (full essay, 17–28).

evaluation of the kind that a guidance counselor might give. If you assigned points, maybe you could make a stronger case for staying in physics, with less uncertainty and with less of a price in other ways. I really wasn't adequately prepared for teaching religion. I had to spend my first few years scrambling to get caught up. I think my choice was based on interest and importance. Maybe importance is a value judgment about what the world needs at a deeper level. But it wasn't a religious call such as some people feel when they go into the ministry."

Ian explained his reservations about using the term conscience to describe his vocational choice and more generally: "I don't naturally fall into the language of conscience myself, simply because it can be easily identified with adherence to a particular idea of right and wrong, rather than a response. I have not myself seen conscience as direct divine guidance. I've tried to meditate on decisions. I know of people who pray for divine guidance in a very specific way, or who feel they have received a call from God to a vocation. I hope I can see my life in a religious context, and openness to God's influence is important. I'm also highly aware of the role of human interpretation in prayer or scripture. I certainly don't expect to find direct guidance from reading scripture that would be clearly applicable to a decision. I don't see conscience as an intuition of a moral order that would be a path independent of my own reflection."

This view of conscience is quite different from his mother's. Dorothy believed that conscience should reflect God's direct guidance, and she was often certain that she knew exactly what God wanted. One influence behind Ian's allusion to conscience as a response is the approach to Christian ethics of his teacher, H. Richard Niebuhr. Niebuhr emphasized the concept of the responsible self and the ideal of responding to what God is doing in the world, which is always a matter of human interpretation. In contrast to several traditional ideas about conscience, Ian defined it "in a more flexible way, as response to need and to one's possibilities rather than according to norms that are more culturally influenced than we have recognized." He distinguished this view of conscience as based on interpretation from conscience as following intuition, obeying God's direct command, or conforming to a society's moral rules. For Ian, conscience is rooted in an individual's capacity for reflective choice. Yet he was strikingly reluctant to use this term for a major life decision about his future direction. Ian was so aware of possible misinterpretations of conscience (especially the belief that one's judgments obey infallible divine commands) that he rarely described either momentous decisions or everyday moral choices as matters of conscience. In contrast, I see conscience more positively and expansively, as the ongoing process of self-monitoring and assessment that is always going on as a person reflects on whether past and future choices reflect fundamental values.

Ian began teaching at Carleton College in Minnesota in 1955. Initially he taught physics half-time and religion half-time in the Philosophy Department. In 1960 he founded the Religion Department and began to teach full-time in it. He had a distinguished academic career, founded the interdisciplinary field of science and religion, and wrote many books.[3] He received many fellowships and awards, culminating in Scotland's Gifford Lectures and, in 1999, the Templeton Prize for Progress in Religion.

Ian searched for both a Christian and a secular philosophical foundation for addressing ethical issues. In 1969, "On to Mars?" challenged America's pursuit of manned space exploration when so many urgent needs on Earth are ignored.[4] Two books and many articles examined the rightful place of technology in various areas of human life and argued against both antitechnological views and belief that technology alone will solve social problems. We need clarity about and commitment to the crucial values that should direct uses of technology, such as social justice, environmental preservation, and sustainability. At Carleton, Ian founded the Science, Technology, and Public Policy program to examine the ethical values at stake in policies for agriculture, energy, genetic engineering, and computer applications. To discuss these intellectual projects would take me too far from Ian's personal story and role in my family. The example of his work was for me a model of how deep ethical concerns—conscience in the largest sense—can motivate and shape an intellectual vocation.

* * *

IAN WAS A SYNTHESIZER of insights from many distinct fields of knowledge. He interpreted the history of interactions between science and religion, including conflicts over evolution and the nature of creation. He analyzed epistemological issues, comparing science and religion as different ways of knowing. Reflecting on the implications of science for Christian belief, Ian argued that science does not determine religious beliefs in any simple

---

3. Ian's most influential books are Ian G. Barbour, *Issues in Science and Religion* (Englewood Cliffs, NJ: Prentice-Hall, 1966); *Myths, Models, and Paradigms* (New York: Harper & Row, 1974); *Religion in an Age of Science*, The Gifford Lectures 1989–1991 (San Francisco: Harper & Row, 1990); *Ethics in an Age of Technology*, The Gifford Lectures 1989–1991 (San Francisco: HarperCollins, 1992); *When Science Meets Religion* (San Francisco: HarperSanFrancisco, 2000); and *Nature, Human Nature, God*, Theology and the Sciences (Minneapolis: Fortress, 2002).

4. Ian G. Barbour, "On to Mars?" *The Christian Century* 86 (November 16, 1969), 1478–80.

way. Yet traditional theological doctrines, especially those concerned with creation and human nature, may need to be reformulated in the light of scientific theories. He used the process philosophy of Alfred Whitehead to integrate scientific theories and theological ideas in a comprehensive worldview. Even in his eighties he continued to work on how understandings of nature and human nature are influenced by evolutionary history, genetics, neuroscience, and the artificial intelligence of computers and robots. His was a truly outstanding record of intellectual accomplishments.

Ian in his office, 1999.

It was also a hard act to follow for a son who chose an academic career. How could I ever measure up? I knew I couldn't, but somehow I've never felt inadequate that I can't match his achievements. I feel only gratitude for his example of commitment to an academic vocation, which was a huge influence and advantage. Ian loved his work and said he felt very lucky to have work that he would do even if he were not paid for it. As his intellectual interests continued to evolve through his career, Ian joked, even in his sixties, that he looked forward to figuring out what he would do when he grew up. He worked long hours but did not seem frantic or harassed. He was preoccupied, thinking of intellectual matters, as we children scurried through the house. He was usually in his rocking chair, reading and underlining, or at his office in the college chapel just a block away. It was not hard for me to understand what professors do: they read, write, and talk about books. It seemed a good life, if you like books. I did not decide to go to graduate school until the year after college, but the basis for that decision lay not only in my intellectual interest in the subject matter, but in the evident satisfaction and joy in his work that my father constantly demonstrated.

My sense of space and place—where I feel most at home outside my home—was shaped by a childhood playing games on a college campus. I grew up as a faculty brat across the street from the Carleton College chapel that housed my father's office. With my pals, I played football, flashlight tag, or "No Ghosts are Out Tonight" on the lawns around the chapel. The college campus was an enormous and intricate playground with climbing trees, hiding places, Margaret Evans hill for sledding, skateboard-friendly sidewalks, Frisbee fields, and the endlessly explorable arboretum. My sense of vocation as a professor and my ease on a college campus took root in those boyhood games and play. In a classroom, too, it can be fun to see down what path ideas lead, to create a cool new game with friends, and to gain confidence by taking risks in a safe environment. Not always, but at their best, childhood games and formal education merge work and play.

Like Ian, I was very lucky to have found work that I enjoy. I have been fortunate and privileged, for I enjoyed huge advantages based on economic and social class, race, and gender. I could afford to spend six years in graduate school with little income; I did not worry much about making ends meet, knowing that I could turn to my parents in a crisis. The meaning of vocation is different for those who must do menial, boring, or dangerous labor to provide for their families.

My father taught me a work ethic by example rather than explicit instruction. Frederick Buechner described the ideal vocation as ""the place where your deep gladness and the world's deep hunger meet."[5] That kind of work both fulfills a person and contributes something to others. Sometimes when the gladness dissipates, you still need to do unpleasant tasks. So having a work ethic includes having the grit to stick with a job when it loses its enjoyable aspects. But the ability to bear down on tasks even when they give no pleasure has a shadow side. The drive to work hard is an aspect of conscience that, in my experience, reflects compulsive psychic forces. I'm a work-lover—of what I thought of as "my own work," anyway, as opposed to sitting on committees or grading student papers. I have to accomplish a certain amount to feel all right about myself. A morning person, I find it difficult to relax and enjoy anything else until I have done some reading

---

5. Frederick Buechner, *Wishful Thinking: A Seeker's ABC*, rev. and exp. ed. (San Francisco: HarperSanFrancisco, 1993), 118–19.

Family Conscience

or writing. My need to base my feeling of self-worth on productivity may have fostered obsessive workaholism at times. Then vocation, the sense of being called to express one's deepest values in one's work, became unrelenting busyness, perfectionist striving, and insatiable ambition. Single-minded focus on my work sometimes meant detachment from or indifference to others so I could be efficient and productive. From a Christian point of view, the anxious work habits of a high achiever often reflect an attempt to earn or prove one's basic worth, rather than understanding the value of human life as based on God's creation.

Ian's life as a college professor was dominated by work in a way that was common for White men of his generation and is still pretty much the norm for professionals of any race and gender. It is an unbalanced life, without enough time for hobbies, friendship, family, recreation, spiritual practice, and other important concerns. After he retired, Ian acknowledged that he had missed some precious opportunities for relationships, and that both he and his family paid a price for his focus on his work. He often expressed regrets about this.

I don't think I ever resented my father's preoccupation with teaching and writing, as my siblings sometimes did. Arguing with them in days gone by, I defended Ian's dedication to his work in terms of what it contributed to an intellectual field of scholarship and in terms of his own personal satisfaction. I explained the trade-offs between being available and responsive to other people and committing to work that demands concentration, solitude, and detachment. My defense of my father's work ethic has a strong element of self-justification. When I evaluate Ian's priorities and vocational commitment, I may be too closely identified with his way of life to see him accurately or to be critical of how he spent his time and energy.

* * *

IAN'S DISCUSSIONS OF SCIENCE and religion have an ethical dimension that I interpret in terms of intellectual conscience. Put simply, it's wrong to believe what doesn't make sense. Many aspects of modern science pose challenges to traditional Christian affirmations and literal interpretations of the Bible. Ian helped clarify Christian alternatives to a secular worldview or fundamentalism. He interpreted relationships between scientific theory and religious claims in terms of a fourfold typology explained in *When Science Meets Religion*. He distinguishes between cases in which there is genuine conflict between the claims of science and of religion, situations in which they are independent modes of reflection, occasions that call for dialogue between these two kinds of thinking, and attempts to integrate science and religion in a comprehensive philosophy or worldview. Long before I read his publications, I learned from my father that religious faith is compatible with certain forms of doubt, and that faith and critical thought can be mutually enriching. This conviction was strengthened by teaching at a Lutheran college where Christian identity and intellectual integrity were equally important. My version of faith has been nurtured in my local congregation of the United Church of Christ, where a series of challenging ministers and a vigorous membership seek expressions of their faith in the arts, intellectual endeavors, and concern for social justice. In my vocation and my understanding of the church, I've been strongly influenced by Ian's combination of intellectual searching and religious conviction.

The interdisciplinary character of Ian's work influenced my basic orientation to academic life, and his example helped give me confidence to pursue my interests and follow curiosity wherever it led. Disciplines, departments, and the various ways in which teaching and learning get organized in institutions are necessary, but these structures should not get in the way of inquiry. When I was deliberating about graduate-school programs, I was torn between studying Christian ethics or an interdisciplinary program in Religion and Literature at the University of Chicago Divinity School. I received very strong advice against the interdisciplinary program from two major figures in religious studies who visited Oberlin when I was a senior. "John," said one of them, "if you do this program, English departments will say you are a good theologian. The hiring committee in a religion department may say you are a good literary critic. But you will never get a job." Their caution was realistic advice, and I would say the same thing to a graduating religion major today. But I followed my intellectual passion and enrolled in the Religion and Literature program. I was very lucky to find a teaching position where I could sometimes teach in my field of specialization and was encouraged to create new courses. This was unusual in the 1980s and is even more rare today in the shrinking fields of the humanities, where many recent graduates can find only adjunct work, if any.

I had to keep some psychic distance from my father in order not to be in his shadow. I didn't read any of his books until the 1990s and avoided discussions of science and religion. A friend told me that my scholarly ambitions reflect an Oedipal struggle to displace the father. Perhaps I illustrate this theory perfectly, because consciousness of this motivation is so deeply repressed that I am not aware of it. I didn't want to displace him, but to be like him, at least as a teacher and scholar.

I also wanted to find my own way. I disliked being with my father in academic contexts such as the annual convention of the American Academy of Religion. In my early career, I was irritated when he tried to introduce me to people he knew, so I avoided him. I had to meet people on my own terms through shared interests, rather than as his son. I didn't want to take advantage of his stature in the profession. I must have benefited from it, though, when I was hired at St. Olaf College by Harold Ditmanson, the Religion Department chair, who respected Ian and his work. I got my foot in the door that way, but, I tell myself defensively, I could only keep the job through my own efforts.

* * *

WHEN IAN DIED, WE received many letters of remembrance and heard many stories from people who knew him. The most repeated motif was about his combination of intellectual brilliance and modesty or humility. He was often reluctant to discuss his ideas or books. Said one friend, "He always turned the question back and asked what I thought." Colleagues and friends recalled how at dinner parties Ian and Deane drew everyone into the conversation, yet changed the subject when asked about their own lives. My parents' shared scruple about talking about themselves made them generous and supportive, yet in some ways hard to know. Not being self-centered was a crucial ideal and aspiration for them. In personal relationships with others, though, it sometimes created an imbalance or one-sidedness.

Ian's desire to avoid self-centeredness influenced his religious life and thinking in several ways. He had decided views about what he should and should not pray for. In 1989 my mother discovered a lump in her breast that might have been cancer. In a letter to his children, Ian described how he turned to God:

> Deane was calmer about it than I was. I found myself praying that it not be cancer—which is absurd, because it already was whatever it was. Even if it had been cancer, I think it would be okay to pray for strength and peace of mind, and to express gratitude for the gift of life, but not to ask God to intervene, which would be playing favorites if it involved helping some people but not others. I remember that after my brother died someone said "It must be comforting to know that it was God's will"; I strongly disagree with that idea, even if it was a well-intentioned comment.

In this case, the issue for Ian was not praying for oneself; he felt he could ask for the capacity to face events bravely and with wisdom. A theological issue was at stake: it would be wrong to expect or ask God to "play favorites." If this scruple were widely shared, there would be a lot less prayer! Yet Ian would never criticize others for offering such a prayer. He appreciated the congregational sharing of joys and concerns that preceded the minister's prayers, and he sometimes expressed concern for particular individuals or a world crisis. To my knowledge, he never shared his own personal worries or thanksgivings.

In the family, Dad rarely spoke about God or his faith. We usually had a moment before meals when we would "say grace," but often we did not *say* it. Dad would request a time for silence like this: "Let's bow our heads, shall we?" Or "First, let's give thanks." Or even, "Let's pause for station identification"! We would hold hands and sit quietly for a moment or two until he whispered "Amen." This form of table grace seems to invite everyone, even the atheist or skeptic, to find a personal way to be grateful. Sometimes Dad would make this explicit: "Let's each say thanks in our own way." He combined reverent piety with respect for other perspectives. And he had a cautious reluctance to reduce to words the subtle movements of the spirit, as was evident also in his and Deane's appreciation of Quaker worship.

For someone who thought and wrote about religion so much, he was remarkably reticent about saying what he actually believed, even to his children. When I asked him about this, he responded: "A parent has to assume some but not too much responsibility. I don't like to preach to my kids, especially about religion. This is partly about respecting your independence, partly because my own search continues, and partly I'm an academic who attempts to see other viewpoints." It was also a matter of humility. In a letter to one of his children, Ian wrote: "I know my own family knows better than anyone else how far I fall short of practicing what I preach, and I am very reluctant to preach to them."

Somehow Ian combined a deep and utterly sincere faith with what many people would consider an agnostic stance. He knew that every statement about God is a human interpretation, and usually metaphorical or symbolic, not to be taken literally. More elaborate and systematic views of God—the "myths, models, and paradigms," as he titled one book—are subject to ongoing debate and revision in the light of critical reflection and further religious experiences. His understanding of resurrection was less traditional than most Christian views, including Deane's. I'm not sure whether or not he believed that a person's soul survives death in some way or becomes absorbed in the cosmic process, even as it influences it. He was a bit cagey about resurrection, in my opinion. Yet God was real for Ian, and he cherished the symbols of Christian tradition. He wrote to the widow of a Scottish cousin who was a minister: "I do not know if there are angelic choirs who welcome a faithful servant. But I think there must be great joy as Maxwell somehow knows God's love in a new way."

Family Conscience

That "somehow" is significant. Ian's combination of faith and agnosticism (perhaps a better description would be openness to further understanding) influenced my own orientation before I could think about religion. When I was a boy, I put a sign on my door that said "In God we trust. All others, strictly cash." I thought this was a hilarious joke, yet it suggests that from an early age I viewed religious people and institutions skeptically. When I was nineteen, I felt that I had found a kindred spirit when I read in chapter 85 of *Moby-Dick* Ishmael's interpretation of the rainbow that can appear in the fountain of a whale's ejected jet of water:

> For, d-ye see, rainbows do not visit the clear air; they only irradiate vapor. And so, through all the thick mists of the dim doubts in my mind, divine intuitions now and then shoot, enkindling my fog with a heavenly ray. And for this I thank God; for all have doubts; many deny; but doubts or denials, few along with them, have intuitions. Doubts of all things earthly, and intuitions of some things heavenly; this combination makes neither believer nor infidel, but makes a man who regards them both with equal eye.[6]

Now I'm more A believer than an infidel, but my version of faith encompasses doubts of all things earthly, including the words and institutions of the church in which I worship. I am grateful to belong to a church where that is possible.

* * *

Dad had a very simple lifestyle and owned few possessions. When he died, his car was a fifteen-year-old Toyota Corolla. He donated nearly all of his million-dollar Templeton Prize in 1999 to establish the Center for Theology and the Natural Sciences at the Graduate Theological Union in Berkeley. My sister Blair, in a letter to our minister as he prepared his eulogy for Ian, described how our father eschewed luxuries and found pleasure in simple things:

> He had a strong sense of environmental stewardship and was disturbed by the materialism of our society and by conspicuous consumption. Decades before remote control mute buttons were widespread, he had figured out how to rig up a switch on the TV and would turn off the volume during advertisements. He would always choose to stay in a YMCA, if possible, over a

---

6. Herman Melville, *Moby-Dick: An Authoritative Text*, edited by Harrison Hayford and Hershel Parker, A Norton Critical Edition (New York: Norton, 1967), 314.

Pros and Cons, Regrets and Grace

hotel. Until his last car bought in 1998, he wouldn't dream of buying a car with air conditioning or a radio, nor did he believe a/c to be environmentally responsible, so only in the last few years in their home on Winona Street did he install one window unit in the smallest room in the house. He wore the same watch for almost his entire life and was oblivious to clothes. He would be as happy wearing a tweed jacket my mom would have found in a second hand clothing store—where she bought most of her own clothes—as a new jacket from Brooks Brothers. On the other hand, he was extremely generous in large and small ways (the donation of the Templeton Prize being the most dramatic example), and he enjoyed simple pleasures such as a piece of peanut brittle, a roaring fire in the fireplace, classical music on the radio or performed live, and reading *Winnie the Pooh* aloud to his children or grandchildren.

To this list OF Ian's pleasures, I must add his total absorption and ecstatic engagement in conducting an invisible orchestra as the radio played Beethoven. And his love of the natural world as he relished a sunset, a mountain outlook, or a seascape. Like his grandfather, RLD, Ian felt strongly God's presence in nature. These experiences grounded and motivated his strong commitment to developing an environmental ethic, a central aspect of his teaching and writing. He knew the authentic sources of human happiness, in contrast to what we so often pursue. What he enjoyed or did not want was based on convictions about what is truly important and sustains life.

* * *

A TYPED NOTE FROM my father, dated August 28, 1965:

John—
   Your bike was out again and unlocked last night. What happened? You came in late, so you knew you weren't going to use it again. Did you forget, or do you figure it isn't worth the trouble, or that someone else would put it in?
   I thought I should put this in writing, so that you would be warned ahead of time:
      1. A brand new Schwinn is a very tempting item.
      2. Insurance does not cover loss due to the owner's carelessness.
      3. I do not plan to buy you another bike if this one is stolen or rusted due to your carelessness, so you'll have to save up to buy any replacement.

Family Conscience

If it is just forgetfulness, I'll be glad to try to help you figure out a way of remembering—like putting a notice by the toothbrushes so when you brush your teeth each night you can be reminded if you haven't done it.

On the back is 25 cents for a 1965 license. Please be sure to get it before school starts.

Dad

He was always in control of his emotions around me, although sometimes he was exasperated by my sisters or brother. He could be thoughtfully critical of a politician's or colleague's views but was almost never angry. Several times he told me, "It takes two to have a fight," as if a person could always make a conscientious decision not to be angry or aggressive. An adjective that describes Ian well is "irenic." Not ironic, for his use of language was crystal clear and straightforward. Irenic: seeking peace. He always sought reconciliation: between people, communities, and ideas, especially religious and scientific ones. Never did I hear him make a mean or cruel remark to or about another person; he had no impulses to sarcasm. Only once did I hear him curse, when, after hitting his finger with a hammer, he cried out, "Hell's bells!" That is just like him: even in hell he would see the bright, joyful, musical side: the bells!

I admire Ian's generous nature and readiness to seek reconciliation. I didn't learn from him how to fight fair, work through angry feelings, or respond to the anger of others. And his calm reasonableness, to which I was readily amenable, sometimes seemed to infuriate my siblings. My brother said it is maddening to disagree with someone who seems always to have a good argument worked out and in place while you are still trying to figure out what you think and feel. Especially when you are a teenager, it makes you wonder whether you are crazy.

* * *

DEANE MARRIED A MAN who would never be tempted to take his own life. In Ian's office in the Carleton chapel in June 2003, I probed connections between depression and conscience in Deane's father and other members of my family. Ian said that although he had felt anxious and sad, he had never in his entire life been depressed:

"I can't imagine contemplating taking my life, even in moments when it has been painful or difficult. I've thought you were more like me in that, compared with your siblings. I take that partly as a very serious indictment of me, because my younger children, who grew up at the time I was busiest, have felt depression more seriously. But I'm also aware that there are genetic factors. We have an inheritance of genetics in relation to depression that is quite serious. Do you think you are somewhat set apart from the other three?"

I responded: "I think I'm less susceptible to depression than they are, although I have had moments of gloom. I see this as related to conscience, self-assessment, judgment of oneself. Depression is often linked to unduly harsh self-judgment. I'm exploring links between a pattern of depression and ethical issues. For example, perfectionism can mean that I can't accept myself, and this turns into depression, and then I start getting depressed about being depressed."

"Do you think it's primarily a kind of genetic, biological, serotonin-related pattern, or do you think it might be that in your childhood I could give you more attention? For a while, you were the only child. I would say bedtime prayers with you, and we made some trips together. There were times I could give you my undivided attention."

"I think in our family there is a biological, genetic factor: a tendency towards depression. But I don't think that's all of it. Culture and family experience enter in. I see three of us, the older kids before Heather was born, as being in the same boat when you were so busy. I would say we had about the same parenting."

"I took more time with you," Ian said. "I went to some of your school conferences. I read to you at bedtime quite often, whereas when David and Blair were on the scene, it was Mom that read to them at bedtime. But back to the question of depression. I hope you know how aware we are of the genetic factor and of the importance of getting medical help. If you felt the need to try out Prozac, you shouldn't wonder if we would disapprove. Many in our family have gotten help, and I think it could have saved Deane's father's life. You have seen the utterly tragic medical report just before his death, when the doctor essentially said: 'You ought to try harder.' The lack of any real insight, much less any medication—that would have so changed Mom's life. And the message that she mustn't talk to anybody about it. All these things make depression something I've taken much more seriously. I've been trying to read up on it. I haven't had it in my own experience and need to understand it."

"There is a link that is not just genetic but is related to conscience," I said. "Depression is often anger turned inward. That is an issue in both sides of my family for different reasons. I don't think expression of anger in a healthy way is one of our strengths. And it hasn't been in Meg's family, either, because her father could be explosive. We've struggled with how to teach our children about anger. I think a tendency to depression is linked to worrying about hurting other people."

Family Conscience

"It gets involved, as in my mother's case, with a religious judgment that anger is unchristian, unloving."

"Do you remember expressing anger?"

"I don't myself," Ian responded, "but I do remember my siblings being angry. I never got spanked. I remember Freeland being spanked."

"Were you disciplined in other ways?"

"I lived up to their expectations and was cheerful. I'm sure I must have been disciplined for some things. But I don't remember any sequence of rebelling and being punished."

For a short time in 1989, I had fantasies of suicide when I thought my marriage was disintegrating. I have been close enough to depression to understand how someone can feel so terrible as to think life is not worth living. I believe that love for my children would prevent me from ever committing suicide, because I witnessed the damage such a death leaves behind. But how can I know how I might react to a series of blows, debilitating illness, or the mind's helpless slide into despair? I don't have Ian's predisposition to constant good cheer and optimism. Yet usually, when in a melancholy mood, I suddenly and inexplicably break out of it. I've experienced mild depression but not crushing despair. I share enough of my father's nature—whether it be hopefulness, genetic factors such as serotonin levels, or capacity for detached engagement in intellectual work—to have escaped severe depression. So far.

* * *

IN JUNE 2005, IAN and Deane are moving out of their home into an apartment in a month. They are out of town for a few days, visiting Heather. With a key to their house, I return to my childhood home at 106 Winona Street, where my parents lived for forty-eight years. I wander through the rooms, remembering incidents that happened there, trying to elicit memories and associations. In my parents' bedroom, there is a deep closet where Ian keeps his clothes. Hanging there are his academic gown, a bathrobe, tweedy coats, his pants and shirts. He sure doesn't own many clothes. When I was a child, there were boxes stored in the back of this closet. What was in the boxes? I push the clothes aside and peer back into the cavernous depths of the dark closet. There is nothing there. What was I expecting to find? A skeleton? Evidence of crimes, vices, or secret obsessions? I am certain that my father has nothing to hide. He seems to me a person with no dark secrets or painful history to conceal. There is no guilt in his past, nothing of which he is ashamed.

Pros and Cons, Regrets and Grace

I look in his dresser drawers. Socks, underwear, two Nalgene bottles, pills, a drawer of gift-wrapping paper. It feels intrusive, even sordid, to do this, so I stop, sit on the bed and muse. When I was a boy I played "monster-with-a-broken-leg" under this bed. Beneath the bed, I'd snarl and crawl around, trying to catch my screaming siblings lying on top, when they dared to poke their legs in the air. If I caught them, I would hold and tickle and pretend to eat them. This game, at once scary and funny, may have acted out our dim awareness of something below the surface that was broken and dangerous. We didn't come in here often.

I move through other rooms. In two upstairs rooms, former bedrooms of Blair and David, there are many boxes of files, photos, financial records, letters, and papers. Ian and Deane are sorting through two lifetimes' worth of memories, discarding, saving, and organizing things for various recipients. I am curious but don't look within the files. It is not only that my conscience finds snooping repugnant; I just don't think that there is much to be found here. Ian and Deane will tell me what I want to know, whatever I ask. But what don't I know enough to ask about? What will I someday wish that I had asked?

This vaguely unsettling inspection of physical objects in the family home feels like the writing project I recently started. There is something unseemly, transgressive, or dishonorable about poking around for I-know-not-what. I sense something just out of sight or flickering at the edge of consciousness that makes me anxious and intrigued. I remember the biblical story of Ham seeing the nakedness of his father and the curse that Noah puts on Ham's descendants (Genesis 9:20–27). Ham dishonored his father, in contrast to Noah's other sons, Shem and Japheth, whose "faces were turned away" (v. 23 NRSV). I think about the fifth commandment: "Honor your father and your mother, so that your days may be long in the land that the LORD your God is giving you" (Exodus 20:12). What does it mean to honor one's parents? In the biblical world, it meant not exposing them to shame, not revealing what would humiliate them, but rather protecting them from such a threat. Shame and honor have different meanings for me. I don't turn my face away; I would know the dark side of my parents' lives. I want to honor Deane by showing how she overcame shame and depression with insight and courage. I cannot honor my father in the same way. I did not worry much about whether writing a memoir might cause him pain, even when I was critical of Dorothy or probed his feelings about being a father. Perhaps like a child I saw Dad as invulnerable, as the protector rather than one who needs to be protected. What is there to say about a father who is perfectly good, rational, and generous? What's the buried secret, where is the flaw that humanizes? I would like to honor Ian, but not by looking away.

Family Conscience

* * *

Ian never expressed guilt, shame, or even regret about the past, with one important exception: he reproached himself for not having spent more time with his children. He did this many times, and he always moved quickly from self-criticism to excuse-giving or justifying his focus on his work. He would explain how difficult it was to change fields from physics to religion with only two years of seminary coursework. This he called "retooling," and I pictured him trying to hammer with a wrench or saw with a screwdriver. He wanted to make the study of religion academically respectable at a time when this new field was widely viewed with suspicion as lacking intellectual substance. At first he was a one-person department, teaching a wide range of courses and staying one class meeting ahead of his students. At the same time, he launched his scholarly career and wrote his first books. He was under great pressure and had a lot of intellectual ambition.

In 1975 I went to see Bob, the psychologist who worked with my family when I was a boy. I recorded in my journal his view of my father during those early years and a question about myself:

> Dad didn't ask about Mom's state of mind but buried himself in his work. With Mom's permission he worked, only came home for meals, smiled benignly, didn't get involved in family affairs. Mom and Dad had a tacit if unspoken agreement that everything was always fine in the family when he came home. He didn't ask questions and she didn't open up. Bob seemed slightly sarcastic about Dad's work and apparent insensitivity. How much of Dad's attitude have I picked up? Doing academic work not as a direct avoidance of conflict but as a focus of concentration that blots out awareness of human relationships.

Bob's view was formed in the early 1960s, when the children were small and Deane had most of the responsibilities of child-raising. Later, Ian faced challenges from his children as in our teens and twenties we rebelled in various ways. I was the least of his worries, going to graduate school, getting married at twenty-seven, and following a conventional academic career path that he understood. I had no serious conflicts with him or my mother, and when I made different choices than they had, such as living with Meg for four years before we were married, it did not create emotional turmoil. My three siblings, however, went through troubled times, personal crises, and periods of anger and rebellion against Ian and Deane. Their searches for meaningful work took them in directions that my parents worried about or could not understand. David and Heather did not quickly settle into the familiar pattern of steady job, marriage, mortgage, and children. David was sometimes explosively angry at Ian, and this was the primary reason my father sought counseling in 1981. In the course of therapy, Ian came to wish that he had been more present and involved in the lives of his children and had supported Deane so that she could pursue interests outside the home.

I think that Ian's relationships to his children affected his moral sensibility in two ways. First, it took both psychological insight and ethical self-assessment for him to recognize the problems in his relationships to his children and to try to change the pattern. Some of his children's anger was a response to his emotional absence from their lives and a desperate attempt to engage him. He realized that he had not been as involved as he should have been, and he tried to connect with them, and later with his three grandchildren. Many times he expressed to me his regret—and perhaps remorse—at his overinvolvement in work and emotional detachment from his family. I think he was also hoping that I would empathize with him and affirm his life choices, because I understand the demands of an academic career and scholarly achievement.

Regret involves sorrow and sympathy for someone's pain and suffering. Remorse and guilt focus on one's culpability for an incident seen as not only unfortunate, but a wrong for which one is responsible. Ian seemed to me to vacillate between these different responses to his limitations as father and husband. Regret and remorse may both be appropriate in a particular situation, and it can be hard to sort them out.

Framing the issue in terms of conscience in 2003, I asked him how he felt about having neglected his children. He responded: "It's both a feeling of regret, and maybe a bit of guilt, that I didn't spend more time with my children, which would also have let Deane spend more time outside the home. But it's not just that I neglected my duty. I realize now that I neglected things that were important to me as well as to the children. I paid a high price for those early years at Carleton, retooling in a new field that I wasn't adequately prepared for. The circumstances required me to teach a much greater variety of courses than any sane person should have. I was beginning a one-man and then two-man department. In those days one's duty was defined in terms of more rigid roles for men and women. I neglected a part of myself. If I had come into a well-established department where I could teach a narrower range of courses, it would have been different than founding a department. It really was a high price I paid in my life and in your lives, more than a neglect of duty."

As when we discussed vocation, Ian did not refer to conscience and spoke of neglected self-development rather than duty. He acknowledged only "a bit" of guilt but regretted missing experiences he could have shared with his children. Ian was averse to using the language of guilt or conscience, which he saw as burdensome, unhelpful, or destructive. Yet I think that he felt more guilt than he admitted. Conscience was at work when he assessed his life, found it lacking, and reoriented his priorities.

A second way in which his children changed his moral perspective, Ian said, was teaching him to appreciate other ways of living. Like his parents, he closely identified the proper work of young adults with an academic path. He came to affirm other ways in which his children found and made meaning in their lives. The theme of tolerance or, more positively, affirmation of the goodness of other ways also shaped his perception of family roles and homosexuality. He learned that there are "a variety of ways of being human and many good patterns." He was very supportive of his granddaughter, Alex, when she came out as a lesbian in 2005. Blair described it this way: "His efforts to build a relationship with Alex made me happy and grateful. He has really been there as she has come out as a lesbian. That required authenticity and open-mindedness on his part. Alex is amazed and happy that she has grandparents who accept her as she is. When Dad was in Chicago, they went to a play about homeless kids who are gay and lesbian and were rejected by their parents. She was sitting in the theatre next to her grandfather, who was one of the few straight people there, and she thought: 'I'm the only one in this queer audience who has a grandparent with them.'"

Ian's therapy in 1981 with the psychiatrist Lynn was a catalyst for these changes. At the end of a tape recording of their final session, he said: "I couldn't have gotten this out of a book. I needed a person." Lynn helped Ian to understand how George had shaped Ian's orientation by making him overly focused on work and expecting his children to follow his example. On the tape recording, Ian regrets what he missed as a father but does not say he feels guilty. I hear again a mixture of excuse-giving and muffled remorse as he recounts the pressures he was under while he changed academic fields, created Carleton's new Religion Department, and wrote his books. I feel uncomfortable as I listen to this confusing confession. Is he stuck in a rut or being honest about an unresolved conflict? Hearing my father talk this way gives me the same pinched, anxious feeling I had when I saw my mother pained by memories of her father. I flinch because of compassion for him and because it touches a nerve: the recording of his therapy session triggers my questions about my own limitations as a father.

I wonder whether we can ever get completely beyond contrition about the past. Would doing so even be desirable? Conscience is not simply rational evaluation of one's actions; it brings up deep and painful feelings. The metaphors for a guilty conscience involve suffering: carrying a heavy burden, feeling the sting or bite of conscience, hiding something ugly from

Pros and Cons, Regrets and Grace

the gaze of others. Conscience gnaws, disturbs, accuses. It is not entirely responsive to logic or rational arguments. When a person remains stuck in remorse, unable to move beyond terrible feelings about the past, self-judgment becomes destructive. Yet to completely forget those feelings seems to me an impossible and questionable goal. A person without regrets seems to me to have learned little or to be in denial.

As he got older, Ian tried to live a more balanced life, make amends with his children, and seek new intimacy and experiences with us. He loved and spent time with his grandchildren. He realized that, as he said, "you don't have to be perfect to be lovable." Ian owned up to regret for mistakes, felt sad about what he missed, and focused on what he could learn for the future. This seems like a good example of a healthy conscience, yet something puzzles and bothers me. Sometimes I think he was too hard on himself and at other times I suspect that he never fully admitted or came to terms with the guilt he felt. Did he learn from his mistakes and move on, or did his conscience linger and get stuck? I am not sure, and that question stays with me.

I was keen to find evidence of a guilty conscience: the flaw that makes my father human, a suffering and emotional side that would balance the dominating rational side that seemed always calm and in control. Given Ian's remarkable clarity about so many things, his unresolved attitude to his past as a father disturbed me. This one area of his life where he seemed troubled and uncertain fascinates me, resonating with my deep sense of moral ambiguity.

* * *

IN DECEMBER 1995, IAN gave a sermon at First United Church of Christ in Northfield, Minnesota, that dealt with the role of forgiveness and self-acceptance in healing. "Brokenness and Healing" begins with exegesis of the parable of the prodigal son: "The son can be found only when he has come to himself and made the decision to return home." When a person feels forgiven, he is enabled to love others, because he is freed from preoccupation with his own status or worthiness. Turning to his own experience, Ian compares this form of religious grace with psychological self-understanding:

> Let me suggest that there are parallels between self-acceptance in a religious context and self-acceptance within psychotherapy. I discovered this fifteen years ago when I belatedly sought help from a therapist in understanding myself. My father was a wonderful person in many ways, but during my childhood he was not very often home or able to share his feelings with us; the

childcare was left entirely to my mother. I perpetuated exactly the same pattern with my own children. I put most of my energy into my work, especially when I was retooling from teaching physics to teaching religion courses. I was a typical workaholic father who was largely absent from the personal and emotional lives of his children. We didn't communicate our feelings with one another very well.

One of the things I discovered in therapy is that we don't have to be perfect to accept ourselves or to be accepted by others. I didn't have to earn my father's love by trying to be a perfectionist in my work. I loved him dearly and I am thankful for all he did for me and meant to me, but I also feel sad for what he did not give me in my childhood. So too I can ask my children's forgiveness for times when I was not present to them. I regret the loss to their lives and to mine. In recent years we have worked on better patterns of communication and can still do so. My point here is that self-acceptance and acceptance by other people are linked together, just as self-acceptance and acceptance by God are linked.

Ian compared the father in the parable of the prodigal son to Jesus Christ, in whom "God has run to meet us while we are yet afar off." He closed by interpreting the ritual of communion in terms of the symbolism of brokenness and healing.

Tears came into Ian's eyes and his voice choked up at several points. The congregation was surprised and moved that morning as this respected intellectual, this calm and dignified elder, made a public confession. Ian did not use the language of conscience to describe his breakthrough, but I would. It takes self-judgment to recognize how self-centeredness has impaired one's life. Conscience does not simply recognize brokenness; it does some of the breaking, shattering one's flattering self-image or illusion of virtue. Such an experience of self-condemnation is crucial in the Protestant understanding of justification by faith, though it can take other forms than Martin Luther's period of terror of God's vindictive wrath. Not every Christian goes through internal conflict and troubling self-scrutiny, followed by release and a sense of being accepted. But the experience of self-judgment and renewal is a crucial experience for many, including my father.

Conscience also plays a role in the healing process. It is not itself the source of healing or forgiveness; that usually comes from other people and from God. Yet conscience involves more than negative self-assessment; it depends on aligning one's heart and soul with the good, with God. Insight and intention help one turn from a purely negative judgment to a source of goodness and affirmation beyond oneself. This turning is experienced by a Christian as grace, which overcomes the self-reproach and even self-hatred that a scrupulous conscience can engender. Contrition and repentance may linger, even many years later. Yet for the Christian, a new serenity is based on the recognition that one does not earn love by being morally perfect or attain peace of mind by satisfying a demanding conscience. Rather, trust in God's judgment and mercy finally overcomes self-condemnation and opens a person to new possibilities. The insights and reorientation of conscience play a crucial role in this transformation.

Ian and Deane, 2007.

* * *

IAN HAD A STROKE on December 19, 2013. He was taken in a helicopter to an intensive care unit in Minneapolis and the family gathered. He never regained consciousness. We thought he would die when the ventilator was removed, but he continued to breathe. For five days, Dad struggled to go on living. Without food or water, he became dehydrated. His breathing came in rapid gasps that went on and on, as if he were running a marathon or climbing Mount Everest. His frail, shrunken ninety-year-old body was surprisingly strong; he was a tough old buzzard. He would not let go but clung to life and what he loved. Those days and nights were a terrible ordeal for me that felt like witnessing a crucifixion. "He's not conscious, he's not suffering," said the chaplain and nurses. But body, mind, and spirit are connected, and I felt his agony as dehydration made his bodily systems shut down.

For a hundred hours my siblings and I hovered around Dad, holding his hand, whispering words of love, speaking quietly with each other, spelling each other for food breaks and phone calls. Music that Dad loved, especially by Bach, was playing on a CD. I went home to sleep the first three nights, then napped fitfully on a cot the final night. In my journal I noted different ways in which Ian's children coped with this vigil: "The ways we enact our family roles: I'm wanting to do something, organize, move on fast from this horrible dying. David is totally into the present moment, nursing Dad attentively. Heather wants to make a death mask, making art out of suffering. Blair is taking care of us all, thinking of what people are feeling." Throughout this waiting time my brother stayed with Ian, sleeping by his bed, caressing him, washing sweat from his body, recalling their life together. He would not leave to get food but snacked on what was brought to him. David and my father had an intense and complicated relationship, with painful conflicts and joyful shared experiences. I think Dad's emotional life was more fully engaged with David than with anyone except Deane.

Late in the afternoon of Christmas Eve 2013, we had just played Handel's *Messiah* and were listening to Bach's cantata *Sleepers Awake*. Heather and her husband, Tom, decided to leave the hospital to get something to eat. David turned away from Dad for a moment to ask Heather to look for some vegetarian food. There was a half minute of back-and-forth about the options. Tom noticed that Ian was not breathing and we turned back to him. He made three wrenching groans or gasps and stopped breathing. We huddled around his exhausted body, weeping, touching his cooling hands, and hugging each other, utterly spent and relieved that his suffering was over.

I found a lot of meaning in the way Dad died. I sensed that he was so intensely involved with David and so concerned about him that he could not leave him. His spirit could not pass on while they were locked together. When David turned away for that moment, discussing what he might eat, Dad somehow knew that his son would be okay without him. I have heard other stories about dying that suggest movements of the spirit when a person is not conscious. An unbreakable connection with loved ones must be broken, and this often happens when there is a distraction or a blessing is given. Then the departing soul lets go and is released.

The manner of my father's dying is significant to me for another reason. Along with the good times and the love, my siblings and I have had our share of conflicts, estrangements, and rivalries. If Heather had left the hospital, she would have missed the crucial moment. But we were together for the final parting, although we each experienced it in our own way. For me, it was as if by the way he died Dad was saying: In the future you will encounter problems and pain. You will hurt each other. But remember this moment, when together you shared love and grief. Honor this memory and bond that unites you.

Dad's dying gift to his children expressed his deepest yearning: to overcome estrangement and seek reconciliation. For me it was an experience of grace, when God's goodness and generosity were mediated through the constant, imperfect, and sustaining love of my father.

CHAPTER 7

Another Elder Brother

In January 2006, I went to visit my uncle Hugh, taking the train up the Hudson River Valley from Grand Central Station to Sleepy Hollow, New York. Hugh and Sirkka had recently moved to a retirement home there. I had read some of Hugh's scholarly writing and corresponded with him about his reactions to my writing about George, Dorothy, and Ian. He responded to my questions about the family and sent me "Autobiographical Notes" on which he was working. I hoped that Hugh would shed some light on my father and grandparents. I quickly became interested in Hugh himself because of the contrast with Ian and because in several ways Hugh's life resembles and illuminates my own. I'm drawn to Hugh, as I often am to people who find that the judgments of conscience conflict with each other or are confusing.

A central issue in Hugh's life was the choice of a vocation in relation to his parents' influence and expectations. In "Spilgrimage," a twelve-page autobiographical essay in a 1992 Festschrift dedicated to him, Hugh describes how for missionaries such as George and Dorothy, the central question was: "If you have a gift, where is it most needed?" Hugh felt a duty to live up to their legacy: "My parents took the world as their parish; Dad's mother's father [George Brown] had been Prime Minister of Canada. Any career which did not change the world would be a betrayal of my heritage. Even now I haven't freed the world from nuclear weapons."[1] After studying science and history as an undergraduate at Harvard, Hugh faced a choice between several medical schools and divinity schools. Looking back at this

---

1. Hugh Barbour, "Spilgrimage," in *The Lamb's War: Quaker Essays to Honor Hugh Barbour*, ed. Michael L. Birkel and John W. Newman (Richmond, IN: Earlham College Press, 1992), 21.

difficult decision, he questions whether it was really his own: "My mother's model won out over my father's; I had not yet found one of my own strong enough to affirm against both."[2] Hugh thought that while many people could practice medicine as well as he would have, he might have something distinctive to contribute to the study of religion: "I told myself I did not want to be a sloppy amateur in religion; many laymen feel their own experience strongly and don't know when their ideas are foolish. My own religious and psychological hunger moved me more than I knew. I went to Yale Divinity School because they seemed to care about personal and congregational life." Hugh wanted to integrate rigorous critical thought and his own search for religious experience and meaning. He spent most of his teaching career at Earlham College and focused his scholarship on the history of the Quaker movement. Ian, Hugh, and I were all professors of religion at liberal arts colleges. In certain ways I feel more intellectual affinity with Hugh than with my father. Whereas Ian was primarily interested in theories and systematic thought, Hugh and I explored personal experience and how the subjective side of religion shapes and is shaped by ideas.

At several "dark times" when Hugh agonized about work-related decisions, he tried to discern God's guidance. When he left a pastorate in Coventry, Connecticut, to teach at Syracuse University, he made a breakthrough: "I tried to quiet my own mind and will, hoping God would give me a clear leading, as my mother had taught me to do out of her background in the movement later called Moral Rearmament. My long periods of paralysis about these decisions tore me up and cut me off from people. When I turned from Coventry to Syracuse, I also began to turn, whether away from neurosis or sainthood, toward accepting responsibility for my own decisions." Without an unambiguous call from God to end his uncertainty, he had to choose for himself. In a letter to me in 2005, he explained the sources of his perplexity when making decisions. Like Ian, he resisted the way I had framed my question in terms of conscience, preferring instead H. Richard Niebuhr's idea of response:

> At several stages of my life I spent weeks or months hoping for leadings or guidance as to God's will for me. In some cases the insight came that it was up to me to say first what I really wanted. Certainly, as you say, these times involved the question of who I was or would become. But these times also involved the need to choose between concrete actions . . . In my case the strongest element of guilt in retrospect involves things I did not do or people I did not respond to. Like H. Richard Niebuhr, I

2. Hugh Barbour, "Spilgrimage," 22–23.

Family Conscience

think of ethics in terms of responses and responsibility. These are the areas where insight, intuition, and awareness are the key determinants, whether or not we translate them into faith language about guidance and being led.

Hugh's introspective focus on evaluating his motives and his search for a clear sign from God prevented him at certain times from recognizing his own deepest desires as well as the perspectives of other people. Periods of brooding introspection isolated him so that he failed to respond to other people. I see myself in Hugh's troubled, introverted self-scrutiny and acknowledgment of gaps between himself and others.

"Spilgrimage" ends rather surprisingly with an account of an incident when Hugh realized that other people saw him very differently than he saw himself:

> It takes much grace just to listen. In 1968 I took part in a two-week encounter-group program at Bethel, Maine. The program drew on skilled methods for letting those who took part see ourselves as others saw us, in an accepting group. It is an intense experience. The middle weekend off gave some of us a chance to drive to the White Mountains. Halfway up Mount Washington I asked our carload to let me out to climb the rest of the way. The foot trail from that point is above the timberline. I had climbed it with my brothers and parents and my grandfather [RLD] had loved it too. Squam Lake was in clear view. It was a time to feel God's presence as Rufus Jones [a Quaker leader] did in the Alps, to be affirmed and to rededicate who I was. But when our Bethel group next met together we were asked to rate each other in terms of how much we thought each person had learned in the program, and I found to my shock that I'd been so wrapped up in my own experience that the group rightly ranked me very low.[3]

When I asked Hugh about this experience, he said it illustrates a "self-centered, almost solipsistic pattern . . . That day on Mount Washington we were looking down at all the places like Squam Lake that my parents and grandparents had loved. I began to feel an identity with them that I had suppressed. I kept wondering who I might share it with. I felt rather liberated, or reaffirmed in my identification with my family. But the leaders of the group thought I didn't respond to the other people in the group."

I resonated with this experience, saying: "In the Barbour family there are very strong bonds with siblings, parents, and grandparents, but they are

---

3. Hugh Barbour, "Spilgrimage," 29–30.

usually unexpressed. Often we feel them most when we are alone, as you did on Mount Washington. Maybe this strong sense of connectedness with the family makes it harder to relate to people outside the family. This is one of the puzzles of my family: the combination of detachment or remoteness with an underground connectedness."

"In Maine," Hugh went on, "I was partly involved in making a young person who had cancer feel accepted, and then I would not let them put him ahead of me in the sequence of who had been most helped. They got mad at me for that. I was trying to identify the importance of my own experience and they were most concerned about my recognizing someone else's experience. I was not sensitive to group psychology."

"You were thinking about your own experience rather than the other guy's. In our family we are sometimes most intensely aware of each other when we are alone or apart, after we may have been emotionally distant when we were with those same people we love. While all these feelings of engagement and disengagement with family go on inside us, we miss actual possibilities for relationship with others."

I asked Hugh why he chose to conclude his autobiographical essay with this incident, which seems unrelated to the Festschrift's essays on Quaker history. He answered, "When I was teaching about the Quakers, I didn't listen to what the students said. I told them what I thought Quakerism was. I didn't hear their personal experiences." That is exactly what I feel is my chief fault as a teacher. For many years, especially the early ones, I lectured too much, relying on notes that outlined my brilliant ideas rather than trusting the insights that would emerge from others. Hugh is right: it takes much grace just to listen.

* * *

HUGH SPOKE OF HIS sense of aloneness as a boy and attributed it partly to his family's geographical mobility. From "Spilgrimage": "By the time I was sixteen I had crossed the Pacific five times and the Atlantic ten, and been the outsider in ten schools. Having been a stranger in each country, it seems an achievement just to be human." One of the chapters in his unpublished "Autobiographical Notes" is titled "Stranger on Three Continents" (referring to China, England, and the United States), an allusion that suggests not only his father's "Memories of Three Continents," but also, Hugh wrote, "both my loneliness as an outsider, like the opening line of *Moby Dick*: 'Call Me Ishmael,' (a 'wild ass of a man' in the Bible), and the surprised joy in the song 'Stranger in Paradise.'" In English boarding schools, he was teased and bullied. Of his kindergarten and first grade years in New York City, Hugh

Family Conscience

recalled: "I remember only pain." Dorothy taught her sons to switch in the middle of the Atlantic voyage between holding a fork in the right or left hand. For many years, Hugh tried to belong to both countries. On a visit to Great Britain in 1948, he realized that by not having lived there during the war years, he "was no longer part of that community." All this travel created an extraordinarily close family but made them "slow to make or keep other friends."

Hugh shows several characteristics of missionary children. Like many "third culture" children who grow up abroad, he felt at home nowhere. "Mish kids" often have a special kind of self-consciousness about their religious identity and their parents' hopes to make the world a better place. Such children, according to David Hollinger, were both "more cosmopolitan, but also, it was often said, more traumatized by the cultural shock of adjusting to life in the United States."[4] Missionary children were often emotionally vulnerable high achievers dedicated to a life of service. Hugh fits this profile. His detachment from any home, school, or culture was painful, and it also fostered a critical perspective on the moral norms of all the cultures he encountered and an extremely strong identification with his parents' values.

Like Ian and Hugh, the third and youngest brother in this family was deeply affected by its many geographic and cultural displacements and a childhood with missionary parents. Robert Freeland Barbour (1926–1953), my godfather, had a long history of undiagnosed fevers and headaches and after he died cysts were discovered in his brain. George's biography, *Free*, is my main source of knowledge about this uncle. Free was the rebel in the family, mischievous and often in trouble as a child at home and at school, where he ran afoul of varying standards of discipline in China, England, and the USA. Two years younger than other boys in his class, he was frequently teased and bullied. He attended ten schools on three continents, two American colleges, and three graduate schools. George astutely discerns connections between Free's early displacements and conflicts and a central concern as an adult:

> At each stage, his differences were apt to be taken by his fellows to be those, not of a "foreigner" who might naturally be expected to be a bit queer, but of a nonconformist native. Perhaps this sense of not belonging wholly to any one background accounts for his keen understanding of the feelings of expatriates, whether the foreign students at the university or the DPs [displaced persons] in Austria to whom he gave one of the last

---

4. David A. Hollinger, *Protestants Abroad: How Missionaries Tried to Change the World but Changed America* (Princeton: Princeton University Press, 2017), 16.

years of his life. It explains also the deep satisfaction with which he learned shortly after reaching New York from Europe in September 1950, that he might take the oath of allegiance within three days, and the peculiar joy with which he welcomed his wife into American citizenship as one of his last acts prior to coming home three days before he was taken to hospital.[5]

Freeland's wife, Doe, was from a Jewish family that left Germany in 1934 for Persia. Doe was a fellow medical student at Harvard when she met Free.

My baptism, 1951. Front row: Dorothy, Ian, Freeland, Deane, Dolly.
Back row: George, Hugh, Doe.

The turning point in Free's life was the year (1949–1950) that he spent in Germany and Austria. Because of his recurrent fevers, he was advised to leave a physics program at Johns Hopkins University to recover his health. He volunteered to work in Europe, where he matched displaced refugees with sponsors in the United States. He held the post of civilian administrative officer for the International Refugee Organization in northern Austria. George's *Free* reports stories that reveal his courage, compassion, and

5. George B. Barbour, *"Free"* (Assen: Royal VanGorcum, 1954), 4

Family Conscience

resourcefulness as he rescued people still homeless nearly five years after the end of the Second World War. He literally gave the coat he was wearing to one man. Free was adept at slipping through the cracks of bureaucracy and official regulations and negotiating with various governmental and military units and international organizations. He helped countless refugees escape devastated European cities and find a new home in America. As a result of this year, he decided that he wanted to work more directly with people as a doctor instead of doing research; he was in his third year at Harvard Medical School when he died. As a memorial to Free, a youth hostel for displaced children was built in Salzburg, funded by gifts in his name. The experience of being displaced was a crucial influence, both on the loneliness, insecurity, and disciplinary troubles of his early years, and on the conscience and compassion that moved him to want to help other people who suffered their own forms of dislocation, homelessness, and fear. Free found himself when he broke out of the family pattern of doing academic teaching and research. He created his own way to express the classic "missionary kid" desire to make the world a better place by translating Christian ideals into secular terms.

* * *

HUGH DESCRIBED HIS HIGH school friendships and dating as formal and superficial. Strong bonds developed in college with fellow members of the Student Christian Movement. A profound experience that he compares to a conversion took place when he was able to overcome intense jealousy: "At one conference in June 1941, there came for me a conversion experience one night walking alone in the mist beside Sebago Lake when I was given grace to break through a wall of jealousy and found power to love more unselfishly. Such an experience has recurred two or three times since. Then 'the whole earth had a new smell,' as George Fox had found, and one could help other students with problems."[6] In his "Autobiographical Notes," Hugh goes into more detail about this incident:

> Middy was too busy being a central committee member to have much time for me. One evening when she had a little time free, she went off to talk to Don about religious problems. I was intensely jealous and walked up and down the sandy lakeshore in the dark for several hours. Then, quite suddenly came an inner voice: "But this is just what you have wanted for her"—to get

---

6. Hugh Barbour, "Spilgrimage," in *The Lamb's War: Quaker Essays to Honor Hugh Barbour*, ed. Michael L. Birkel and John W. Newman (Richmond, IN: Earlham College Press, 1992), 22.

such help. It came as a crisis experience for me, as if the mist glowed or had lifted and God had spoken. With it came a huge outburst of joy, which was evident in my voice to the first person I met as I came up from the beach, and seemed to affirm our call as a whole group to help each other find God. I think it also represented a breakthrough of my own ability to be self-giving and caring about others, as Middy had always been. I was able to tell her the next day that "the patient had taken a turn for the better." I never told her nor anyone else the details until here.

Hugh's jealousy may have reflected a romantic attraction and/or a wish that he, too, would be sought out as a leader of the Christian student group. In any case, this story reflects the Quaker understanding of how God addresses a person in the depths of conscience. It involves recognizing one's selfishness and feeling released into a more free and loving relationship with others.

Hugh hoped for this kind of clarity when he wrestled with vocational choices, as he explained in our taped conversation: "That time at Lake Sebago when I was given a breakthrough and a voice came was a liberating experience. It was a time when by waiting in the darkness I got an answer that was not what I wanted or expected but was what I needed. It was not slow but very sudden. I kept hoping for something like that, an opening of light as early Quakers called it, as I struggled for so many dark nights waiting to see if that kind of opening would happen. And it didn't in the vocational context. There wasn't a dramatic moment of insight with regard to vocation, the way there was about the jealousy situation." Instead, he had to take responsibility for a concrete choice between alternatives: to decide rather than wait to be transformed. The more I talked to Hugh, the more I wanted to understand the Quaker experience of discerning an "opening" or "leading" that offers a way out of a troubled or perplexed conscience.

* * *

IN A 2005 LETTER, Hugh attributes his attraction to the Quakers to his mother. After describing Dorothy's involvement in the Oxford Group and her daily practice of self-examination, he stated: "I suspect this is why I became a Quaker." He joined the Cambridge Friends Meeting while he was a student at Harvard. He was active in Young Friends activities and with this group discussed the urgent question of how to be a pacifist during World War II. He filed as a conscientious objector and applied for ambulance or relief work overseas, but a law passed by Congress made it impossible for COs to serve abroad. He remained in divinity school at Yale during the war and wrote a dissertation on the early Quaker movement.[7] "Spilgrimage" describes what appealed to him about the Quakers: "The directness and human equality of every person's relationship to God seems to me more basic than denominations; Quakerism seems to me to witness to this centrally ... The early Friends seemed to me then, and within human limits still seem to me, the purest examples of direct testimony to personal religious experience without traditional channeling."[8]

I turned to some of Hugh's historical writing to learn how Quaker tradition understands conscience.[9] For seventeenth-century Friends, an experience of Light, Spirit, or Christ was crucial in "the Lamb's War," the conflict between God and human sin. The Lamb's War, wrote Hugh, is "the power of the Light to show moral truth and self-deceptions to tender consciences." God's "leading" to a new way of life resolved an individual's ethical struggle to renounce self-will. According to Hugh, conscience is not itself the Light: "The Quaker's appeal to his hearer was 'to the Light of God in thy conscience.' He knew that the Light could shine through the conscience like a light in a lantern, though that conscience alone was not the source of man's power."[10] One early Friend compared the Light of Christ to a candle and conscience to the candleholder.

The Quaker view of conscience gives a central role to intuition as a source of moral guidance. A "leading" is an intuitive response to a concrete problem, when a "way opens" or one can respond to others' needs. In a 2007 paper on Quaker ethics, Hugh wrote that "often intuitions turn out wiser than conscious wisdom," and that sudden flashes of insight "are in fact complex syntheses of past experience, personal relationships, and actually given data, often created in the subconscious mind." Sometimes intuitions are manifested as a voice speaking, "because our fullest and most complex human experiences are interpersonal, not simply rational."[11] These sudden

---

7. See Hugh S. Barbour, "The Early Quaker Outlook upon 'the World' & Society, 1647–1662." PhD diss., Yale University, 1952.

8. Hugh Barbour, "Spilgrimage," in *The Lamb's War: Quaker Essays to Honor Hugh Barbour*, ed. Michael L. Birkel and John W. Newman (Richmond, IN: Earlham College Press, 1992), 8.

9. Hugh's revised dissertation was published as *The Quakers in Puritan England*, Yale Publications in Religion (New Haven: Yale University Press, 1964). He coauthored or coedited several volumes about Quaker history. See the Selected Bibliography in Birkel and Newman, eds., *The Lamb's War* (Richmond, IN: Earlham College Press, 1992) 31–37.

10. Hugh Barbour, *Quakers in Puritan England*, Yale Publications in Religion 7 (New Haven: Yale University Press, 1964), 112.

11. Hugh Barbour, "Quaker Ethics: Purity and Persuasion," unpublished manuscript of a lecture at Earlham School of Religion, June 2007, 7.

resolutions of problems are often accompanied by an outburst of emotional excitement. Hugh's holistic understanding of conscience encompasses intuition and emotion as well as reasoning.

Because a "leading" incorporates so much of a person's identity, it can include bias, error, and distortion. It therefore needs to be compared to the insights of other people. A central issue for Friends is how to distinguish between genuine "leadings" from God and wishful thinking or willful self-assertion. Unlike the seventeenth-century Ranters, who claimed that because they were led by the Spirit they could do nothing wrong, the Quakers insisted on a process of communal testing or discernment. In dialogue with others, a person was expected to examine whether he was rightly led. Hugh delineates four Quaker tests for the genuineness of a leading.[12] First was the criterion of moral purity as opposed to self-interest: "The true Spirit was always contrary to self-will and led to righteousness." A second basis for evaluation involved patient waiting, for "self-will is impatient of tests." The third standard in the discernment process was consistency with the Spirit's actions in scripture and with the witness of other Quakers. A fourth test of the Spirit was whether a leading brought the group into unity. To determine this, Friends searched for "the spirit of the group." In silent meetings, Quakers sometimes came to believe that the Spirit of God had unified their community.

On the basis of these tests, Friends might warn each other that they had not truly understood the Light. One early leader, James Nayler, rebuked another Friend: "Richard Mires, thou getts above thy Condition. Mind the babe in thee and it will tell thee soe. And friend, thou that calls thy selfe a prophett art run up into the ayre; lowlie consider it . . . I saw many dangers cominge through looking out, but if thou waite upon the Lord to be guided by his feare, all will be well, husht and Calme."[13]

Can these Quaker tests of a true leading be translated into criteria for evaluating intuitions and judgments of conscience? If so, an assertion of conscience should be self-denying rather than self-serving; one should be patient while others learn to understand and accept it; it should be consistent with other moral beliefs and exemplars in scripture and history; and it should help bring a person into unity with others rather than into divisive conflict. I don't think any one of these tests is either sufficient or necessary in discerning whether conscience is trustworthy or in error. For instance, conscience is not always self-denying but may sometimes insist that one

---

12. Hugh Barbour, *Quakers in Puritan England*, Yale Publications in Religion 7 (New Haven: Yale University Press, 1964), 119–22.

13. Quoted in Hugh Barbour, *Quakers in Puritan England*, Yale Publications in Religion 7 (New Haven: Yale University Press, 1964), 121.

Family Conscience

be given one's just rights, and conscience may dictate a radical break with moral practices in the Bible or one's community and therefore lead to conflict. Still, these general considerations are a starting point for reflection and help check self-righteousness. The Quaker insistence on self-restraint and patience contrasts starkly with the strident assertions of many would-be prophets.

The Friends insist both on each individual's unique experience of moral clarity and on the need to seek truth in dialogue with others. Even a person's best intentions and deepest convictions are usually mixed with egotism, contentiousness, and biases learned in a family or social group. Conscience should not produce imperturbable certainty and blind confidence in one's own opinions; it must be open to correction and guidance from beyond itself. The difficulty lies in knowing what to do when an individual's conscience differs from what others tell him is right or wrong.

Hugh and Sirkka discussed the strengths and limitations of the Quaker moral sensibility. Hugh said that President George W. Bush used ideas very similar to the Quakers, such as the sense of being led by God: "This language came to Bush through the Baptist tradition, which also traces its roots to Puritan England." (Since Bush grew up in an Episcopalian family, I think Hugh meant that Puritan history influenced Bush's experience of being born again.) I asked how Bush's feeling that he was being guided by God is different from the Quaker orientation.

Hugh responded: "Bush is self-righteous. He doesn't see his limits. He is not alert to the dangers of his confidence. The early Quakers understood that self-righteousness is not only personal, but social: it is expressed outwardly in relation to other people. This was the reason for the plain language of the Quakers, for 'thee' and 'thou' were the way one addressed servants. Similarly, the Quakers' plain dress was intended to avoid class distinctions. Today we need another Reinhold Niebuhr to point out the self-interest and pretension in appeals to God's guidance."

Quakers question the testimony of an individual's conscience and interpretation of God's will. I wondered aloud whether this testing process ever leads to control or manipulation. Sirkka responded that Quaker parents sometimes told their children where they thought God would lead them, for instance, to take a nineteenth-century issue: "Isn't God telling you that you don't really enjoy dancing?" She saw her mother-in-law engaging in this kind of subtle coercion: Dorothy wanted you to come to your own conclusion, but she wanted to make sure it was the same as hers. It is sometimes hard to draw the line between manipulation and appropriate parental guidance or education about a family's or group's values.

Sirkka pointed out another resemblance between Quaker history and the Barbour family: "The Quakers have their blind spots. They saw as 'worldly' most interest in the arts and music. The aesthetic was always subordinated to the ethical. It was the same with Hugh's mother. She never read Tolstoy or great literature, but only didactic things. Hugh's reading habits are similar, in contrast with my love of Kafka and other imaginative writers." Often the spouses of Barbour men are better able to integrate ethical concerns with aesthetic and imaginative experience, as well as emotion.

* * *

Sirkka, Hugh, and I were sitting in their living room in Sleepy Hollow. Sirkka did not want to be tape-recorded but permitted me to take notes as she freely shared her perspective. She remembered meeting Hugh when she was a young Finnish student at Earlham in the late 1950s. She described Hugh as heavy-laden and brooding about the state of the world. From his mother, Sirkka said, Hugh had gotten the sense that he had to "set the world straight." Out of his colossal sense of responsibility came indecision, uncertainty, and finally depression when he could not find a way to solve enormous problems. Both Hugh and Dorothy had a disproportionate sense of moral responsibility that made it hard for them to choose and act, in contrast to each of their spouses. Sirkka thought that some of the difficulties of Hugh and Dorothy were rooted in a distinctively American tendency to psychologize: "They could examine their motives endlessly." As they debated complex moral issues, they often didn't notice small but significant actions they could have taken.

Sirkka's Finnish perspective throws a different light on my father's family. Her candid and sometimes harsh comments on the Barbours were refreshingly incisive, though they sometimes made me wince. She resented her mother-in-law's continued dominance of Hugh's emotions. When Hugh was an infant and a boy, he went through several life-threatening illnesses that required Dorothy to nurse him back to health. The tight bond formed between mother and son persisted in the form of Dorothy's anxious demands to which Hugh could not say no. Sirkka described Dorothy as "a mother-goddess constantly demanding tribute. Hugh responded to this. He always had to be the perfect son and never rebelled. He never drank his first bottle of beer because Dorothy did not approve of it."

I looked over at Hugh and my heart went out to him. I, too, am a son sometimes seen by my siblings and spouse as too closely allied with my parents. I wanted to argue with Sirkka, or rather to defend Hugh, yet I admired her outspoken criticisms and honest acknowledgment of feelings of anger.

Family Conscience

She never felt fully accepted into the Barbour family and decided very early that she did not want to be enmeshed in it. She wrote to me that she had a "kindly, quiet-spoken relationship with George, with a shared sense of kinship that neither of us was American. But Dorothy parceled out her favors according to who paid tribute to her." The Barbour family was "a maze of both intriguing and intimidating complexity to me."

In his *Confessions*, Augustine uses the jealousy of a baby who sees his foster brother at their mother's breast as his first example of the sinful nature of humans. Whether sibling rivalry is a form of sin, an evolutionary trait with survival value, or just the way children are, comparison and competition among brothers and sisters seems to me a central reality and drama in most families. In a letter, Hugh described tension between Dorothy and her sister, Jean: "They competed to be RLD's favorite: Dorothy as the oldest and better student who rode in RLD's electric auto (the first in Brooklyn) as he made his night house calls as a doctor, and she sailed with him, but had an injured leg for years. Jean could hike and lay out trails with him and sailed, too." Tension persisted in the sisters' adult lives as Dorothy, with her usual forthrightness and need to pronounce judgment, commented on the lives of Jean's children.

Ian's academic career was more outwardly successful than his older brother's, at least in terms of public recognition, although Hugh was highly respected among Quakers and church historians. Several times, Hugh made self-deprecating or apologetic remarks about his career. Sirkka recalled that when Ian decided to shift from physics to religion in the mid-1950s, Hugh said wistfully, "Ian stole my field." He did not remember this. When Hugh wrote in "Spilgrimage" that "two or three" times since 1941 he was "given grace to break through a wall of jealousy and found power to love more unselfishly," perhaps he was thinking of feelings about Ian. I, too, am an older brother who sometimes felt displaced or overshadowed by a younger brother who seemed to absorb most of my parents' attention. We are birds of a feather: me, Hugh, and the elder brother in the parable of the prodigal son.

Hugh and Sirkka were more exposed to Dorothy's interference than my parents, partly because of Minnesota's greater geographical distance from my grandparents' home in Cincinnati as compared to Indiana, and also because of Ian's more cheerful and detached personality. Sirkka said with assurance: "Of course Ian was always the favorite child." I argued vigorously against this claim. I asserted that the two brothers received different forms of attention and affection: Hugh got Dorothy's anxious concern and fussy solicitude, while Ian received her highest praise for achievements. But, I claimed, there were no favorites in the Barbour family. This is a bedrock belief for me. It is what my parents told me, and I saw it confirmed in the way they treated their children: not the same, but with equal love. I asserted fervently that all children have been loved equally in the Barbour family, as if appeal to this fundamental article of faith, the common denominator of our collective conscience, would end a painful discussion.

Perhaps this family ideal or ideology blinds me to reality. A few nights later, when I compared these impressions with those of Hugh's daughter Celia, her husband, Peter, said matter-of-factly: "Of course parents have favorites. Some children are more fun to be with." My mother once admitted to me: "Sometimes you can *like* one of your children more than another at a particular time."

So much of my identity was forged in early conflicts related to sibling rivalry, by lessons learned about vulnerability and reconciliation with brother and sisters, and through experiences of my parents' steady love and consistent fairness. Ian's earliest memory was of a brother being punished unfairly. The power struggles and bonds among siblings in various branches of my family formed many a conscience.

* * *

AT HUGH'S MEMORIAL SERVICE, held on the Zoom platform in 2021 during the COVID-19 pandemic, many of his former students and friends described how fully present, sensitive, and compassionate he was when they sought him out for advice or insight. He counseled conscientious objectors during the Vietnam War. I remembered how intensely engaged Hugh was when, during my senior year in college, my Jewish girlfriend, Cheryl, and I shared our struggle to discern whether our relationship could survive our religious differences. I think Hugh's internal conflicts and contradictions helped him connect with people trying to find their way out of ambivalence and uncertainty. At the same time, I know from his daughters that Hugh's parenting involved harmful patterns he learned from his mother: manipulation of guilt, playing the martyr, disparaging condescension, and (unlike Dorothy) barely suppressed rage about small things. I have several times encountered a similar discrepancy reported by the children of ministers or professors, who are at once proud, saddened, and puzzled when they hear from others grateful reminiscences about a parent they knew as narcissistic, judgmental, and harsh. A stern conscience can express itself in starkly contrasting ways within and outside one's family, in sudden flashes or long-term patterns, in unrelenting demands or understanding sympathy.

* * *

Family Conscience

HUGH IS A MENTOR and a warning to me as a fellow writer of memoir. He valued not only his memories of family members but the written record of their actual words. He gave me a list of more than forty boxes of family records that he kept in a storage unit near his home. In these boxes are financial transactions, manuscripts, slides, photographs, movies, academic course outlines, travel diaries, "treasures," and many letters, including those from the courtship of Robert Dickinson and his future wife, Sarah. Hugh hoped that someday Celia or I or someone interested in medical history would write a biography of RLD. To go through all this material carefully and interpret it would take years. Hugh kept every scrap of paper. His instinct as historian and as an eldest son was to preserve everything from the past as potentially meaningful. It's too much, only the raw material of memoir.

Hugh's unfinished "Autobiographical Notes" contain moving passages, but for someone outside the family there is too much description of the accomplishments of ancestors and the famous people they knew. Hugh wrote for family members whom he assumes will be interested in their forebears, but the accumulation of factual detail about so many people is wearying. No unifying theme or narrative arc ties it all together or draws the reader to care about these individuals. This will be some readers' response to my memoir, too: why would anyone outside your family care?

Another way that Hugh's example is a warning to me is that his preoccupation with the past sometimes cut him off from the present. I sensed Sirkka's ambivalence about Hugh's immersion in family history. Even after she died, Dorothy continued to dominate her husband's attention. Sirkka does not have forty boxes of files. As a girl, she was an internal refugee within Finland, her family displaced by the Russian occupation of Karela. Sirkka came to the United States on a scholarship to Earlham with two suitcases. She said Hugh was held too tightly by the grip of the past. In this, too, I sense my own temptation and danger. Digging into archives of letters, construing unknowable motives, and theorizing about conscience to explain family history, I miss opportunities in the present. A price is paid for living so much of one's life in the lost world of the past, for dwelling in a castle made of ink and typescript. Yet although Sirkka was ambivalent about Hugh's preoccupation with family history, she affirmed wholeheartedly my work on this memoir: "You are trying to do justice to the living and the dead as they continue to interact in our lives in powerful ways. It is good that you are airing out these musty closets."

I empathize with Hugh's struggle between full disclosure and privacy. He wanted to tell his own story and at the same time to preserve his own and others' privacy. Several times he said, "Don't quote me on this," or "This is off the record," and I've adhered to these requests. In the preface to his "Autobiographical Notes," Hugh says that he is "not sure who will see these notes." He often skips over events and refers the reader to documents such as George's biography of RLD, *In China When . . .* , and Hugh's biography of a Chinese colleague of his parents. He states that there is no crucial information about him that remains unknown: "I have no buried diaries or important unpublished works. In this, as in so many other ways, I have been very fortunate." Like Ian, he seems to be an open book. Unlike Ian, his life story involves a good deal of internal struggle and self-doubt, both as a recurring theme and as he reflects on the process of narrating his life.

A chapter of Hugh's "Autobiographical Notes" titled "Med to Div, Harvard to Yale: Turning Points in Darkness," depicts agonizing deliberations about his vocation, loneliness, and awkward relationships with women before he was married. In a 2005 letter, Hugh described "the most painful and one of the most liberating moments of my life. I hope it too will not go beyond my family for a few years if ever." I will not quote or discuss this writing. Yet I am struck by the fact that Hugh chose to write about intimate matters and share his writing with me when, as a professional historian, he knows that family records often become public documents. His "hope" and that vague "if ever" indicate an openness to quotation that could easily have been negated by a straightforward request or by not giving me his private writings. The readership of a family memoir or private letters is always uncertain. What can I reveal about Hugh's life? Do I betray his trust if I pass on even this much of his story, "beyond the family," more than "a few years" later?

The title of Hugh's chapter, "Spilgrimage," in the published Festschrift compiled for him is intriguing . I think Hugh meant it as a contraction of "spiritual pilgrimage." Yet to me this amalgam or pun also suggests the involuntary, accidental, or chaotic nature of both a life journey and its narration, as in "spilling one's guts" in confession. Hugh felt an urge to reveal secrets and tried to discipline that urge. He wrestled with the ethics of memoir writing. He wanted to tell the truth about himself, to confess. At the same time, he knew how much could not be said if he was to protect vulnerable loved ones. As a historian, he knew that "the truth" is different for various people. Given these uncertainties and ambiguities and his deep ambivalence, what should I say about stories he freely shared with me?

Hugh responded generously to my inquiries and early drafts of chapters about his parents and Ian: "I am impressed with your honesty and openness and I do not find any errors of fact and learned about a number of experiences, especially Ian's decisions in wartime." He also cautioned me, saying that to understand my project, "I would need to know for whom you are writing, and what kind of publisher you have in mind . . . I may lean too much to caution in saying nothing about anyone living except Ian in my notes thus far. How far you have been able to write up chapters on Deane, Blair, Heather, and David without hurting them, I will hope eventually to find out." Hugh was rightly concerned about the vulnerability of family members as he tried to tell a personal story that is inextricable from relationships. About his view that the living are off-limits, I'll say more in the final chapter.

I resonate with Hugh in many ways: as an elder son, a fellow professor of religion, a scholar of others' elusive religious experiences, a self-doubting introvert, and a hesitant autobiographer spilling (some of) his guts. In his self-thwarting scruples and longing for wholehearted conviction, I recognize myself. I honor Hugh's confession, his scruples, and his essential mystery. I'm grateful for his candor and courage in revealing his struggles and vulnerability. Only Hugh can tell his own story. But I, too, tell a version of it: how his life touches mine, bringing insights, moments of identification, and questions about the role of conscience in our family and in writing memoir.

Chapter 8

Early Scruples and Quandaries

The roots of conscience go deeper than thinking, beneath memory, to my need for control and instinct to please my parents. I clamored for food, attention, toys, or sleep and learned to curb these desires. As well as conforming to expectations, I was trying to create order and control in my life. Going to sleep was a complex ritual. I had to arrange my stuffed animals in their proper order, lined up on each side of the pillow. I wanted to be tucked in as tightly as possible, like a papoose. "Tighter, please!" As I lay in bed waiting for sleep, I had to scratch my body symmetrically: if my right shoulder itched, I had to scratch not only that one but also the left. At last I got too tired to care and fell asleep. I had number fetishes and had to eat five, eight, or fourteen grapes or French fries. The first task of conscience, the ordering and shaping of instinct, brings self-imposed scrupulosity. I learned to regulate my body's demands, create pattern in my life, and conform to an ideal of how I should be. This capacity in a child can develop into self-discipline or into obsessive-compulsive behavior; it is sometimes hard to tell the difference, then and now.

As well as clear convictions and certainty about some things, I experienced scruples, doubts, and quandaries that made me question what it was right for me to do. These interest me more than the certainties. The etymology of "scruple" is a sharp stone. This word came to be used for a source of uneasiness, a reservation, or an obstacle that inhibits action. A quandary is a state of perplexity or doubt when conscience is uncertain or conflicted so that choice and action are blocked. When I didn't know what to do and had to deliberate and reconcile conflicting values, conscience became, at least in part, an expression of agency and individuality.

Family Conscience

* * *

My siblings played important roles. Two photographs seem to me to symbolize aspects of my relationships with them. One picture shows me with David and Blair, sitting in the grass. I think it was taken in 1957, the summer when I turned six, Blair was four, and David would soon be three. I am wearing cowboy boots and holding a toy pistol, pointed at my brother. I look down at it and say something serious, as if giving a lecture. David has an insistent look on his face as he holds his right arm fully outstretched, demanding the gun. The look on his face is firmly determined, adamant; he will not be denied. Blair looks towards David, her hand open, palm up, as if offering something to him, patiently explaining what is plain to see. She is mediating a conflict between her brothers, perhaps telling David to wait for his turn. Her head turns, and she gazes intently at him, trying to fathom his feelings, wanting to reach him.

David, Blair, and me, 1957.

This photograph bothers me because I look pompous, if that is possible for a six-year-old. The little professor drones on, oblivious to other people. I'm looking at the gun, so wrapped up in my lecture that I don't notice what's going on around me. I embody the rational side of conscience and its possible abstractness and remoteness from others. David just wants the gun, and it is probably his turn; he insists that would be fair. The photograph previews Blair's role as mediator in the family and foreshadows her career as a social worker. She shows another dimension of conscience: its concern for other people. In 2005, Blair said that she, too, was ambivalent about the photo:

Early Scruples and Quandaries

"I have mixed feelings when I think of myself in that picture. I'm trying to help everyone get along. I was so earnest in my desire to help everyone be happy. It makes me a little bit sad, too. I could never do that, make things all right. I couldn't take away the grief Mom felt when her mother died. I couldn't change you and David so that you would be happy to see each other and play in a nice way."

I said to her: "That photo shows something about your role in the family. You wanted to mediate and bring people together. You have always been generous, compassionate, and concerned for other people's pain. Conflicts between people upset you and you want to take away the pain and heal people. That is a deep part of your character, more so than the rest of us."

How different we are from each other and from our youngest sister, Heather. For a college sociology course, I wrote a research paper on sibling birth order. The only finding that was statistically significant was that first-borns tend to identify more with their parents and be more achievement oriented. (More recent research suggests that younger siblings are often more adventurous and imaginative.) Gender, age difference from other siblings, personality, and many other influences make any generalization simplistic. Yet in countless fascinating ways, sisters and brothers play an enormous role in how individuals become who they are. We became our distinct selves by playing and arguing with each other.

When I asked what kind of big brother I was, Blair responded: "At different ages you were different things. From the time I came to visit you in Chicago during that blizzard and we got socked in—it must have been 1975—I felt like I had a brother. Before then, when I visited you at Oberlin, I didn't feel that you were interested in getting to know me. You were remote. I don't have many good memories of you. I have some bad memories. I do have a wonderful memory of the time when I was in seventh grade and you were in ninth grade. It was May or June and we were in your room, and you taught me how to dance to that Beatles song, 'You Better Run for Your Life.' I remember you playing with your men, your toy soldiers, on the floor. And at family dinners. I was sort of scared of you. You could burp better than me. And you would slug hard. You made it clear: don't mess with me."

"I wish I'd been a better big brother. I was interested in my own world. 'Don't mess with me.' I think older siblings want to forget where they have been recently. Some brothers must be less narcissistic than me, more involved in their younger siblings' lives. I don't think I was ever abusive."

"You were a little abusive. You had a hard punch. That's not good. Some things could have used improvement."

I asked: "Do you have other memories? You said you don't have many good ones. That could mean you just don't remember them, or it could mean there aren't any because I was always distant and remote."

"I could come up with positive ones. In fifth grade it was such a thrill when you would invite me up to your attic room the year we lived in Belmont. You had a cool room with windows looking over the street. On your record player you would play 'The Monster Mash.' One day you had this recording of Eliot Ness and the Untouchables. You played the shooting sounds out the window for passersby."

"I wonder if that's revealing. Here I am now imagining broadcasting family stuff to an audience. I'm trying to interest people in something happening inside the house. And there in seventh grade, in a bizarre humorous way, I was broadcasting not family secrets, but gunshots." I made childish shooting noises and we laughed.

"You could make great gun noises. You would sit in the car on long trips, shooting targets for hours. I guess it's a boy thing."

"A very boy thing. But David didn't do that," I said. "So it's not all boys."

"You were usually in the front seat with Dad."

"Riding shotgun."

When I think about how much time I spent playing with toy soldiers or imagining gunfights, I wonder where those aggressive instincts have gone. Mostly into self-criticism, perhaps, but I can still make cool shooting noises.

With Heather, 1964.

Early Scruples and Quandaries

Another photograph shows Heather and me in a swimming pool. She looks about four years old and I must be thirteen. She rides piggy-back on me, reaching tightly around my neck. She looks down at the water and her mouth is open as if shrieking, but her eyes say, I hope, that she knows that she is safe and this is fun. My arm goes back to hold her securely to my back and I squint into the camera, smiling, confident, proud of my reliable strength. This is the big brother I would like to be: a capable lifeguard. In fact, though, I couldn't swim very well and did not learn until I was almost ten. In the pool with Heather, I'm just standing on the bottom and there is no real danger as we splash around.

Born in 1960, Heather is nine years younger than me. I left home for boarding school in 1967, then was gone for college and every summer, so I didn't see her much. Heather has always been extremely independent—that's the first word my parents used to describe her. Talking to her in 2005, I was surprised by her ambivalence about this role in the family; she said it came as much from us as from her. She suggested that we wanted her to grow up quickly so that we could get on with our lives. Is even independence from the family not freedom from it but itself a role in a family script? Who wrote that script? Did we each choose our part or accept a role assigned by others?

During my teenaged years and when I was starting a career and a family, I was focused on my own goals. I did not help her deal with the issues in her life. I wish I had reached out to her more often, been a better big brother, a more alert lifeguard. This confession, an acknowledgment of negligence and plea of engagement in work, sounds like what my father said about his relationship to his children. Ian asserted that he didn't feel guilty, but rather regret. I find it harder to separate those feelings.

The four siblings have different ways of getting what we want. We were baby robins in a nest, each with our beak open, screeching for attention, wanting our share and more. Now we have left the nest but still squawk in the way we learned there.

* * *

I MUST HAVE ABSORBED a lot from church without realizing it. I went to Sunday school for many years and didn't particularly enjoy it, even though several of my friends were in the class. I didn't dislike it either; I'm sure I told my mother: "It was okay." When I sat in church during worship, Dad gave me paper on a clipboard and his mechanical pencil to doodle. The pews, with little racks for communion glasses, were warm brown wood. When it was time for prayer, my mother did not close her eyes or fold her hands; she lowered her gaze and became very still and intent, as if listening for a faint sound. I don't know what I got from sermons, but I felt comfortable during worship; it was okay. Once, when I expressed ambivalence about dragging my reluctant children to church, my mother said: "It doesn't matter so much if a child understands the theology or believes everything said in church. It is good that they know that church is a safe place where people care about you." Feelings of togetherness and peace in that sanctuary have stayed with me, and it is still my spiritual home. I'm glad I had childhood experiences of worship and community, which kept drawing me back when I had times of doubt or criticism of the church.

Blair described our parents' role in our early religious experiences: "Religion was fairly private in our family. Mom and Dad didn't quote the Bible or try to influence us directly. They didn't ask 'What would Jesus do?' Yet you knew that theology was important to them. I could see Mom's devoutness, her spirituality. She had a personal relationship to God. But there wasn't a single right way to worship. I grew up with a sense of the sacred, but I don't think I got it from church. Mom and Dad said prayers with us when we were little."

"I wonder when they stopped," I said. "I remember Mom telling me it was up to me now, whether I would pray or not. It became no longer a habit, but an occasional choice. I guess that's still the case."

Blair shared another memory: "I remember Dad saying grace at dinner. Often it was just silence. Sometimes we said that prayer RLD loved: 'Father of all, God, all we have is of thee. Take our thanks and teach us, that we may learn to do thy will.' I also knew that the depth of Dad's faith made possible questioning. He didn't talk about it, but we knew he was thinking about creation, science and religion, and such things. Also, sacred music was very important to both our parents."

My siblings and I have gone in various directions religiously. Blair worships in a Methodist church and does Buddhist meditation, David practices meditation and devotion to a guru, and Heather has attended Quaker meetings and a UCC church. We share certain things that we inherited from our liberal Protestant upbringing: concerns for social justice, affirmation of diverse paths and traditions to meet different religious needs, appreciation for music and aesthetic expressions of spirituality, and the tendency to question or doubt the official institutions of religion. We have all been drawn to meditation and communal silence in Eastern religions and Quaker worship. We are not the same in our religious orientations and seeking, but there are family resemblances.

* * *

Early Scruples and Quandaries

SKYE, THE COLLIE-MUTT WHO was the first of our three dogs, was the one I was most attached to. We had her for about a decade, from the time I was three. I didn't have to take care of her; Mom did most of the pet-raising chores. I just played with Skye. One night she lay on the living room floor while logs crackled in the fireplace. I stroked her fur for what seemed like hours, gazing into her half-open eyes and whispering, "Good dog, good Skye doggie." I wanted her to know that she was loved.

Skye was with my gang of friends roaming farm fields at the edge of the Carleton arboretum one cool autumn Saturday when I was about ten. We were spread out, playing at some heroic military fantasy, when someone yelled that Skye had been shot. My buddy Jim carried her to the road, soaking his coat with blood. He looked like a fireman carrying a limp victim out of a blazing house. I ran to find a phone to call for help. My memory of running as hard as I can and tasting blood blurs into childhood dreams in which I am unable to run fast enough. I still have them: not *running-away-from* nightmares usually, but rather *can't-get-to-urgent-business-fast-enough* dreams. We never learned whether the shooting was a hunting accident or a farmer's revenge for trespassing. This traumatic incident was my first encounter with mysterious, random violence, in contrast to the black-or-white bad guys and good guys on television.

Skye died not long after that, after choking on a chicken bone. When Mom and Dad told us that she had died, I cried and Mom comforted me. When Dolly (Gam) died soon afterward, I felt guilty that I couldn't cry about losing her. Wasn't it wrong to care more about a dog than my grandmother? Once, in my bedroom with my mother, I tried to fake grief for Gam by thinking of Skye and worked up a few tears. Mom gave me a hug and seemed a little comforted, so I felt better, but also false.

We had other dogs, as well as gerbils, chameleons, turtles, and mice. It's hard to understand why Deane added more chores and messes to her never-ending workload. I think she believed that loving these creatures would be good for her children, but, surprisingly, she did not link this to our learning to take responsibility for them, except for occasionally walking the dog. For several years my mother led a children's worship service after Sunday school. The only sermonette I recall from her in one of these services was a story about a group of kids who were mean to an old dog, in contrast to the boy who comforted it.

Deane's concern for and love of animals had a big impact on Heather. She saved a 1970 letter that Heather wrote, adding this prefatory note: "Heather wrote this out and read it aloud to the manager of the Ben Franklin store."

Family Conscience

I would like to make a complaint about the way you are keeping your turtles. Turtles do not normally get chalky white shells. It is not from "hibernating," as one of your assistants said. Turtles should be kept in a fairly large container. You have about 20 in one tiny aquarium and they are climbing on top of each other so not to be squished by others. They also have no room to swim around. Healthy turtles do not have clammy and bulging eyes. The water as I noticed was grey and dirty and barely enough to keep 20 turtles alive. I suggest that you clean it daily. I should not have done so, but I touched the turtles' backs and found out that only two are living. I hope you take this seriously.

It took courage for a ten-year-old girl to confront a store owner. Heather's relationships with helpless creatures expressed a vital part of her character. She had many pets: mice named Benjamin Shadow and Crispin, gerbils, and a golden retriever called Layla. She nursed wounded animals back to health and in her adult years has taken care of feral cats, feeding them and paying for them to be neutered. In 1994, Heather wrote a birthday card to Deane that lists some of the things she appreciated about her. Included in this list are "your love of dogs and their humility" and "your loving the stuffed animals no one else would love."

* * *

I AM ABOUT TEN years old, standing in the kitchen with my mother. I ask her how much money Dad earns.

"I don't know exactly how much," she replies.

"Well, about how much? Just a guess. How much in a year?"

"I really couldn't say, honey."

I want intensely to know how much money we have. I suggest a figure: "Do you think Dad makes, like, about fifty dollars a year?"

She laughs. "More than that. I don't think fifty dollars would even pay for the milkman's bill."

"Well, how much, then? A hundred dollars, or a thousand?" I think we can't be millionaires, mythical figures on television, but I have no idea. She steadfastly refuses to give any specific figure.

In school and church, I learned about poverty and hunger, but those people were far away, in Africa or Appalachia. Our church gave offerings to relieve their remote miseries. In small-town Minnesota, everyone seemed to have about the same amount of money. There were farm kids and town kids. I was dimly aware of a difference between the college-related families and other ones, but it wasn't based on money. I picked up unspoken messages about actual or potential friends when my mother asked: is the television usually on in that boy's house? Are there books in their family living room?

At some point I noticed that there were people in Northfield who looked a little different. They had dirt on their jeans that didn't come from playing outside and was greasy or oily. Some people in the grocery store had a hard, tense look. Occasionally a woman would yell at or even slap her kids in the checkout line.

In my family, we did not talk about how much things cost. Mom removed the price tag on gifts and cut off the price listed on book jackets. It was rude to mention money; it seemed to make my parents uncomfortable, so it was better to avoid the topic. I think Deane's main concern was that her children not make someone else feel ashamed. And she believed that the most important values are not economic.

"Are we rich, Mommy?"

"We're rich in love, darlin.'"

The result of this downplaying of economic facts was to make financial matters a closed-off and slightly shameful area. Not an exciting and alluring secret like sex, but an unpleasant part of reality that we didn't need to discuss, like going to the bathroom. Money wasn't a taboo subject; it just wasn't interesting or important to my parents and was best ignored.

Where did I learn about otherness and difference? I've led a very sheltered life. Most of my early friends were children of Carleton College faculty or staff. The class or caste consciousness that I developed was based not on race or money, but rather on whether education was the highest value. This priority was reflected in details like where a family took vacations and what they watched on television or talked about at dinner. Starting in junior high school, I made friends with kids whose parents were farmers or worked in a store. Steve had serious chores like milking cows at dawn; I didn't even make my bed very often, and I got paid to mow the lawn. Some friends' homes had lots of books in them and others had very few. The homes that felt similar to mine had wooden rockers and Persian or Turkish rugs in the living room; the other ones had a La-Z-Boy or two and an overstuffed couch. Although I didn't feel superior to the noncollege folks, some of them must have thought the college families were pretentious, or at least eccentric, with our antique furniture, ponderous conversations at dinner, and living rooms set up for discussion rather than watching television. It slowly dawned on me that the pursuit of a liberal arts education at Carleton or St. Olaf College was not an aspiration that everyone shared.

My first memory of racial consciousness is of a visit to Washington, DC when I was about seven. I was in the yard of Gam's house while an African American man did garden chores. He was raking leaves and he stopped, smiled at me, and said a few gentle words. Later my mother said: "I'm glad you didn't say anything about his color. That was the first time you've seen a colored person. It's good not to mention the difference in the way his skin looks compared to yours."

There was nothing my mother cared about more deeply than treating others fairly, kindly, and as equals. She wanted me to see the humanity of this humble gardener, not his skin color. The message I absorbed was to not call attention to race, to pretend I didn't notice it. I was more afraid of doing something wrong, of being a racist, than I was drawn to other ways of life. Northfield was for the most part racially homogenous in the 1950s and 1960s, and I didn't interact with the few people of color who lived in town. At Oberlin, where most of my friends were Jewish, I first became close to people with a significantly different background. But we were all at this progressive college and shared many values and experiences.

It is sometimes a challenge to acknowledge how race shapes American experience—to neither deny the existence of race nor make it the only important quality of another person. Once when I was teaching *The Autobiography of Malcolm X* in the 1980s, a student got defensive about Malcolm's claim that all White liberals are covert racists. This student, a young woman from a wealthy suburb of Minneapolis, said to the class: "I see everyone as equal and the same. When I look at an African American or Asian American, I don't see their skin color. I see an individual person."

There was a moment of silence while we considered this statement of an ideal we all believed in. Then an African American woman, the only one in the class, said, "I hear what you're saying, and it sounds good. But if you don't see my skin color, you don't see *me*."

In the name of idealistic aspirations, we were denying reality. In my privilege, I can come to think everyone is equal and basically like me. Yet I also know that race, gender, and social class shape my life and the lives of people I encounter more than I realize. One part of me says that these aspects of identity aren't the most important traits of another person. Yet a different inner voice warns: "That's easy for you to think. This person might see the world very differently than you do." How to reconcile or integrate these conflicting perspectives and scruples is a challenge and—in the aftermath of Black Lives Matter, the murder of George Floyd in Minneapolis, and the election of 2024—an ongoing process.

* * *

I DON'T THINK I was ever a bully, but don't ask my siblings. I recall only one time that I was deliberately cruel to a younger person. I don't know why I

Early Scruples and Quandaries

was with this boy, whom I'll call Tim; it was the only time we were together. I was about ten, and he was perhaps six. My memory kicks in with us running across the Carleton College campus. Tim couldn't keep up with me; he whined and grumbled and I urged him to go faster. I kept moving on and turned our situation into a game, pretending to ignore him as I ran ahead, but staying close enough that he tried to catch up. Tim started to cry and begged me to wait. What an irritating kid, I thought, pathetic in his eagerness to please. I commanded him to go faster. This went on for only a few minutes, but when we arrived at his house he was sobbing and blubbering. Mucus ran from his nose and he was soaked with sweat and tears. I said: "Well, we're home. See you around," and left him there. I made sure he got home but felt no compassion for him, just disgust. What a sniveling little runt, I must have thought, he really needs to toughen up.

Perhaps I wanted to test my power or took a secret pleasure in being cruel. Most likely, I was punishing my own fear of weakness. I did not feel guilty during my sadistic game, but it bothered me afterwards. I never did anything like that again. I avoided Tim.

I witnessed several disturbing incidents of bullying, the ordinary cruelties of boyhood. Although I didn't participate, I permitted them to happen. In my gang of friends in elementary school were a couple of guys who loved to dominate younger kids in the neighborhood. Bob claimed that Eric, known as "Icky-Ick," was his personal slave, and ordered the younger boy to pull him around the block in a wagon. "Mush, Icky-Ick!" he would command. When Eric balked, Bob organized mock trials and invented ingenious punishments for disobedience. There was a pseudolegal dimension to this form of play, with the members of our gang (the Coolie Cats Club) acting as prosecutor, defender, and judge. We had a "jail" in our clubhouse in the attic of my family's garage, where we threatened to imprison younger boys. It was a wooden pen with a roof and door that could be locked. Once, Icky-Ick was cajoled or coerced into the jail, and for a few minutes Bob pounded furiously on the walls. This was necessary to "break the boy," he asserted. Eric was complicit in this situation, desperately hoping for friendship on however twisted a basis. The whole relationship bothered me, and I preferred to play only with kids my own age and ignore younger boys, including my brother.

Bob was a master at creating odd, usually insulting nicknames. In a series of free associations, my brother Free became Freetle the Beetle, then Beetle Bailey, and finally Bailey. Bob called an intimidating big guy "Twenty-Tonner." He got even with more athletic and physically dominating boys by using irony, wit, and sarcasm. With cutting words, he defended himself, humiliated other kids, and struck back at tongue-tied "goons." Bob grew up to be a generous person to friends and family and an active participant in artistic and environmental causes. His cruelty did not survive childhood, and his wit and intellectual interests enliven our ongoing friendship.

Bullying was most vicious in junior high school. Karl, a frail, mousy kid, was utterly meek and harmless, with no muscle or will to fight back or defend himself. He actually looked like a mouse, with big ears and eyes and an anxious, placating demeanor. Several of the best athletes in my class relished humiliating this poor fellow. When he was naked in the locker room after physical education, they would whack him with a wet towel. They pinched him in class, trying to make him cry out and startle the teacher. They stole his mittens, played catch with his hat, and knocked his books off his desk. Karl pretended that this was great fun, that he was one of the guys. His pleading eyes told a different story.

The wolfpack of Karl's tormenters had two ringleaders. One was a small guy who was an outstanding wrestler, who delighted in practicing takedowns on Karl at unexpected moments. The other bully's parents had come to Minnesota after the Second World War as refugees from Eastern Europe. Both boys may have been compensating for some sense of inadequacy by humiliating Karl. They hounded him until he cried and then mocked his tears: "What a sissy. You wimp, you pathetic loser." Karl made visible and punishable the weaknesses we denied in ourselves.

Although I never joined in this relentless bullying, I didn't intervene to protect Karl. I could have defended him or at least criticized my schoolmates' pitiless domination. I was never teased, and my actions would have made a difference. I was a silent witness, a culpable bystander; I passed by on the other side of the road. I don't remember feeling guilty about this when I was thirteen or fourteen, but it got under my skin and deep into memory. I am ashamed of my complicity in junior high school cruelty.

At this time, in ninth grade, our class read "The Rime of the Ancient Mariner," the poem that moved me most during my youth. Coleridge's tale of inexplicable violence—the Mariner's unmotivated shooting of the albatross—must have resonated with my own sense of puzzlement about the sources of bullying. Perhaps, too, the Mariner's search for peace through confession appealed to me at a time when I could not find words to express what I felt. And now, Gentle Reader, you may wonder: "By thy long grey beard and glittering eye / Now wherefore stopp'st thou me?"

As an adult, I sometimes feel ashamed of things that didn't bother me as a child, like not protecting Karl. About other matters, I no longer feel the anguish I once did. For instance, when I was twelve, I purchased a book in a drugstore in Belmont, Massachusetts, where my family lived for a year. *The Scourge of the Swastika* was a history of Nazi war crimes. It had a red cover and contained grainy black-and-white photographs of corpses, naked prisoners going into gas chambers, and gaunt survivors of Auschwitz. I considered reading this book about the Holocaust to be shameful, as if it were pornography, which I discovered, in the mild form of *Playboy*, at about the same time. I hid it behind a row of books and never discussed it with my parents or friends. Knowing about the Nazis' acts of horrendous cruelty made me feel as ashamed as my growing awareness of sexuality did at that time, during my seventh-grade year.

Shocked by what I learned, I read on helplessly. It was like witnessing a gruesome car accident: physically nauseating, yet I could not turn my eyes away from unimaginable suffering and incomprehensible, cold-blooded cruelty. Learning about Nazi concentration camps was a guilty secret; by reading about the Holocaust, I felt like I was endorsing it. This was a fall into the knowledge of good and evil. Now I don't consider there to be anything morally wrong in this distressing new awareness, but I remember the feeling of shame vividly. Different layers of conscience—as it spoke then and speaks now—sometimes confront and challenge one another, vying for control.

* * *

ONE EVENING IN AUGUST 1966 I wandered the streets of Northfield with my friend Rich. We had just turned fifteen and were bored, bored, bored. "There is nothing to do in this dumb little hick town." Rich peered inside the windows of cars parked outside the movie theater. A big station wagon's keys were still in the ignition and the door was unlocked. "Let's go for a ride," he said.

"Do you know how to drive?"

"Sure, I drive tractors and cars around the farm all the time."

Soon we were racing along country roads. Rich took the car up to ninety miles per hour. It was a beautiful late summer evening for a joyride. We didn't wear seatbelts, although I was anxious about Rich's driving. Whump! A wheel went off the pavement and we hit something. "It's okay," my friend said with authority, "no damage done." We drove around for an hour and carefully returned the car to its original parking spot. The owner of the theater was standing outside, smoking. No one else seemed to be around. It was the perfect crime: no victims, witnesses, or consequences.

We walked a couple of blocks. Suddenly a police car screeched to a stop beside us, and two officers ordered us to get in; we were under arrest for car theft. A woman in an apartment window had noticed us snooping around, reported us, and acted as a lookout to identify us when we returned.

Family Conscience

If we had parked the car a block away, we would never have been caught, but we put the car back where we found it. Such considerate criminals!

The policemen took us to the station and booked us for car theft. My father was out of town that weekend, so it was my mother who came to get me. Behind our restrained manner, we were pretty upset. I did not feel particularly guilty about what I had done. It was just a stupid prank, a mistake of judgment, and I felt foolish. Deane wanted to interpret this act in a larger context, understand its deeper meaning. She wondered whether my choice of friends played a role, or the influence of Tiny's Smoke Shop, the local pool hall, where I occasionally bought a snack. I insisted that the joyride was an isolated incident that meant nothing. I was angry when she considered aloud what the consequences should be, including no more hanging out at Tiny's. Why did there need to be more consequences? Wasn't dealing with the police enough?

By an uncanny stroke of luck, the car we had stolen belonged to the local social worker who worked with juvenile delinquents in Rice County. Mr. Miller must have seen things like this frequently. I'm sure that he played a decisive role in how our case was handled. We had to pay for the damages to the car, which meant aligning the wheels and replacing a hubcap. We had to meet with Miller and talk about what we had done. If we kept out of trouble for three years, until we were eighteen, all evidence of the incident would be erased from our records. The police impressed on us that had we been adults, we would have been charged with car theft and probably served time in jail.

I didn't make much of this incident at the time; it seemed disconnected from the rest of my life. I never decided consciously to reform my ways. But that year, my tenth-grade year, I suddenly got serious about school. For the first time, I studied and received A's instead of B's. Some of the books we read, especially in English class, started to interest me. Perhaps working hard at academics was a sort of atonement to my parents for the trouble and worry I had caused them. Did I get interested in literature to understand my own puzzling behavior? I may have been alarmed at a deeper level than I realized by what I had done and what might have happened.

Rich and I were both involved in wrestling and track, and for a while we still hung out together. But we drifted apart. Rich continued to be a wild kid who often broke the rules. He had an unlucky tendency to get caught and got kicked off sports teams several times for smoking or drinking. He became a farmer who lived three miles south of me until he retired and moved into town. We were racquetball buddies for decades and are still friends. His brother used to be married to my sister Blair, so we are in some sense family.

Early Scruples and Quandaries

I went to see Rich in July 2007 to get his reaction to a first draft of the car theft incident. He said: "Well, as I remember it, it was your idea and you drove." My jaw dropped, he kept a straight face for a second, and then we both cracked up. Later, sitting on his back porch over a beer, Rich challenged my portrayal of him: "I wasn't a wild kid, compared to some. I wanted to be liked and got talked into doing whatever others were doing. The really wild ones didn't care what other people thought and would come to school drunk or high. I wanted to please everyone, including my parents, and I always felt guilty."

Looking back on his high school days, Rich is amazed that he survived. One of his exploits involved three guys in the front seat of a station wagon, driving fast down a country road. The middle guy holds the steering wheel and keeps his foot on the accelerator. The guys on the left and right each climb out of their side window, crawl over the top of the cab, and jump in the other window. A more elaborate variation of this stunt involved four people crisscrossing a car roof, all at once. Another competition was acting as a "hood ornament" while the car was moving.

I was not in those cars. I became a straight arrow, and my experiments with alcohol and drugs were few, restrained, and discreet. I wasn't a model citizen, but I never again got in trouble with the law. I made a new best friend who was the intellectual type; a studious introvert who started a high school paper called the *Idealist*. When we drove his car into the Carleton arboretum to drink beer, we discussed existentialism.

Augustine meditated upon a youthful transgression—his theft and destruction of some pears—not because it did great damage, but because of what it revealed about him. He was horrified by the pleasure he took in doing something forbidden and discerned that it was his desire to be liked by friends that motivated him to smash the pears. He thanked God for sparing him from other sins he might have committed, given how easily he could do an act that was purely destructive. Augustine makes a lot out of an incident that he once—like some of his readers—considered insignificant.[1]

The stolen car was my pear tree. It wasn't a terribly wicked act; I didn't want to harm anyone. But my life might have veered in another direction at that point. Beyond the obvious fact that Rich and I could easily have been hurt or killed someone, the ways in which adults reacted might have embittered me or made me see myself as an embattled rebel. Mr. Miller was calm and thoughtful; he knew that teenaged boys do stupid things. Something was more important than punishment: that we turn a corner, the right

---

1. Saint Augustine, *Confessions*, 2.4.

Family Conscience

corner. I wish that I had gone back to Mr. Miller later to thank him for the way he treated us.

In 2006 I asked Deane what she remembered about the Incident of the Stolen Car. She said that at dawn after a sleepless night, she thought, "This is the end of innocence." She preferred to describe what we did as "borrowing a car without permission" rather than stealing it, and she recalled that the policeman used both terms. She must have brooded, as I did later with my own children, about how much to make of a youthful misdeed. I asked her how I responded, and whether I seemed to feel guilty or ashamed.

"I think the literature you were reading made you think a lot about choices. Jean Valjean's theft of the silver candlesticks in *Les Misérables* is such a powerful story; you remember how when he was caught with the silver, the priest from whom he stole it told the police that he, the priest, had given it to Valjean. Ian and I once talked about what we would most hate to have stolen. What would make it hardest to say: 'We gave it to him'? It would be that antique silver teapot on the table, a wedding gift to us. Another book you liked was *Beau Geste*, which describes how some young men went into the French Foreign Legion as an act of atonement. And, of course, there was Dickens' *Christmas Carol*, which shows Scrooge's transformation."

I don't remember thinking that those works of literature illuminated my own life. I didn't consider joining the French Foreign Legion—at least, not as an act of atonement! But maybe the appeal of certain books was more personal than I realized, and I was trying to understand myself obliquely, as seems to be my wont. If my awakening interest in fiction grew out of the car theft, I was thinking in an indirect or metaphorical way about my experience of crime and punishment. The joyride with Rich was at once a trivial episode of delinquency and a catalyst that started me thinking seriously about why people do what they do, how they are treated, and how they learn to take responsibility for their deeds.

* * *

DURING THE SUMMER OF 1968, before my senior year in high school, I took part in a humanities program at St. Olaf College. We read some philosophy, including a few snippets of Kant's *Critique of Practical Reason*. I was fascinated by this strange new way of thinking, so utterly abstracted from specific moral situations. Kant discussed not which specific actions are right or wrong, but what makes an act right or wrong. When making a moral decision, I was supposed to think about whether everyone in my situation could make the same choice. A verdict of conscience is not simply a private intuition or opinion, but should be based on what ought to be done by anyone in that situation. I should treat other people as ends in themselves. Respect for human reason, not obedience to God's commands, is the basis for ethics.

This was heady stuff, in several senses. Intellectual passion is falling in love with an idea or subject matter; in some ways, it resembles being swept off your feet emotionally. For certain people it happens with lichens, for others with the theory of evolution, Bach's fugues, or ancient Greece. For me it was ethics. It wasn't just that Kant appealed to my intellect; this way of thinking had an austere aesthetic beauty. It was so clear and free of mess and muddle. This ethical orientation was inspiring, as worship should be. What an amazing and wonderful thing it would be to live according to this idealistic philosophy! What a noble act: to sacrifice self-interest to the demands of the categorical imperative! I read slowly, assimilating Kant's ideas sentence by sentence, in awe of this vision of how humans should live. But how could I translate this philosophy into my life as a high school student? Did studying and being inspired by philosophy make any practical difference in my life? Was this just an academic "subject" or genuine wisdom? What would Kant say about touching a girl's body, cutting weight for wrestling, or deciding where to go to college?

A few months later, in an essay for a college application, I described the effect of discovering moral philosophy: "I realized how narrow my views were and how often I acted without rationally deciding what the right thing to do was." Yet at the same time, I think through literature, I had become aware of the limits of reason; I wanted to study "psychology as it influences the ways that men make ethical decisions and the ways that men can rationalize their deviations from a moral code." I hoped to become a professor of philosophy or psychology and to change students' attitudes through education: "I believe that nearly all men will change their attitudes when they are rationally convinced that to do so would be the best thing for themselves and society." This assertion seems ridiculously optimistic about the possibility of reasoned choice, given my awareness of rationalization and covert self-interest. Another essay question asked what the applicant would someday like to write a book about. I said that I would write on the theme: What is a good man? I would look at modern novelists (Dostoevsky, Camus, Alan Paton, Graham Greene, and Arthur Koestler) whose works show how psychological knowledge makes it "hard to distinguish between what is the right thing to do and what the subconscious mind would like to be the right thing. This is an age-old problem about which I am always uncertain." What happened to my supreme confidence in reason?

In a ragged manila file marked "College application essays," I found a piece of paper dated October 1968. It is a list of people I admired:

Family Conscience

twenty-four men including my father and grandfather, ministers, teachers, a wrestling coach, and friends. They had diverse characteristics, some of which had less to do with moral virtue than good humor or keen intellect. I wonder if any of the people on my list thought about universalizability or the categorical imperative. I included only people I knew, so Kant is not in the cast of characters. Almost the only thing I remember about the life of the great philosopher is that in Konigsberg you could set your watch by his daily walk. My list shows a very different approach to ethics than Kant's philosophy, and perhaps a dim awareness that moral goodness is more than a matter of how one reasons. A note scribbled on the side of the page, dated July 1973, shows one way in which college had changed me: "All *men*. Why no women?" Where did this new perspective come from? I had no female professors in college, and only one in graduate school. I had read no works of literature by women. Yet somehow, I had begun to assimilate feminist thinking, largely through the influence of friends.

I initially thought that I would major in philosophy in college. The papers I wrote in my first class are embarrassing: not analysis or persuasion, but mere assertions of a point of view, my personal "philosophy." In those days, most of my peers asserted that their primary purpose in going to college was to develop a meaningful philosophy of life. In an essay called "The Circle Game," I described how I usually return to my original beliefs after examining other points of view. It is anecdote, not argument. Another paper, no doubt influenced by Aristotle, says that virtue is a mean between extremes, but moderation in all things is boring and prevents intense experience. I was dimly aware that for me, moderation was based more on fear than on wisdom.

I soon learned that my mind is not very good at the rigorous academic discipline of philosophy; I just wonder a lot about certain things, especially ethical questions. I also thought that philosophy (as I then understood it) left out too much: stories, the unconscious mind, feelings, and the religious faiths that shape convictions. The next semester I took a course in world religions, and during my sophomore year, courses on the Gospels and ethics. I decided to major in religion. In that field I hoped I could consider rational arguments like those that so moved me in Kant's thinking and also take account of all the things that make it hard to be logical, precise, and certain that reason is always the best guide.

* * *

ONE AUGUST DAY IN 1969, I stood by a campfire in the Boundary Waters Canoe Area, near the Canadian border. I was a "swamper" or assistant

Early Scruples and Quandaries

counselor, and my brother, David, was a camper; we were with a head counselor and four other boys. This was the last of four two-week canoe trips I took that summer. About noon the sun finally came out after several long days and nights of intermittent rain. We hadn't been able to cook supper the previous night or breakfast that morning because the wood was so wet. Now, with a brisk wind and bright sun, we decided to cook lunch and dry out our soggy clothes. From a tiny island in the midst of the huge lake, we surveyed a spectacular panorama as sunlight sparkled on the water. We clustered around the fire, ravenous for a hot meal.

David had become a vegetarian within the last year. His initial motivation was simply disgust at the quality of meat in the student cafeteria. He gradually saw other reasons to continue as a vegetarian, as he has done ever since. There are many good arguments for vegetarianism, including health, economy, environmental impact, and religious reverence for life. I find these rationales overwhelmingly persuasive, yet I continue to eat meat, though less and less.

To be a vegetarian on a canoe trip creates a little more work. Often you can set aside a portion of the usual one-pot stew before adding meat for those who want it. But sometimes you must dirty another pan to avoid getting the meat grease into the vegetarian portion. Whatever we were cooking that day took a little extra preparation, so the other boys began arguing with David, trying to persuade him to eat the one-pot stew, meat and all, with the rest of us. The argument became an end in itself, an episode when boys learn to think and to skirmish verbally instead of physically. People get defensive and aggressive around vegetarians; at least they did in 1969 in Minnesota. Soon we were vigorously debating various hypothetical cases. It was a memorable introduction to moral casuistry, ethical argumentation about specific situations. The carnivores wanted to know what David would do if he were starving to death. Would he eat an animal that had not been killed by humans, but was already dead? For instance, what if he witnessed a turkey struck by lightning and cooked just right?

The debate turned to the use of leather. If it is not okay to eat meat, how can one justify using leather for boots or a belt? After considering this argument, David removed his belt. He used a piece of rope for the rest of the trip, his pants often slipping down his hips on portages. I may have imagined another detail as I fantasized about the likely consequences of rigorous moral consistency. Did David remove his boots and wear sneakers with no ankle support, risking injury on portages? It would have been like him to suffer for an idealistic principle. He argued with the rest of us, adamant, determined, fully committed to his convictions and their implications. He thought carefully about his views, not trying to persuade anyone but only to be consistent. The rest of us were fascinated by this eccentric moral position—or was it integrity, and we were moral slackers? David's rigorous ethical stance was closely bound up with his nonconformity, his adamant disagreement with the rest of us. Our debate on the island was at once a serious discussion of a moral issue, a conversion of adolescent testosterone into rhetoric, and great entertainment, a drama of wills and ideas. We were at an important stage of moral development, an initiation into independent thinking about a matter of principle. While sincere deliberation was operating on one level, many other things were going on. That's the way it usually is with conscience, in my experience.

* * *

THE VIETNAM WAR WAS at its peak of intensity during my senior year in high school. I knew that I would have to register with the Selective Service System on my eighteenth birthday the following summer, in August 1969. I was opposed to the war and had to decide whether to file as a conscientious objector. I was not a pacifist opposed to all wars, but a "selective objector" who believed that this particular war was unjust and immoral. Today I would appeal to the long tradition of Christian thinking about just and unjust wars to argue that American engagement in Vietnam, like our invasion of Iraq in 2003, did not satisfy the criteria for a just war. But local draft boards did not want to go into ambiguous debates about how the conditions and criteria of just warfare apply to particular conflicts. The rules of the Selective Service System granted CO status only to individuals who were opposed to all warfare for religious reasons. A standard question of local draft boards was whether an applicant for CO status would have fought in World War II. If the answer was yes, the man was drafted into the military. I wrestled with this dilemma for several years: What should I do as one opposed to the Vietnam War, when the rules of the system did not allow for conscientious objection to a specific war?

This ethical question was the subtext of a story I wrote during my senior year in high school. In the winter of 1969, my English class explored "the good man." I wrote a first-person narrative entitled "Thoughts of a Priest at War." I was greatly influenced by Camus's *The Plague*; my priest, like Dr. Rieux, speaks with heavy weariness as he steadfastly persists in his duties because of his "belief in man." My priest thinks that although the war he is involved in is immoral, he must serve the soldiers fighting in it. He feels inadequate, yet that he is doing the right thing. He affirms a form of humanism: "There have been good men who believed in God and good men who didn't; there have never been good men who didn't believe in the worth of mankind." Yet the priest also asserts that, given the limitations of human goodness and rationality, he must believe in a higher ethical standard rooted in God's will. He struggles with his faith and wonders whether he is in a false position as a priest. In addition to the ethical dilemma of a person caught up in an unjust war, I was beginning to think about three issues about which I would later write books: the loss of faith, solitude, and conscience. The theme of deconversion lurks in the background as the priest questions the authenticity of his faith, given his doubts. As a monologue with very little plot or interaction with other people, the priest's confession reveals both his solitary detachment from others and his yearning for solidarity with them. The seventeen-year-old author of this story was interested in ambiguous ethical questions and thought that the drama of a conscience at work was itself a compelling story.

To get the CO classification, I had to show that I met three requirements of the law: I had to have a religious basis for my objections, show that I was sincere in what I believed, and oppose participation in war in any form. In applying for CO status, I explained my Christian belief that "to deny one's conscience is to deny God." I had signed petitions, demonstrated, and nonviolently protested our country's war in Vietnam. The problem was the third criterion, opposition to war in any form.

My way of justifying my position seems very odd to me now. I wrote: "I am opposed to participating in war in any form because to serve in an army I would have to be untrue to my conscience. To serve in an army one must follow orders." Obeying commands would mean denying my personal responsibility for my actions. Although nonviolence is always morally superior, I did not rule out violence absolutely and allowed that a police force or an individual might have to restrain others. If I ever decided that I had to use physical force on another person to prevent him from harming another person, I would "accept the consequences of my actions." What was central in my thinking in 1969 was not opposition to violence, but rather objection to the collective nature of a military organization, when "men lose all control and responsibility for the consequences of their actions." I thought that my conscience would be harmed not by committing violence but by following orders. This is not exactly the teaching of the Sermon on the Mount! I had come up with what now sounds like an anarchist's view of social institutions to explain why I was opposed to all military service. I'm not sure whether I misrepresented my real beliefs in order to present myself to the draft board as a conscientious objector. Perhaps I was just naïve.

I felt uneasy about my situation and guilty in a muddled way for what I sensed was a feeble basis for my selective objection to the Vietnam War. Moreover, I had an undergraduate student deferment (class II-S) while I

Family Conscience

was in college, a privilege available only to certain Americans. I benefited from a system I wouldn't defend.

I explained my CO stance to Ed Long, a sometimes-cranky professor of ethics at Oberlin whom I admired. He had penetrating eyes and a mind that quickly detected weak thinking. He was known as "the conscience of the faculty" and had written a book about the ethics of war. I should have read it! I think that I was afraid of being overwhelmed by his arguments; I wanted to come to my own conclusions. I went to see him during his office hours. The walls were stacked to the ceiling with books. When I explained my position, Long didn't push our conversation deeper. Other students were waiting; piles of papers and bluebooks waited on his desk. I remember only his brief remark: "So you are an opportunist." This comment puzzled and disturbed me. I believed that the war in Vietnam was wrong and that I could not participate in it without violating my sense of integrity. But I couldn't articulate my views clearly or persuasively to this formidable authority on ethics.

In private moments I raged against the system that put me in this false position. In March 1971, after watching a documentary on the Pentagon's conduct of the war, I wrote in my journal: "It really makes me wonder about the morality of applying for a C. O. These maniacs are going to judge whether I am sincere or not?!?! It might be better to leave the country." Draft dodgers, resisters, and exiles refused to cooperate with the Selective Service System. Several friends said: "The Vietnam War is evil, there's no way in hell I'm going, and I'll do whatever is necessary to avoid the draft." In contrast, I thought that I should try to follow the rules and regulations, hoping that somehow my convictions would be accommodated by "the system" that I criticized.

I participated in antiwar demonstrations at Oberlin and, several times, in Washington, DC. After the May 1970 shootings at Kent State University, only forty miles away, Oberlin shut down for the final month of that academic year. We joined thousands of people who marched through Washington's streets, listened to speeches, and argued about our country's future. Many of the marchers were angry at America, and a few burned flags or hurled insults. After a long hot afternoon of marching and imbibing impassioned antiwar rhetoric, I felt discouraged. I helped a group of people handing out water bottles from a truck. The benefits of this action felt more tangible and real than the demonstrations.

Young men did whatever they could to avoid the draft. One friend stayed awake for several days before his physical examination and then took an amphetamine, which resulted in an irregular heartbeat that got him a physical deferment. A high school classmate claimed that he was addicted

Early Scruples and Quandaries

to LSD and suffered recurring hallucinations. Another fellow, a music major, faked the hearing test several times. Thousands of Americans went to Canada to avoid the draft. Some men pretended to be homosexual, which counted as a disqualifying "moral defect." Others stuffed or starved themselves to fall outside the army's standards for body weight. Enrollments in divinity schools and seminaries ballooned because studying for the ministry counted for a deferment. In 1965, some guys got married to stay out of the military; then that deferment ended. Some resisters suffered for their beliefs in prison. A man I later worked with in a frame store in Chicago was a CO who served as a medic in Vietnam; he described standing in a pool of blood in a helicopter, watching soldiers die.

I filed my CO application and took the student deferment while I went to college. The local draft board would decide about my draft status when I graduated. A lottery was to determine which eligible men would be called up each year. During the summer of 1970, I stood listening to the radio on a day off as a camp counselor in Maine. Three hundred sixty-five dates were randomly assigned a number, and every young man born in 1951 was given one according to his birth date. That year the first fifty numbers were scheduled to be drafted. An inflectionless bureaucratic voice droned on through the year's dates, determining men's fates, until it got to my birthday: "August 8, number 49." I gazed into space across a field of boys yelling fiercely as they played. My future suddenly seemed both decided for me and totally unpredictable.

With that low number, I expected to be drafted as soon I finished college. I hoped I would be granted the CO status and do two years of alternative service: civilian work that the Selective Service System approved for conscientious objectors—work that "contributes to the maintenance of the national health, safety, or interest." During my senior year, I applied for the VISTA program, a domestic equivalent of the Peace Corps.

In the spring of 1973, just before I graduated, the war in Vietnam was winding down. President Nixon scaled back the American military presence there and created an all-volunteer force, formally ending the draft. In March, the last United States combat troops returned home, although Saigon was not officially evacuated until April 30, 1975. In June 1973, I received a letter from Rice County Local Board No. 102 that informed me: "Under current directives, you are now eligible for assignment to a Reduced Priority Selection Group . . . Class 1-H is a holding classification for registrants not currently subject to processing for induction."

All my troubled reflections about the morality of the Vietnam War and how to deal with the Selective Service System were hypothetical and disconnected from the death and destruction in Southeast Asia that claimed the lives of more than 58,000 Americans and uncounted Vietnamese people. There is an element of survivor's guilt in some men in my generation who lived through those years and saw so many lives lost or damaged. My two ethical questions—whether to serve in the military and how to respond to a system of regulations that does not make room for my position—were critical issues for me during those formative years for my conscience. I can criticize my arguments then and discern their self-serving nature. But I would also like to support this kid, my former self, as he starts to think for himself about what is right. My experience with the draft left me with a gut-level knowledge that moral decisions are often an ambiguous mixture of conscientious scruple and self-interest.

* * *

QUITTERS ARE LOSERS, SAID the coach. For me, decisions to quit a group have generated more soul-searching and self-knowledge than joining or persisting in one. Such choices call forth a sort of "here I stand" individuality that mingles obstinate selfishness with the call to realize a nascent identity. At certain points in late adolescence or early adulthood, one may do one's communal duty at the peril of one's integrity.

I've always liked the ideals of service and community better than the reality. Ian and Deane encouraged me for many years to participate in a Quaker work camp. Unlike my siblings, I never did. In college, I tutored in an elementary school, taught a church confirmation class, worked in a day care center, and did other short-term projects with children. These activities did not bring me much satisfaction and I probably wasn't very good at them. The contemporary equivalent is serving on church committees, which I have done several times with good results but a lot of grumbling. The jobs I've felt best about are being a camp counselor and a college professor. These roles sometimes brought me a sense of accomplishment and intermittent moments of joy, although the possible benefits to other people are more indirect and uncertain than what I once aspired to.

Rarely do I recall joining a group or organization. Instead of these decisions, which now seem to me full of significance for understanding conscience, it is two choices to quit a group that stand out in memory. At these moments I asserted something important to my individuality but felt guilty. I had a vague but insistent yearning that conflicted with a group's claim on my loyalty. At Oberlin, I was on the wrestling team during my freshman year. In the highlight of a mediocre athletic career, I won the 158-pound championship in a weak conference, the Great Lakes Colleges Association. The next year after wrestling during autumn semester, I decided to go for

Early Scruples and Quandaries

the January term to Mexico. A friend and I would backpack around the mountain villages of Michoacán, studying the handicrafts of the people we called Tarascan Indians, who today are known as the Purépecha. It was an academic scam, but it promised to be a grand adventure. I told the coach that I wanted to take a month off to go on this junket and then return to wrestle in the end-of-season tournament.

"No," said the coach, Joe Gurtis, a crew-cut Southerner of the old school. Still fit at fifty, he stood there impassively with well-muscled arms folded across a massive chest. "You can't skip out on the hard work of practice and then show up at the end of the season. You wouldn't be in shape, and you won't have worked with the team. You have to choose: Mexico or wrestling."

For once, I didn't agonize. I was a little sorry to lose wrestling, but eager and excited to travel. Wrestling required an awful lot of grunt work and sometimes being gone entire weekends. I complained in my journal: "Coach expects you to dedicate your life to the sport, which not many people at Oberlin are willing to do these days." Wrestling was the least appealing sport imaginable in a college full of East Coast hippies, and it has since then been eliminated by Oberlin and many other liberal arts colleges, including St. Olaf and Carleton.

I quit the team and had a fun adventure in Mexico. It was, I suppose, irresponsible and self-indulgent, but something told me that I had to explore a new part of the world and of myself. Violating my sense of a duty or obligation was necessary for an emerging new sense of identity. Becoming myself meant breaking with a group, in this case the wrestling team.

Another decision to quit a group I cared about came in 1974. After I graduated from college, I went to Philadelphia to live with my girlfriend, Cheryl. After we broke up, I moved into a house of American converts to 3HO, a movement that combined Sikh religion with Kundalini yoga. We rose every day at 4:00 a. m. to practice yoga and meditation for two or three hours. We ate an ascetic diet, worked at various day jobs, and did yoga again in the evenings. I loved the yoga practice and enjoyed the intense little group of eight residents. I had a demanding and rewarding experience of religious community for about two months.

I wanted to maintain contact with old friends and pursue various other interests. I could only do this in the evenings since I worked during the day. Getting up at four o'clock meant going early to bed, so it was a challenge to fit in any activity or friendship outside the yoga house. One night I went to see the movie *Death in Venice* and didn't return until midnight. The next morning, the community leader woke me up at four o'clock for the cold

Family Conscience

shower before yoga. He was a gentle, patient man a few years older than me who wore a long beard and the Sikh turban.

"I can't do this today," I said.

"Why not?"

"I'm too tired. I didn't get home until midnight."

He let me sleep in that day, but the tension was thick. No one looked at me. I had violated the communal ethos in a way that upset everyone. I felt like an adulterer being shunned in Puritan New England. I realized that I did not want to live in a place where I had to sacrifice something important to me. The right to see a late-evening movie seems a trivial occasion on which to say: "Here I stand; I can do no other." But this little incident was a symbolic turning point for me, a mini-deconversion that decisively shifted my interests from that tight religious community to miscellaneous secular pursuits. I wanted to go to the cinema or practice yoga when I pleased, as the spirit moved me. Now this attitude seems to me the epitome of American individualism, and I would argue with my former self that any religious community worthy of commitment sometimes demands a little sacrifice, such as giving up late-night popcorn. I might scold that young man and preach the virtues of community. But he wouldn't have listened, and he wasn't ready for commitment. And though I can criticize my individualism of those days, I'm not much different today. My left-leaning liberal idealism about community is an opinion or ideal that is largely theoretical rather than lived out in action. Oscar Wilde quipped that the trouble with socialism is that it takes too many evenings.

When I resisted the demands made by the wrestling team and the yoga house, these decisions involved conscience in an unconventional sense. I had to reconcile what I owed a group and what I thought I needed, including the sense of a call to new experience and self-discovery. If moral duties to others have no limits, they become heteronomous and oppressive. A deep part of my being, my capacity for agency and choice, must integrate commitments to others with things that morality fears as dangerous rivals, such as passion, spontaneity, aesthetic beauty, and pleasure. When a person struggles to integrate and order conflicting desires, conscience is at work. Sometimes it denies or overrides moral claims that come from a particular community. Then you may decide that it's all right to do what you want, even if you must neglect the duties required by the group. There is usually a cost to following that intuition, and it may be a loss of solidarity with other people. When I quit the wrestling team and said goodbye to my friends in the yoga house, I felt selfish, alone, and free. It was exhilarating, much more than when I joined a community or did something that helped others. I wish it was the other way around, so that I enjoyed being generous or a good citizen more than doing what I want.

Now I can criticize my decisions to leave communities that were important to me. I was like an adolescent or an anarchist who thinks that all rules are stupid. Yet I wasn't just being pigheaded or selfish. When I decided to quit, I was intuitively seeking new perspectives and pursuing other kinds of goodness than moral virtue or duty: what ethicists call "nonmoral goods." Sometimes it's hard to balance and reconcile the needs of individuality and of community. Three decades later, I explored this issue in a book about the ethics of solitude. Aloneness isn't just selfish indulgence, I argued; it can make possible undistracted attention to things outside myself such as books, the natural world, or music. But I can't lose myself for very long in solitude—or anything else, either-—without thinking about whether the activity can be justified ethically.[2]

---

2. See John D. Barbour, *The Value of Solitude: The Ethics and Spirituality of Aloneness in Autobiography*, Studies in Religion and Culture (Charlottesville: University of Virginia Press, 2004).

CHAPTER 9

Choosing a Life
Work, Marriage, Money, and Buddha

During the year after I graduated from college, I made several decisions that shaped the course of my life. In the summer of 1973, I lived at home and worked for a seed company building greenhouses. With my ponytail poking out of my hardhat, I labored at a minimum wage construction job, pushing a shovel and hammering nails. In late August I would be going to Philadelphia to live with my college girlfriend, Cheryl. I had no other plans or job prospects, though I was thinking seriously about going to graduate school in some field of religious studies.

Blair came home in June from her sophomore year at Earlham College. She was deciding whether to move into an apartment in Chicago with her boyfriend, Joe, for the summer. This was a time when I felt great tension with Deane and Ian, who disapproved of their living together. I thought my parents had a double standard, because they didn't seem to mind that at the end of the summer I would move in with Cheryl. Although I was two years older than Blair and had finished college, I thought that my sister was not being allowed the same independence as I was. I encouraged Blair to go to Chicago despite my parents' reservations. Looking back at the extensive journal I kept at that time, I see more anger at my parents than I felt or expressed at any other time in my life. We conflicted about two things. One was my generation's different attitudes to sex, living together, and marriage. I argued with Ian that it was not "exploitative" of women for men and women to have a sexual relationship or to live together without being married. My parents' views, it seemed to me, reflected an outdated, paternalistic attitude toward women. For the only time in my adult life that I remember,

I yelled at my father as we stood in the living room one evening. I told him to back off and let Blair make her own decisions. I asserted the right of my generation to explore relationships and sexuality outside the boundaries of traditional marriage. As often happens in my family, feelings came out sideways in the form of an intervention on behalf of someone else.

Ian and me, 1974.

The other flash point that triggered my feelings was planning for the future and finding work. Blair was undecided about what to do after college, and I did not know what I would do in Philadelphia or whether I would enroll in graduate school. I was vicariously defending my own uncertainties as I sympathized with and encouraged Blair. I confided to my journal: "Although intellectually Mom and Dad say it is fine that kids today are so open to the future and have escaped some of the preoccupation with planning the future characteristic of their generation, they still have a hard time dealing with the unsettled states of their own children. We don't know how things are going to work out in the long run with Cheryl or Joe, we don't know about career and school and plans farther away than the next few months. I am very ambivalent about academic pursuits in the future. They are anxious that we won't have any meaningful experiences or long-term motivation. Those are real concerns, but pressure from them to give definite answers only makes it more difficult to decide what's next." Anxious about my own future, I tried to support Blair while she gave herself time to make crucial choices about work and love. The outburst at my father was a mild rebellion, but it felt momentous.

Family Conscience

That same summer I fell in love with Meg, who lived a few blocks away and was Blair's good friend. Meg worked in the fields for the same seed company as I did, weeding and watering vegetables. One day it started raining and she headed home. She saw me working and offered me her thermos of lemonade. I looked into her blue eyes. She smiled. I asked if she wanted to go for a walk that evening. For the next two months, we wandered the dark, deserted streets of Northfield, the night breeze cooling our skin burnt by a day in intense sunlight. Like children, we threw twigs at each other's second-story window and called: "Come out and play."

I was strongly attracted to Meg but conflicted because I was involved with Cheryl. I felt giddy and guilty as I became infatuated; I was falling, out of control, exhilarated. I told Meg a little about Cheryl, and she knew I was leaving in August, so she was guarded about our relationship. I was torn between my conscience and my feelings. How could this be wrong when it felt so right, so good?

Some of my euphoria about Meg was feeling liberated from intractable problems with Cheryl, who was Jewish, and whose parents strongly opposed our relationship. I went to Sabbath services with her and briefly considered converting to Judaism but realized that for me this would be the wrong motivation for a religious commitment. After we broke up in November 1973, I stayed in Philadelphia for the rest of the year, working odd jobs. I joined the house of people doing yoga and living as Sikhs. After the incident when I went to a late-night movie and wouldn't get up the next morning for yoga, I moved into another house where there was a lot of alcohol and marijuana consumption, going from strict discipline to hedonism and another girlfriend. During that chaotic year I began writing to Meg, who was going to Carleton College. She was a connection with home, childhood, and Minnesota, yet she was also new, different, and mysterious: an artist, a lover of nature and poetry, and a person with a kind of spirituality that, like my own, was both related to Protestant tradition (the same UCC church) yet searching outside Christianity for meaning and orientation. When I returned to Minnesota in August 1974, Meg and I went on a canoe trip in the Boundary Waters. After that, we were together for 46 years, marrying in 1978.

Choosing a Life

Meg and me on the evening before our wedding, 1978

During the year in Philadelphia my vocational direction became clear. I had originally intended to work after graduation as a conscientious objector at some form of alternative service. When the Vietnam War ended and I didn't have to deal with the Selective Service requirements, I found other jobs. As a lab rat, I sat in a tank of hot, lukewarm, or cold water, wearing on my head and hands tubes through which flowed water of various temperatures. My reactions to this experiment provided evidence about the body's adaptation to heat and cold. I was a substitute teacher in the junior high schools of West Philadelphia, enduring stressful encounters that left me exhausted and depressed. As a volunteer for an agency defending the consumer rights of poor residents of the neighborhood, I spent many hours unsuccessfully trying to get a landlord to refund someone's security deposit. None of this work did any good or felt satisfying.

Family Conscience

I also worked as an orderly at Philadelphia General Hospital in a project investigating links between alcohol, tobacco, testosterone, and aggression. Some of the subjects, who were all alcoholics, were allowed cigarettes, liquor, or both, and some had to abstain. My role was to be a bartender and scribe who measured and recorded the drinks of the ones who could have as much alcohol as they wanted. When they got irritable or angry, especially the ones who had to go cold turkey, I noted their tantrums. These guys told marvelous stories, some of which may have been true. But I found myself mentally checking out of this job, too. I was more interested in reading literature I hadn't had time for in college: fat novels by Proust, Joyce, and Thomas Mann. I wished the research subjects would turn down the daytime TV soap operas so I could concentrate on *Ulysses*. I hoped they would wait to ask for their next drink until I finished the chapter.

During that year, the only one I spent outside an academic institution until retirement, I decided to go to graduate school to study Religion and Literature. I did not feel called to be a teacher. In fact, the work of a professor seemed at first only tangentially related to my intellectual interests. Before I arrived at St. Olaf College, I had no experience teaching undergraduates and only a vague sense of how to construct a syllabus, lead a discussion, or advise a student about a paper topic. It was the subject matter that hooked me. I wanted to understand how literature conveys religious meaning. I wanted to read, write, and talk about books.

I did not hear an external or internal voice calling me to be a professor. To condense a long process of vocational discernment into a moment of recognition, a scene: I'm sitting by a window in a locked ward of Philadelphia General Hospital, reading Mann's *Doctor Faustus* by the light of a gray winter sky. The TV blares in the background as the ward's residents fill the dull hours with card playing, banter, naps, or restless pacing. I look up from my book and observe my surroundings. I'm not doing anyone any good here. This novel is so interesting and complex that I want it to go on and on, and I want to understand all its subtle meanings. How can I keep doing this?

I entered the University of Chicago Divinity School's program in Religion and Literature in 1974. This choice of an academic field synthesized my mother's love of literature, my father's theological and philosophical interests, and my keen interest in ethics. In addition, my relationship with my brother had a big influence on what I chose to study. In 1972, David joined a new religious movement that emphasized meditation practices and commitment to its adolescent leader. I will not describe my brother's religious experience or trajectory, for reasons I discuss in the final chapter. Yet his religious conversion and commitment shaped my life and story in many ways, including focusing some of my intellectual pursuits and ethical concerns as a scholar and teacher.

I appreciated the important role of meditation in religious life. I had participated in an intensive monthlong religion course at Oberlin that involved several hours a day of meditation practice led by a Theravada Buddhist monk or a Zen monk. During my senior year I began to do yoga, and the next year in Philadelphia I lived with American devotees of a Sikh leader named Yogi Bhajan, who taught his version of kundalini yoga. I studied Eastern religions in an academic way as part of my college Religion major and was drawn to their understandings of human existence. I recognized that David had a powerful and profound experience of something sacred.

Mixed with my appreciation of meditation, however, were two related doubts. To my Protestant sensibility, David's devotion to a guru was idolatry. The leader of this new religious movement encouraged his followers to worship him as the current incarnation of a divine lineage. (In later years he de-emphasized worship of himself as a divine figure.) The fervent devotion of his followers seemed to me to view something finite as God. To my Protestant conscience, this total commitment to a human being was not simply misguided, but dangerously wrong. I was also angry and sad about the growing rift between David and me and his estrangement from our family. Perhaps it was I who was the idol-worshipper, outraged by this challenge to my ideal and myth of family unity.

Not only did I abhor idolatry, but I was also critical of this movement's understanding of the relationship between faith and reason. Its devotees seemed to me to demand blind faith and did not allow challenging questions to be raised. I was detached from any religious community at that time, and freedom of conscience was one of my central values. The rights of the individual were sacred, and I saw strict religious communities as a threat that compromised not only the intelligence but also the integrity of anyone involved. The antagonism between me and my brother was a conflict between a Protestant sensibility focused on the Word and Hindu-inflected piety displaying fervent love of the deity, which I now recognize as *bhakti* devotion. Our tensions expressed the temperamental differences and contrasting commitments of an aspiring intellectual and a religious practitioner offering gratitude for an overwhelming experience of bliss.

I envied David's capacity for intense religious experience and ecstatic emotion, which I thought my more prudent outlook and steady temperament prevented me from knowing firsthand. I felt something like the wistful yearning that William James reveals in *The Varieties of Religious Experience* when he implicitly includes himself among those who could never be converted: "Such inaptitude for religious faith may in some cases

Family Conscience

be intellectual in its origin. Their religious faculties may be checked in their natural tendency to expand, by beliefs about the world that are inhibitive, the pessimistic and materialistic beliefs, for example, within which so many good souls, who in former times would have freely indulged their religious propensities, find themselves nowadays, as it were, frozen; or the agnostic vetoes upon faith as something weak and shameful, under which so many of us today lie cowering, afraid to use our instincts. In many persons such inhibitions are never overcome."[1] Some scholars of religion long for the spiritual experiences they study, even as they question their nature or value. I am one such ambivalent student of religious experience.

The events related to my brother's conversion were crucial not only for his emerging sense of identity, but also for my own. A vivid memory of this period is when David said to me: "John, you and Dad study religion. I *do* it." David saw me and Ian as intellectualizing about religion, pondering it in abstract and theoretical terms that missed the real heart of religion: the ecstatic experience of encounter with the sacred. In contrast to judicious weighing of pros and cons, and to constructing an intellectual house of cards built on finely balanced distinctions, David threw himself into the more-than-rational aspects of religion, the emotional fervor and mystical sense of self-transcendence through participation in a larger consciousness. I devoted my energy to studying religion and evaluating its positive and negative effects on human life. I remember thinking: If religious faith can be as dangerous as I have seen it in the life of my brother, and if it can be as disruptive and painful as it has been in my family, then religion is not simply a good thing. I have seen this not only in studying religion's role in human history, but in the lives of the people I love most.

More positively, choosing the Religion and Literature program expressed my desire to understand the vitality of religion in a way that was not abstract and theoretical. I saw attention to literature as a way to comprehend aspects of religion that were crucial in David's life. I am impatient with systematic theology and well-organized conceptual theories. I didn't like the way many of my fellow graduate students argued about hermeneutics (the theory of interpretation) without engaging specific texts. Or they talked endlessly about method and how one would do theology if, hypothetically, one was ever to do it. My disdain reflects my own intellectual limitations, but I also knew that religion is not just philosophy. It is messy and ambiguous; its power and meaningfulness are not simply a matter of logical clarity, but expressed in symbolism, metaphor, and narrative, which

---

1. Wiliam James, *The Varieties of Religious Experience* (orig. pub. 1902), with an introduction by Martin Marty, Penguin American Library (London: Penguin, 1982; repr., Penguin Classics, Harmondsworth, UK: Penguin, 1985), 204.

have a different kind of coherence. My sense of vocation as a scholar and teacher owes a lot to David and the ways we differentiated from each other. Although I was critical of his religious commitment, I saw it as profound, authentic, and mysterious. I wanted to understand what happens when people have intense religious experiences such as conversion or a vision. I thought that the best way to do this would be to read stories by or about people like my brother.

For many years I was estranged from him. I felt that he was breaking up the family's unity and hurting my parents. I was part of The Establishment, the Old Guard, wanting to keep things the same. Yet a small part of me may have been rooting for him, vicariously wanting someone to bust loose, rock the boat, find a new way to be. My conflicting feelings about David—yearning, resentment, jealousy, rivalry, and love—reflected ambivalence about a brother who seemed free from the scruples that bound me to the family. He was attempting to escape, while I was a loyal subject of a kingdom that constrained me and gave me an identity.

David's involvement in a new religious movement, personal troubles, and angry rejection of the family caused a lot of turmoil for my parents, sisters, and me. He was the primary catalyst for change in the family; he shook things up and helped us all to grow. For Ian and Deane, David's estrangement brought profound sadness and soul-searching. It was hard for me to see them agonizing about his suffering as they asked themselves in what ways they were responsible. I think this family situation influenced my choice of a dissertation topic. "Tragedy as a Critique of Virtue" explored the ways in which tragic protagonists sometimes suffer and bring suffering to others because of their most admirable qualities. A professor asked me why I felt compelled to write about tragic characters. He intuited a personal source of my engagement in this topic. I couldn't articulate the connections between family trauma and my intellectual interests. Now I think that I was trying to put my family's conflicts into a larger context. For me, scholarship was a way to "tell the truth, but tell it slant," as Emily Dickinson did in poetry. David's search for self-transcendence struck me as tragic as it sometimes veered towards extreme asceticism, renunciation, and rejection of everything in his past. I also saw in my parents' suffering a sense of responsibility for their son that was admirable yet perhaps excessive or misplaced. They could not help trying to understand how the family had influenced him and trying to do whatever they could to support him. As I saw it, David, Deane, and Ian suffered partly because of their virtues, their best and most admirable qualities. In my dissertation, I argued that literary tragedy offers insights about how people sometimes bring about suffering as they pursue their ideals and try to do what they think is right.

Family Conscience

Many of the religious topics that I pursued in teaching and writing reflect my relationship with my brother: conversion; the relationship between faith and reason; and the tension between communal ideals and an individual's quest for religious experience, which may involve solitude, asceticism, renunciation, or deconversion from inherited beliefs. As much as my parents, my brother influenced my vocation as a teacher and writer about religion, motivating me to try to understand its ambiguity, power, and mystery.

* * *

A COMPARISON WITH EACH of my siblings reveals different ways in which our parents influenced our attitudes toward work as well as some common themes that reframe how I see my own career. When in 2005 I asked Blair about her sense of vocation, she stressed Deane's role:

"Mom really emphasized looking after other people at times when I might not have. Like inviting a lonely girl who lived next door to my birthday party. That only happened once and Mom regretted it. She gave me that kind of message: not to hurt other people's feelings. And the Christian message of humility and not making yourself center stage. Later she got me interested in the American Friends Service Committee and their ten-week work camps. She found out about Friends Hospital in Philadelphia. That's how I got interested in working in a psychiatric hospital. Mom had a lot to do with my choice of social work. I remember watching *The Three Faces of Eve* with her. She told me about *I Never Promised You a Rose Garden* when I was in junior high school. That book described therapy situations for families and multiple personalities. Mom's influence was really important."

"Once you said that for some therapists, their motivation has something to do with fixing their own families."

"That's common knowledge," Blair said. "Whether they realize it or not at the time, many people go into it with the hope of being a therapist to their own family. It doesn't work."

"Was that true for you?"

"I had an awareness of some brokenness in the family. It wasn't conscious at the time that I got into social work. But when you are learning about psychological development and doing treatment with people who have this or that problem, it's inevitable that you think about your own family and psychology. If it isn't a motivation when you go into the field, it becomes one."

"You have been interested in family systems psychology. Does that theory make the most sense to you because of the family you came from?"

"Most of my career, my approach has been psychodynamic. This kind of therapy emphasizes the relationship between the therapist and the client, to become more aware of how the past continues to color relationships and the client's expectations about the world and himself. I'm interested in how people change and get to where they want to be. Family systems theory looks at family myths that get established and passed down through the generations, and at how one person's actions affect the whole family. The training program I'm in now, called Internal Family Systems, combines these approaches, looking at the client's internal world as a system composed of parts that can be differentiated and listened to and brought into better balance."

"Do you use the metaphor of family to understand the psyche? Do you say, 'this is the mother inside'?"

"Sort of. But it's not that literal. I may have a mother part that's very nurturing, and another part that's polarized with that nurturing part. Let's say it's a part that feels compelled to be perfectly skilled and competent in all aspects of parenting. These parts may or may not be related to our mother. But experiences with family members are formative. As an example, you taught me how to fast dance to the Beatles *Rubber Soul* album in seventh grade. So maybe I think I can dance with boys. I can see myself as worthwhile enough for someone I admire to take the time to teach me to dance. That experience with you may give rise to a part of me that feels hopeful about managing feelings of insecurity or klutziness in social situations."

I'm glad that incident had a positive impact on my sister; I know I've had a negative influence, too. Family experiences shaped the ways Blair understands her vocation, and she brings that history into her work. She knows she can't be a therapist for her own family. I wonder if I am foolishly trying to be a scholar of my family.

David studied at Carleton and Macalester Colleges and the University of Minnesota, as well as on his own at computer science. About medical issues, genetics, and nutrition, he is a walking encyclopedia and master of internet research. He has an amazingly diverse work history, including being a painter, a waiter, a handyman, a taxi driver, a computer specialist (both salaried and freelance), an information-systems consultant, a salesman, a layer of tiles, and a school bus driver. David has many talents and learns quickly; he's easily bored and for many years changed jobs frequently. When the learning curve leveled off, he sought a new field to master. He immersed himself in projects with great energy and concentration, forgetting about everything else. When his interest flagged or something else became more engrossing, he moved on. He avoided authority figures, preferring work that he could do in his own way without supervision from a boss. His restless moving from job to job and periods of unemployment were very different from my own work history as I slogged through graduate school and the predictable stages of a college professor's career.

David didn't receive the outward recognition and institutional support that go with an established career track. His sense of meaningful work focused not on a defined social role, but rather short-term projects that he threw himself into with great intensity. Once I found him laboring on a car that he had torn apart and rebuilt. When I visited, often he would be constructing a sculpture or painting. One summer he went windsurfing every day that the weather allowed, then quit for good. He plays guitar, composes electronic music, and practices with other musicians. David has worked hard with several counselors, psychologists, and therapy groups, often going several times a week to sessions. He knows a lot about himself and the human psyche. He once said that for him the spiritual meaning of work is "falling in love with the effort of work and not worrying about the result." I can't do that very well; I want a payoff, recognition, readers.

Seeing David follow his shifting and varied interests, I sometimes doubted my own path. I felt like a drudge and a drone, plodding on stolidly even when a task had become dull or frustrating. I don't have many sudden insights or mercurial flashes of creativity, but rather a steady and persistent interest in certain topics. I work at a level of intensity that I can sustain for a long time. I developed only a narrow range of the spectrum of abilities and forms of intelligence with which David explored the world and his own nature. For jumping through various hoops and putting on blinders to prevent distraction, I was rewarded with the salary and status of a white-collar professional. We chose different forms of freedom and limitation.

A tape-recorded conversation in July 2004 probed how conscience influenced our vocational choices, work ethics, and frustrations and satisfactions with work. I asked him: "What is your view of work? Dad had a strong work ethic. You have worked very hard on a lot of different things, and on some of them, like therapy, for years. Your music isn't for money or the outward marks of prestige. You didn't do a career track. I envied your freedom as I followed a traditional career route, and I wondered how you can do it."

"It's pretty simple," David reflected. "We're all in the same boat. The outward markers of success, in the end, don't mean anything. If I spend my whole life making art that nobody sees but me, that doesn't mean anything. When work is being done, the natural order is being served. When I'm performing a function like making a floor, or doing something for somebody, that's work, whether I'm paid for it or not. Because it has value. Anybody who looked at it would say: He's doing something useful. The other stuff—whether I have a degree or not—doesn't mean anything. It doesn't matter if I get paid for it. It comes down to conscience and confidence: that I know when I'm doing something good. And I know when I'm just tooting my horn. That's boring. Nobody wants to see art that says: 'Look how great I am, look what I made.' People want to say: 'that's beautiful.' If I'm an artist and it's just about pumping up my own ego, it's stupid. The work that Dad has done is his life. I respect that work. I honor him for his good work, not his awards or recognition. He could have been helpful as a bus driver. He's an honorable man, but not because of the markers. Our family trades in a certain currency: academic markers. I've never been anything in those terms."

I responded: "When I think about conscience and work, I think about the Protestant work ethic. I don't think any of us are working out our salvation, but I see in myself a desire to work that is sometimes healthy. I want my sons to have a work ethic, to be useful to other people and to keep going when the going gets tough. I also think my work ethic has dimensions that aren't healthy, such as feeling driven and anxious. Maybe all the outward markers of success are ways of trying to reassure myself that my work has meaning."

"That comes from trying to inject value into yourself from outside."

David analyzed Ian's influence on each of us: "I can't have any self-worth from trying to please him. It has to come instead from this sense: I made something here that did someone else good. I participated in the drama of the universe, in the economy of energy. I was in the flow. I used my mind and body and it felt good. None of that has come from Dad. He taught me a few things, like how to hold a hammer. He never gave me meaningful work. So why do I feel that he has anything to do with my work life? He really doesn't. You, maybe, because you are in the same field. But ultimately you must have a sense of yourself as a good teacher. It doesn't matter whether Dad thinks you are a good teacher. The thing that impresses me about Dad is the students who say 'He's the best teacher I ever had. He listened so well.' I'm sure he gets tricked by the illusions of fame. There's going to be a time when he is not here anymore. If he's my big motivator for working, then I'm going to have a crisis. A lot of guys have a crisis when their father dies, apart from the loss of the person. They don't know who they are anymore."

"Like Everett," I interjected. "His crisis came soon after his father's death. Maybe he was working just to please his father."

David asserted that belief in the value of one's work must come from within, and also that our family influences our attitudes and our temperaments: "We do have these genes. You have a brain and a constitution similar to Dad's. It doesn't surprise me that you are in the same line of work and have some similar gifts. When you actualize yourself, lo and behold, you have a lot in common with Dad. I don't think you made a choice either to be yourself or to follow in Dad's footsteps; I think they are one and the same. And it's not unusual for the second son to go into something radically different. I don't think that we are that different from most families. The first son goes into the family business and later sons have to create something new. We played the hands that were dealt to us."

David, Blair, John, and Heather after skiing, 1980. Photo by Meg Ojala

My youngest sister, Heather, started classes at Macalester College in September 1979. She wanted her education to give her practical skills to help her address social concerns. During the spring of her first year, Heather volunteered in a program called the Bridge, which helped runaway children and teens. At the same time, she took an academic course on critical theories of social services. From this academic perspective, the helping professions and welfare institutions were viewed as ways of shoring up an oppressive economic system. This theoretical orientation seemed to Heather to call into question or undermine any attempt to address social problems. She told me in 2004: "I was baffled by this approach. What do you do with all this radical theory? How could I connect this kind of education with my ideal of service to others? I wanted to do something useful and clear-cut. I was trying to avoid ambiguity. Choosing an academic program can be like choosing an evangelical church: you want to grab onto something absolute and certain. I wanted a connection to my having been a cook in Alaska. I didn't want to be in an ivory tower, but to be with different kinds of people. Mom and Dad seemed unconnected with the real world, and so did this kind of college. My friend Frederick had worked on fishing boats and he disdained academics. I had intellectual abilities but I wanted to get my hands dirty and do something concrete. I couldn't see a way in college to combine intellectual pursuits with practical skills." At the end of her freshman year, Heather withdrew from Macalester and moved to North Carolina, where she worked as a cook at an experimental farm, the beginning of her first career as a nutritionist. She finished college at the University of North Carolina and completed a graduate program at Emory University to get that practical knowledge.

Heather was dissatisfied with the theoretical speculations and ambiguity-mongering of the academic world and with the gap between a liberal arts education and the immediate needs of the world. Her experience challenges my belief in the value of the kind of educational institution in which I have spent my entire life: as a child observing my father's work at Carleton College, as a student at Oberlin, in graduate school preparing to teach, and as a professor at St. Olaf College. I taught a course on conscience in which we read Freud, Nietzsche, feminist thinkers, and other critics of traditional ideas of conscience. For some of my students, this academic study must have seemed utterly irrelevant to their own moral questions and concerns and their own experience of conscience. I may have undermined rather than nurtured their moral commitments as we studied the ways conscience can be twisted by self-deception and rationalization. When they finished with my course, students may have mistrusted their own ethical judgments. I'm not sure whether this helped or harmed their sense of themselves as moral agents.

Heather wanted to address social problems and make a difference in the world. Yet her temperament is drawn to creative work that she does alone. In April 1979, she took a career and personality test and, in a journal, described her reaction to the results: "I was surprised to find that I scored very low in the social services area when all along I've thought it was an area I was cut out for. My advisor suggested that perhaps my family had impressed this on me. It's true that both Mom and my sister are involved in social work and all my life my parents stressed the importance of serving others. In the personality test I did not come out with the strengths associated with the service area. Rather I prefer a lack of structure over structure, process over results, and working with ideas." In the 1990s, Heather left her work as a nutritionist, went back to school to get a Bachelor of Fine Arts in painting, and for several years tried to support herself as a commercial artist.

Heather and I each internalized from our parents an ideal of service to others that informed our sense of vocation but was hard to realize. We wanted our work to address the needs of others and to bring personal fulfillment. Yet I think that both of us turn inward for energy and get satisfaction from working on long-term projects that do not directly and immediately engage other people. These activities—Heather's artistic work and my writing—are not only somewhat remote from pressing human needs, but difficult to rely on as a source of income. All the money I earned from many thousands of hours of writing over a half-century is less than the pay I received for teaching summer school for a month. Yet the college where I worked supported my writing in many ways, whereas Heather continued to search for work that would satisfy her intellectual curiosity, practical disposition, need for an income, and desires for service and self-expression. After the economic downturn of 2001, she decided to become an art teacher, and since then has worked in public schools in Atlanta and Virginia.

The settled and secure career of a tenured professor is an anomaly in the United States, where most people change jobs several times during their working life (though academics may "retool," too, as Ian put it). Many people put most of their time, energy, and passion into hobbies, avocations, and temporary interests. They may do manual or menial jobs for pay and get most of their satisfaction from music, theatre, visual arts, fishing, triathlons, or church commitments, for example. Thinking about Heather's and David's varied work histories, I realize that my own career only appears natural from within the context of academic life—and even there, a tenured perch in a stable institution, especially in the humanities, is increasingly rare in the downsizing, bureaucratized economy of higher education.

My work life involved continual searching for independence and connection, creative expression and service, personal satisfaction and steady income. I wanted to feel competent while also being challenged to keep on learning. I enjoyed exceptional freedom and privilege to look for work that meets all my criteria. The earnest and eager students I taught at St. Olaf similarly hoped to find a vocation that would integrate all these things. They wanted to change the world and they hoped for paid vacations and good medical and retirement benefits. We privileged few want our work to reflect our deepest values, give meaning to our lives, and pay the bills. Our search for the perfect vocation reflects high ideals and the call of conscience, but we chafe at the constraints of every form of employment and the anxiety and dissatisfaction that come with demanding work. I whined about grading papers or attending committee meetings while many Americans were going bankrupt, losing their homes, or struggling with a medical emergency that they couldn't pay for. Our lofty ideals and aspirations may distract us from an elementary truth: "By the sweat of your face you shall eat bread until you return to the ground, for out of it you were taken; you are dust, and to dust you shall return" (Genesis 3:19 NRSV).

Two things seem contradictory but are both true. One: I was extremely lucky to have found work that usually satisfied me, sometimes helped other people, and put food on the table. So I should count my blessings and shut up. Two: Something was always missing, and I was dimly aware of this and right to want more. There is so much that did not fit into my academic career that would have enriched my life: learning a second language well, playing my dusty guitar, engaging with any number of people outside my academic bubble, and so forth. Perhaps a sense of dissatisfaction about work can be a good thing, if it alerts one that the meaning of life is more than one's career.

Yet in retirement, I'm more at peace with the choices I've made—or I have lost some creative spark or restless energy. There is always a price to make a choice, and I would gladly make the same vocational choices again.

* * *

THERE IS SOMETHING PRIVATE and precious about a marriage, even when it is over, and I would not expose much of it to public gaze. Only insofar as it reveals some things about conscience do I offer a glimpse. On the positive side, my relationship with Meg was based on common values reflected in how we raised our sons, spent our money, and used time and energy for work, rest, and recreation. But listing the values we shared would sound ridiculously self-righteous. More interesting and revealing are failures to practice ideals, and the ways the best intentions miscarry. I won't criticize my ex-spouse, but only my own habits and tendencies as they are related to conscience.

Always needing to be in the right prevents intimacy, vulnerability, and empathy. I can usually find high-minded reasons why I acted as I did. Preoccupied with self-justification, I don't listen to my partner. A kind of neurotic self-protection that masquerades as conscience lures me into a well-defended, walled-off stance. A therapist asked, "Would you rather be right or be married?"

My prickly conscience is hypersensitive to expressions of dissatisfaction. Then a partner's feelings feel like attacks. I shrink from criticism, yet constantly imagine it, as if my conscience has a life of its own. As if it needs to seek out an external stimulus to react to but is running on its own Eveready battery. As if self-judgment needs a little exercise occasionally, to keep it limber. Guilty, self-righteous, and often both at once, I'm focused on myself.

When my spouse was unhappy, depressed, or angry, I felt responsible to fix her mood, and when I couldn't, I became depressed. An inflated sense of responsibility for her emotional condition got in the way of simply being present.

I seemed to her a little judgmental. Okay, a lot. Especially in the early years of our marriage, Meg would ask: "How can you make that statement? Who are you to judge?" What I thought was a harmless evaluative opinion seemed to her a simplistic verdict about something I didn't understand. Sometimes she would just say: "According to you."

"Well of course," I responded. "Who else? Do I have to add the phrase 'according to me' every time I give my opinion? And aren't you being judgmental about my judgmentalism?"

Good grief! Why couldn't I just lighten up, spare her my nobility, laugh at myself, and let the pressure out? Why does everything turn into a matter of ethical principle? A relentless need to defend myself inhibits other kinds of awareness and understanding.

Every year Meg made a Christmas card, often with a quotation. One year the card included this saying by the Persian poet Rumi: "Out beyond ideas of wrongdoing and rightdoing, there is a field. I will meet you there."[2] Sometimes my spouse or lover has helped me see that; she takes me to the field.

A low time in our marriage was in 1989, when Meg and I were emotionally estranged and fighting a lot. Someone in the family was sick continuously from Thanksgiving to April that endless winter. We were exhausted from the demands of childcare, teaching, getting tenure, and trying to find time for my scholarly writing and her art. It was all work and no play, frantic busyness and not enough intimacy. We somehow made time for everything except each other; our family-maintenance industry had no heart or soul. Meg thought that we should have a trial separation and I should move out.

At that time, I was writing an essay about suicide that discussed William Styron's novel *Sophie's Choice* and a theological analysis of suicide by one of my teachers, James Gustafson. Thinking about suicide so much started to affect me. To take "one's" life started to seem justifiable in certain situations. Then *my* life, if things kept getting worse. I began to imagine driving into a truck. It would only take a split second of thinking this way at the wrong time for it to happen. I didn't want to die, but it seemed like

---

2. "Out beyond Ideas of Rightdoing and Wrongdoing," in *The Essential Rumi*, by Maulan Jalāl al-Dīn Rūmī, translated by Coleman Barks et al. (San Francisco: Harper, 1995), 36.

the only way out of misery. I was thirty-eight, close to the age when my grandfather, Everett, killed himself. In my case, too, the thought of being separated from my wife and small children, who were aged five and one, was devastating, and imagining my life without them unbearable. Yet I contemplated the ultimate abandonment. Part of what stopped me was that I knew how Everett's death had affected my mother. I couldn't do that to Meg or our sons. A half century after he died, my grandfather's negative example steeled me to go on living.

I went into therapy, first with Meg and then alone. I suspect that many memoirs attempt to dramatize in a vivid scene or two a slow and undatable growth of awareness that came about while working with a therapist. As in Christian conversion narratives, the writer condenses a process of gradual and subtle change into an incident of sudden transformation and startling insight. It makes a more dramatic story, whether it really happened that way or not. For me, the results of three separate periods of marital therapy and three series of meetings for individual therapy produced subtle incremental changes, but no dramatic revelation or turning point.

Our marriage did not always run smoothly, but the bond was tried, tested, and endured for forty-two years, plus the preceding four years of living together. We did not give up easily. We struggled to find the right kind of connectedness, neither enmeshed nor detached. I have trouble with boundaries, as is evident in this memoir.

What is a good marriage? A good enough one? Once I was on a camping adventure in the Canadian wilderness, my annual kayak trip with buddies. The four of us were on an island off the north shore of Lake Superior, sitting around the fire on a cool evening, drinking scotch and smoking cigars. Two friends who had recently been through a painful divorce recalled quarrels and conflicts in vivid detail. Searing words and violent rages caused wounds that scarred but never healed. Another guy said that he had never struggled with or in any way doubted his marriage, which was all sweetness and light. After many years of happiness, he had nothing to say about marriage: no wisdom and no powerful stories, just an affirmation of contentment. I said that my marriage was unlike theirs and involved a lot of struggle, but was good. I didn't share many details that evening around the fire, and I won't now either.

Finally, the struggles were too much. Our hard work and effort to stay together as we changed over nearly half a century may reflect a Calvinist work ethic or some tough Minnesotan determination to suffer through all the seasons. One of Meg's proverbs from our early years: you've got to hoe the hardest row. We did that. But there needs to be fun and enjoyment, too, and silliness and sleep. When you cross-country ski, each leg must kick, then glide. In marriage, too, there are moments of pushing, sometimes uphill, and moments when you just coast, slide along, and enjoy the easy motion. Over the decades we both changed, or "grew apart," as they say, until the effort to stay together was too much. In 2020 we divorced. I have been sad about that, and my conscience is not clear about my mistakes. But I moved on and found love again.

* * *

ONE DAY IN JUNE 2004, I went to visit David in south Minneapolis. We rode bicycles along the lakeside paths and Minnehaha Parkway, stopping for supper at a noodle restaurant. We sat outside and talked about money. I asked David about renunciation of wealth as a repeated motif in family history.

"Yes," he said, "I think that is a recurring issue. The family motto, written on the wall at Bonskeid [the Barbour ancestral home in Scotland] is something like 'Live lightly on the earth.' Grandfather inherited land on the family estate and gave it to the tenants. Dad gave away a million dollars, almost his entire Templeton Prize. And Mom had an aunt whose family inherited slaves and freed them."

"Why do you think there is this pattern? How does inherited wealth affect our identity?"

"My theory is that the Barbour brothers in Manchester exploited child labor. Succeeding generations pissed away the money. They also gave it away for reasons of a guilty conscience. Inherited wealth gave them a feeling of moral superiority because they didn't earn the money by exploiting anyone. They went into professions rather than industry or business, so they felt pure. But they also felt guilty because they didn't earn what they inherited."

Two Barbour ancestors acquired wealth from cotton mills in Manchester, England during the late nineteenth century. This industry was based on cotton imported from the Sudan, so it was enmeshed in the colonialism of the British Empire as well as the terrible working conditions and child labor practices of the Industrial Revolution. The family fortune must have been substantial, because enough of it remained, even after being spread out over many branches of the family through several generations, to help pay my way through college and graduate school and purchase a home. The small inheritance that my mother passed on to her children had been invested in real estate in Washington, DC. My Barbour and Kern forebears were thrifty and prudent; they spent the interest while preserving their capital for the next generation. Ian told me that while I could do whatever I wished with my modest trust fund, he had used income from inherited investments primarily for expenses related to education, travel, and emergency health needs. In a 1974 letter, Deane suggested another use: "Some funds, quietly given, sometimes anonymously, may make all the difference to another person's hopes and fears, or their chance to make choices."

Compared to many other families, our inheritance was not substantial. Yet it generated ambivalence as well as gratitude. When he was in his late twenties, David gave his trust fund, which was worth about the cost of an education at a private college, to his religious community. As we sat at the sidewalk café slurping noodles, I asked him whether giving away his inheritance was an act of conscience. Was the money somehow tainted or a burden?

"It wasn't a conscience thing," he said. "I wanted to be unencumbered, to be light and free. I was also afraid of growing complacent. I wanted to put myself in a position of need so that I would have to work hard. The inheritance did not feel like it was authentically mine. I wanted to possess nothing that was not really my own. I had to find my own way in the world, because so much that had come from the family hadn't worked for me."

Donating his inheritance was also an act of devotion to his guru. All the members of the movement were encouraged to give their wealth to the organization. This was an act of worship as well as a move away from materialism toward simplicity.

I have not given up much of anything. I saved a chunk of my salary that is invested in TIAA-CREF retirement funds, so I am deeply entrenched in a capitalist economic system about which I have many reservations. So-called ethical investing is intellectually interesting and morally ambiguous. Criteria to consider about the organizations we are invested in include their environmental impact; if they profit from addictive activities such as smoking, drinking, or gambling; if they value racial and gender equality in the workplace; if they are involved in making weapons; and if they contribute to public goods such as education, health, or children's welfare. Often a company that is good at one or two of these criteria fails at others. In a global economy, many corporations are dependent on questionable labor or environmental practices in other countries. After some inconclusive research, I threw up my hands and invested my savings in mutual funds spread through the whole economy, although some of them adhere to ESG (environmental, social, and governance) criteria. My conscience is uneasy about the impacts of the wealth I accumulated. When I hear older activists and tenured academics rail against neoliberalism, globalization, and environmental degradation, I usually agree with them in theory but wonder how their retirement assets are invested.

David remembered a moment thirty years earlier when he and I were organizing food and gear for a backpacking trip in New Hampshire's White

Family Conscience

Mountains. He mimicked me weighing in my hand a can of tuna and asking: "Do I want to carry this all those miles? Or toss it?" That camping philosophy appealed to us: The question to consider is not "what do I need?" but "what can I get by without?" One outdoorsman advised filing down the handle of a toothbrush to eliminate a few grams.

I had a steady income, a house and mortgage, cars (often low-end Fords), a retirement fund, and insurance on everything. Lots of stuff: three bikes, two kayaks, two canoes, and more books than I could ever read. In contrast, my brother had very few possessions. His apartments in Minneapolis were practically bare. One day I opened his refrigerator; it was empty except for ten pounds of carrots, a lot of vitamin supplements, and an enormous pot of beans. David has a knack for recycling discarded tools, machines, and miscellaneous pieces of junk. He salvaged a chair that massaged your back; it sat like a throne in a nearly barren room. He is a sort of Rube Goldberg inventor, often rigging up an elaborate system to perform a task that he needs to do only once. There were exceptions to his general disregard for material possessions: one room was full of computer and audio equipment. He traveled light, but sometimes with a few high-tech, state-of-the-art gadgets. David has an aesthetic sense as well as an ethics that expresses the philosophy that "less is more." He is a later-day Thoreau, trying to live simply, unencumbered by possessions and job commitments. He stepped off the treadmill of working more and more to buy and consume more and more. He renounced material possessions, ownership, stuff. Focusing on what he did without, I didn't recognize the positive goal he sought: the attraction of being unencumbered, light, and free. A decade later, I wrote a novel exploring the ambiguities of various forms of renunciation: fleeing-from and striving-for, pain and spiritual aspiration, self-laceration and soul-work.

On this June afternoon, David was wondering whether to accept a walnut dresser that our mother wanted to give him, an old family heirloom built by her great-uncle. David thought that he would take the dresser, partly as a favor to Deane, who was searching for the right home for cherished possessions as she and Ian prepared to move from their house on Winona Street to an apartment. I was surprised that he wasn't more eager to have this fine old piece of furniture, but he asked: "How much energy should I put into taking care of Things, when there are so many problems in human relationships that I should be working on?"

"Things" had a capital *T*, like Sloth or Vanity for the Puritans. David's rhetorical question echoed similar statements made or implied by our parents over the years, to the effect that Things are not as important as People. He had learned the lesson that Deane internalized when she told her mother that of everything in their house, it was her mother's desk that meant most to her—and then her sister said to Gam: "You. You mean the most."

Deane treasured certain heirlooms not for their monetary value but rather because of their association with people whom she loved. Several of her autobiographical stories deal with an object that symbolizes a truth about human relationships or a bond of connection—for instance, her father's Annapolis class ring and her mother's walnut writing desk. David seems to have inherited my mother's way of thinking about the priority of people over things, but not her sense of the symbolic value of certain objects. He is not attached to anything material, so far as I can tell, and would relinquish any possession that ties him down.

David was working that summer as a tile-setter, doing repair jobs for friends. He had to remove a lot of debris. As we bicycled through the streets of Minneapolis, he told me that he was searching for a machine called an articulated boom, which is like a cherry picker. We found one in an alley and David explained it to me, caressing it gently. With this extended mechanical arm, he could lift supplies to a second-floor job and more easily remove rubble. It would require a large investment of many thousands of dollars, and he didn't know how long he would be setting tiles. But he looked at this piece of machinery longingly, coveting it the way I would admire a Porsche I'll never own.

Several times during our ride, David launched his bicycle off a curb and came down hard on the pavement. I laboriously stopped, gently lifted my bike up or down the curb, and pedaled on, now half a block behind him. I felt old, overly cautious, and fussy about my bike. At the end of our ride, David noticed two broken spokes on his bicycle. He would have to get them fixed. Or perhaps he would invent an original way to repair them himself; he might devote a day to inventing a spoke-fixing tool. I thought to myself, "Ha! You see what happens when you don't take care of your stuff. You spend even more time and energy on repairing them. Who is really unencumbered?" So did this elder brother congratulate himself on his different way of trying to reach the same spiritual goal: being free from preoccupation with Things. We inherited the same ideal and pursued it in different ways. My brother renounced material things, while I justify or rationalize living a conventional American life with an uneasy conscience.

* * *

CHOOSING A LIFE HAS meant choosing two religious traditions. I need all the help I can get. I continue to worship in a Christian church, serve on its committees, and interpret the world with Christian beliefs. Since 2005 I

Family Conscience

have also been drawn to Buddhism. For me it is a wisdom tradition whose understanding of the human condition makes a lot of sense. The daily practice of meditation now feels necessary as a practice of mindfulness in the present moment and a renewal of my intention to free myself and others from suffering. One aspect of Buddhism that resonates with my experience is its perspective on conscience.

Buddha's teachings begin with the universal human experience of *dukkha*: suffering, unsatisfactoriness, and discontent. We experience suffering from encounters (including imagined ones) with death and illness and from the fleeting nature of our pleasures. Dukkha is also a recurring component of my experiences of conscience when retrospective judgment of past actions brings guilt or shame, and when I worry too much about making the right decision. I suffer because I think that I haven't been as good as I could have been, should have been. I haven't lived up to my ideals for myself as a father, husband, son, teacher, writer, citizen, Christian, Buddhist, or compassionate human being. Even meditation can become an exercise in self-criticism. I become impatient, frustrated, and angry when my actions and thoughts do not measure up to my ideal. It's a challenge to aspire to a higher standard and also practice self-acceptance.

Buddhism gives me glimpses of an outside perspective on my Western obsessions related to conscience. As a result of taking in teachings and practicing meditation, I can sometimes understand my habits of judgment as forms of narcissism and self-inflicted dukkha. Buddhism offers insights into the value of patience, kindness, and tolerance for what doesn't conform to my moral judgments. An important part of the practice is *metta*, the cultivation of loving-kindness, which should extend to every sentient being, including oneself.

The Buddha insisted that his followers live in accord with the dharma (the moral law, the nature of reality) by following the Noble Eightfold Path and practicing virtues such as patience, humility, equanimity, and loving-kindness. Although there is no exact term that corresponds to conscience in Sanskrit or Pali, Buddhists assume that individuals can recognize what is truly good, strive for it, and assess their actions in its light.

In my local sangha, many persons drawn to Buddhism are fleeing Christian churches where they were taught to feel sinful or fear a harsh, judgmental God. I, too, want release from useless self-flagellation and regret, but I don't want release from Christian faith. I find a lot of convergence between Buddhism and Christianity in their realistic understanding of the human condition: our egotism and self-induced misery. These two religious perspectives also affirm both our capacities to recognize a better way to live and our abilities to make persistent efforts toward living better. There are important differences between the two traditions, for instance on whether faith in God helps one to live a good life and practice compassion.

I wrestle with the Buddhist idea of *anatman* (not self), which seems incompatible with my Christian belief in a soul or self. Trying to make sense of this puzzle, I wrote a book about how travel to Buddhist lands helped Westerners understand no-self and changed them.[3] The sense of self is impermanent and elusive. I can't identify my essential being with my body, feelings, thoughts, beliefs, memories, or any conditioned thing because these all go on changing throughout my lifetime. There is wisdom and potential liberation in the Buddhist insight that suffering comes from intense attachment to acquired opinions and personality habits that arise and cease like all conditioned phenomena. To cling less tightly to beliefs about my identity, to see that my sense of self could be different, invites greater ease, freedom, and openness to other people and experiences. Living this way would help me respond more out of generosity and compassion, and less from a need to be right.

I preach to myself a little Buddhist sermon or pep talk about conscience. My goal is to reduce suffering in myself and the world. I want to form the right intentions and consider how my future actions will reflect them and affect the happiness or suffering of others and myself. Sometimes I will blow it. Then guilt and shame may play a role, but only momentarily, to motivate me to do better. A conscience that goes on rebuking the self does not help; to obsess over faults is a toxic form of egocentricity. Instead, I need to observe my actions without attachment or aversion, reflect on their consequences, and either accept the situation or try to change it. I can resolve to mend my ways and be at peace with myself.

I also believe (or, on certain days, try to believe) that I was created by God, that God cares about each unique person, and that there is no coherent basis for morality or human rights without a concept of the individual self. Conscience is the call of my true being, a God-given capacity that allows me to judge myself and make free moral choices. I don't have a coherent theory that reconciles my Christian beliefs with Buddhism. Insights from each tradition ring true to my experience, and each religion has taught me forms of self-assessment and monitoring. They both help me live with my impermanent, suffering, fallible, and undeniable conscience. When I worship in church or sit with the Buddhists, each of these communities feeds my hungry soul, reorients my perspective, and inspires me.

---

3. John D. Barbour, *Journeys of Transformation: Searching for No-Self in Western Buddhist Travel Narratives* (Cambridge: Cambridge University Press, 2022).

CHAPTER 10

Professing Religion and Traveling with Students

Many aspects of college teaching have ethical dimensions. When writing letters of recommendation for students or evaluating colleagues for tenure, how do I balance the desire to help them with honest and fair assessment? How do I present topics related to race or gender in ways that will both challenge and support students? As a teacher of religious studies, how do I respond to a student whose faith is shaken—rightly so, in my opinion—by biblical criticism or feminist insights? Decisions about what and how I should teach are shaped not only by curriculum and pedagogical goals, but by fundamental convictions about what is most important, given limited time and resources. Of many aspects of teaching that mix ethical considerations with other matters, two in particular raised issues of conscience for me: the question of how teaching religious studies is related to explaining my own beliefs, and the ethics of travel, especially in study-abroad programs.

As a professor of religion, I rarely professed my own beliefs, that is, openly declared or affirmed my religious views and why I have these convictions. Once in a while, though, it seemed important to do so, sometimes by telling a story. I wrestled with the question of when it is appropriate for a teacher to describe personal religious experiences and beliefs.

According to many theories of religious studies and many views of religious commitment, academic study and personal faith are utterly different, and sometimes irreconcilable. In contrast, I think these perspectives on religion are distinct yet often related. St. Olaf College calls itself "a college of the church," not a Bible college or secular institution. I felt free to encourage explicit discussions of how learning and faith can influence each other. It can be pedagogically valuable for a professor to speak of his personal faith, just as it can be illuminating for a political scientist to explain her political opinions, for an art historian to justify his assessments of works of art, or for a scientist to espouse a particular energy or environmental policy. In any academic field, teachers must learn to balance critical distance and passionate engagement with their subject matter.

However, there are peculiar challenges inherent in teaching religious studies that complicate matters. There are good reasons to conceal or "bracket" one's views in a religion class, where students need to learn to think critically and not simply confess their faith. Very few students have any prior experience of studying religion in an academic context. Nonetheless, some of them think they already know all about the subject, or all they need to know, and some students think that all other views are wrong. Still others think that all views are equally valid; because they see faith as a subjective, irrational experience, they think we cannot reason about or assess religious claims. In the name of tolerance and being open-minded, they dismiss normative arguments about the adequacy of various claims.

Students differ greatly in the degree to which they are willing and able to profess their own religious convictions. Some people feel confident about their faith and qualified to speak with authority about the Bible or their experiences in church or prayer meetings. Other students are tentative and uncertain, and some are alienated by what they see as false piety or attempts to convert them. It is a challenge for a professor of religious studies to establish a classroom environment where all students feel empowered to speak and write about their personal response to the subject matter and all students are encouraged to question their prior beliefs, doubts, and evasions of critical thinking.

Most professors of religious studies in the United States consider personal references to faith (or lack of faith) to be out of place in an academic context. At public universities, professors must honor the separation of church and state. At private institutions, too, teachers may not want to open the door to proselytizers and those who only accept one religious position as valid. Furthermore, practitioners of religious studies have been anxious to prove that we are as tough-minded and academically rigorous as our colleagues in other disciplines. The history of this field, which grew out of biblical and theological studies in Christian seminaries, has made many scholars cautious about revealing their personal convictions. Some teachers try to be as detached, scientific, impersonal, or value-neutral as possible. Or they may relentlessly analyze the problems in various patterns of belief without revealing their own position. A teacher will rightly stress the need to bracket or hold in suspension one's own beliefs in order to understand the worldview of an ancient Israelite, a medieval mystic, a Muslim theologian, or a Buddhist monk. Although the St. Olaf Religion Department was housed in the basement of Boe Chapel for sixty years, until 2012, we made it clear that this was not Sunday school. We don't use religious language in the same way as those worshiping in the sanctuary.

I'm not worried about converting anyone, a highly improbable event. The issue is rather that when students know my views, some of them might stop thinking, either because they share those views and think that having the professor's approval is a sufficient justification for them, or because they disagree with my views and withdraw because they don't want to be criticized. Some students might be swayed into parroting my ideas or beliefs in hopes of a higher grade. In all these cases, what is at stake in a professor's choices about self-disclosure is the consequences for students in terms of their academic engagement with the study of religion and their learning to become more thoughtful and articulate about their own deepest convictions.

Although I share these several concerns about the pedagogical dangers of a professor's personal remarks about religion, I also think that something important is lost when a teacher is not able to articulate an individual response to the religious issues at stake. Teachers can show students how intellectual and religious convictions are deeply connected to who we are as persons. Students don't care for self-indulgence, proselytizing, or bias in the classroom. They do welcome candid statements about what a professor thinks, including what he believes about some matter of faith, especially if he compares his position with other possibilities and invites discussion and contrasting views. This kind of teaching can stimulate students to think about how their own experiences shape and are shaped by their religious beliefs and practices.

Many of my most vivid memories of my teachers are when I got a rare glimpse of the personal concerns and experiences that motivated their teaching a particular subject matter or book. My graduate school advisor, Anthony C. Yu, labored for decades on a four-volume English translation of the Chinese classic *The Journey to the West*, a sixteenth-century narrative about a monk who brings Buddhist scriptures from India to China. One day Tony told me that, when he was a young boy, his grandfather had read him this narrative as their family sojourned in China during the Second World War. My teacher's bond with his grandfather and the circumstances of this harrowing journey helped me understand his devotion to that travel narrative and his desire to make it accessible to today's "West." Such self-disclosure was an infrequent event, partly because I didn't ask for it. In

Professing Religion and Traveling with Students

dozens of courses in college and graduate school, I almost never learned what my professors believed or how they worshiped. A rare exception was Langdon Gilkey, who recounted vivid stories, both orally and in his memoir *Shantung Compound* (which I frequently taught), about how he came to appreciate the theologies of Reinhold Niebuhr and Paul Tillich because of experiences in a Japanese internment camp in China during the Second World War. I saw how my teacher made sense of his life with these ideas; I realized why theology matters.

As I got older, I became more comfortable with revealing my views to students. It was easier for me than for many other professors to get autobiographical. The subject matter of my primary field, Religion and Literature, lends itself to comparisons with one's own experience more easily than some other disciplines. Being tenured made it far less risky for me to reveal my own beliefs and experiences. Yet the power dynamics of the classroom and students' vulnerability mean that a professor's self-disclosure about matters of religious faith is always a questionable enterprise.

My scruples and uncertainty about waxing personal as I profess religion may reflect preoccupations of my generation. I visited a class in a younger colleague's course for majors, What Is Religion? After I explained my interest in the question of how autobiographical concerns influence the scholarly study of religion, my colleague said, "Of course everything is autobiographical." Well, yes, I thought, but there are better and worse ways of being autobiographical. Perhaps the next generation isn't wrestling with my question, at least not in the same way. After several decades of postmodern theory, the ideals of objectivity and disinterestedness appear to many to be discredited Enlightenment myths that disguise power moves. There was a huge change in academic culture during the time of my career, so that scholars are now free to "own" their location and perspective. Indeed, if they are not forthright about their "positionality," they may be suspected of naïveté. But owning a location is not the same as disclosing autobiographical narrative; describing a position is not telling a story.

The tensions between disinterestedness and commitment, and between critical distance and transparency about one's own views, are controversial and crucial in pedagogy and scholarship. In class, how much should I say about what I think about a particular religious topic? In discussing apocalyptic themes in biblical times and the contemporary world, should I reveal my dismay at the dualistic, world-denying, and judgmental attitudes often fostered by this worldview? Perhaps, but I must also try to show students why eschatological ideas appeal to people in certain cultures and situations, especially to those suffering persecution. In a seminar on conversion, I showed Robert Duvall's film *The Apostle*, which depicts the ambiguity of a certain strand of Southern evangelistic piety focused on sudden conversion. This movie evokes memories and convictions about intense emotion in religious worship. How much should students and I explain the experiences that led each of us to our views? How autobiographical should we get when, in a course on conscience, we explore rationalization, self-deception, or paralyzing guilt?

There is no simple answer to the question of when autobiographical statements are appropriate and helpful. Two convictions shape my thinking about this issue: beliefs about the value of the subject matter I most love to teach and about my vocation as a professor.

Much of my teaching and scholarship focused on Religion and Literature, and I was especially interested in autobiography. The great autobiographers—such as Augustine, Dorothy Day, and Malcolm X—reveal how what they think about God and faith grows out of their suffering, searching, and discernment of how God worked in their lives. Martin Luther claimed, in his usual dramatic way: "One becomes a theologian not by understanding, reading, or speculating, but by living, no, rather by dying and being damned."[4] Luther's example shows that "living and dying" can be integrated with understanding and reading, so this is not an either/or choice. I interpreted autobiographers as theologians who model some of the ways personal narratives shape and are shaped by ideas about God. The attempt to understand one's own life is not a narcissistic, self-absorbed endeavor, but a search for history, culture, and God. Experience is personal, but not merely personal; understanding oneself discloses all that shapes the self. And autobiography is not only about the past; it is often an attempt to find meaning that will orient the writer's future living. In addition to studying theories, doctrines, and systems of ideas, college students need to hear individual voices speak about a search for faith.

When studying religious autobiography, we ought to practice self-scrutiny and narrative self-reconstruction, both to appreciate the skill and integrity of the great life writers and to follow their example of "faith seeking understanding." I saw my role as not only teaching about religion and fostering conceptual understanding of Christian thought and other religions, but also engendering a habit of thoughtful reflection about one's own religious beliefs and personal values. For this educational goal, it is hard to imagine a more rich, challenging, and inspiring subject matter than the genre of life writing.

---

4. Martin Luther, *Luther's Werke* (Weimar) 5.163.28, as quoted in Daniel L. Migliore, *Faith Seeking Understanding: An Introduction to Christian Theology*, 2nd ed. (Grand Rapids: Eerdmans, 2004), 7.

Professing Religion and Traveling with Students

Teaching autobiography, I taught autobiographically—occasionally. I described how a specific book engenders my own reflections or self-scrutiny. I wanted students to think about connections between their own lived experience and religious ideas. I hoped to encourage them to be creative readers of texts and of their own lives by giving them an example that they could react to as they chose. In the classroom I might suggest that Augustine's account in his *Confessions* of stealing pears may prompt us to remember our first awareness of wrongdoing. Or I might pose that Kathleen Norris's ideas about spiritual geography make us think about what spaces are sacred or formative for each of us—for me, it was the vast and intricate playground of the Carleton College campus. I tried to connect the texts with our own lives, starting with my own. These autobiographical or confessional moments were only a small part of what went on in class and usually passed in a minute or two, but they often seemed charged or significant. Students' eyes seemed to turn inwards, and I think they were reflecting on their lives, making comparisons, and probing dark recesses of memory. I hope the autobiographies my students read gave them touchstones that they will remember later when they try to understand their own experiences. We learn to read ourselves by reading how others have written their selves, their lives.

One instance stands out in memory. Augustine's *Confessions* was always the first text studied in my course called God and Faith in Autobiography. Students do not usually respond with enthusiasm to Augustine's ideas, and they find some of his beliefs troubling—for instance, his understanding of sin as the bondage of the will. I tried to show them the value of Augustine's views for illuminating our lives. Once I described a situation involving my relationship to my brother. When he was about twenty-five, he decided that he wanted to be called by his first name, David, rather than by the abbreviated middle name (Free) he had always used until then. For several years I resisted this change and continued to call him by his childhood name, which I loved. One day I was visiting a twelve-step group with him and was struck by the way in which Augustine's ideas about habits both illuminated and were confirmed by this group's dynamics. In this kind of support group, one admits that one is in the grip of a destructive addiction and unable to change compulsive behavior by relying on sheer willpower. Only by relying on God (or one's "higher power") is one freed from dependence on alcohol, drugs, sex, gambling, or whatever is controlling one's life.

Augustine asserts that "the rule of sin is the force of habit, by which the mind is swept along and held fast even against its will, yet deservedly, because it fell into the habit of its own accord."[5] He portrays a loss of freedom in his failed struggle for chastity, in his mother's drinking problem, and in his friend Alypius's addiction to watching gladiator fights. Although we form habits freely, they may eventually cause us to lose our freedom. Augustine speaks of this paradoxical situation as the bondage of the will by itself. I choose to take those first drinks, but eventually I may be unfree to stop drinking. I will have freely lost my own freedom as a bad habit binds the will. And yet in a mysterious way, just when one's own agency fails, a person may suddenly feel enabled to change by something beyond the will. It is as if an outside power has taken hold, and he is freed from the old habit and can respond to life in a fresh way. The will is enabled to assert itself and to form better habits. A psychologist has one way of explaining this change, but for the Christian, it is ultimately God's grace that frees me from compulsive habits and allows me to embrace new possibilities.

I suddenly realized, in that twelve-step meeting, that my clinging to my brother's old name was trapping him in a past from which he wanted to escape. And it was trapping me in a dead past that I had to move beyond not only for his sake but for my sake. Something moved and something melted inside me and I decided I must now call him by his new name. I had to break out of a habit that prevented new growth for me. For a while I still forgot and slipped into my old habit; it's not as if grace forever frees me from having to exert my will or from mistakes. But there was a turning point that day, and something more than my will was involved in breaking an old habit. I realized the truth of Augustine's insight into the bondage of the will. I understood how God's grace can release a person from enslavement to habit and restore freedom. After sharing this story with students, I asked them: Are there other situations you know of that might be illuminated by Augustine's view of sin as bondage of the will? That class now seems a highwater mark of my teaching. I wish I had taken more risks to make a vital connection between what we read and our own lives.

Stories about myself usually came at unpredictable moments while teaching, rather than being planned. I find off-putting the kind of ritualized confessions of "social location" that many academics rehearse as, with the best intentions, they acknowledge their particular point of view: "I say this as a straight, White, male, middle-class, Protestant, Midwestern, educated, blah blah blah." Perhaps it is my scruples about too much self-disclosure, or a struggle between more flamboyant and more reserved parts of myself, that explain why many of my personal remarks come out in a spontaneous

---

5. Saint Augustine, *Confessions*, 8.5, trans. with an introd. by R. S. Pine-Coffin, Penguin Classics (Harmondsworth, UK: Penguin, 1961), 165.

way that surprises me. There must be more going on psychologically than I fully understand in my fascination with both autobiographical texts and the issue of a professor's personal disclosures. I'm struggling with the role of ego in teaching, as ambiguous, inevitable, and worth watching carefully. I am drawn to greater openness, even intimacy, with my students, yet suspicious of teachers who make themselves the center of attention instead of the subject matter. An instructor's reference to his own views or life is not an end in itself, but should be a matter of pedagogy, a strategy to explain the significance of a text or topic or to show students how one's background influences one's interpretation.

My understanding of vocation shapes my thinking about expressions of personal faith in the classroom. I believed that my work as a professor included helping students to become more thoughtful and articulate about their own religious convictions. In our society there are many kinds of "calling" for each of us to do this, whatever our faith or ultimate concerns. I may want to explain how my beliefs or religious values influence how I cast my vote, assess a book or movie, or think that my work situation should be organized or reformed. A liberal arts education should prepare students for these demands and opportunities, which require one to be at once personal and engaged with a pluralistic audience holding other values. In this way, one component of my vocation as a teacher was nurturing my students' developing sense of vocation. That role includes helping them learn to respond to callings to explain their deepest beliefs in a thoughtful and articulate way.

Professing religion isn't simply a matter of declaring *what* I believe; it's also demonstrating *how* I believe. Professing is performative action, a way of engaging with ideas and other people. It may or may not involve moral integrity and rhetorical persuasiveness as one brings one's convictions to bear on some controversial aspect of life. The way in which I avow my beliefs may reveal a capacity for self-criticism or the lack of this virtue. When I profess my own views, I may demonstrate imagination and empathy for other perspectives or else lack of interest or disregard for alternatives. I espouse what I believe with some distinctive combination of epistemological humility and assertive advocacy. I may profess while acknowledging ambiguity and overarching mystery, and/or with a confident claim that "here I stand" as I avow some fundamental conviction. I may explain the reasons for what I believe while also acknowledging the limits of reason. I may demonstrate the value of encountering ancient traditions and difficult texts and allowing myself to be influenced by them even as I argue with them. In all these ways, how I profess my beliefs is often as significant as the substance or content of what I believe.

Family Conscience

Most people have core convictions and values without which their lives would not make sense and without which they would lack a coherent identity. Even if a person does not belong to an organized religious community, she needs to learn how to explain to others how she brings values to bear in personal decisions, and why these values are relevant to the world. I am grateful that I taught at a Lutheran college that encourages appropriate discussions of faith and belief in the classroom and in many other contexts. My vocation as a teacher was to help students and myself gain increased clarity and articulateness about religious beliefs and their expression in our lives. In that broad sense, I wanted each of us to be a better "professor" of religion.

* * *

ON THE MORNING OF September 11, 2001, nothing was scheduled for St. Olaf's Global Program. We were in Cairo: my wife and I as field supervisors, our two teenaged sons, and twenty-seven eager St. Olaf students. After several days in Geneva learning about the work of United Nations organizations, we had been in Cairo for several days. After breakfast in the Cosmopolitan Hotel on 9/11, we decided to take advantage of the morning free time to take field trips as small groups. Meg and I decided to visit Khan al-Khalili, an enormous covered market. With our younger son, Reed, who was then twelve, and two students, we took taxis to Khan al-Khalili.

We wandered through the market's narrow lanes, checking out stacks of tourist souvenirs: stuffed camels, little statues of a Pyramid or the Sphinx, reproductions of tomb paintings on papyrus mats, scarabs, mummies, and miscellaneous knickknacks. There were few Western tourists in this labyrinth, which was primarily patronized by Egyptians, who have been buying and selling there since the fourteenth century.

As we strolled along, we were stopped by a striking-looking man of about sixty who was observing the market scene:

"Hello, are you enjoying Cairo?"

I responded politely, "Yes, very much," and kept walking. He joined me and seemed concerned that we find good quality merchandise and get a good deal. He said he wasn't selling anything. I was immediately suspicious, for most of the people who approached me, not only in Egypt, but everywhere in the world, sooner or later tried to sell me something. I'm not particularly surprised or dismayed about this, but usually I don't want to hear a sales pitch. This guy was friendly, but with a gravity and thoughtful dignity that appealed to me. He attached himself to our little group and offered to take us to the spice market "where tourists never go" and we could take good photographs. "I don't want any money," he said solemnly, "I do this for friendship." It wasn't long before we found ourselves in the depths of Khan al-Khalili. There were mounds of fresh fruit and huge barrels and burlap bags full of freshly ground spices: cardamon, cinnamon, pepper, and saffron. The colors were gorgeous, the smells tantalizingly aromatic. We took photographs and wandered on. Soon we came to an empty shop that sold perfumed oils, and our guide suggested that we try some. Strangely, the shopkeeper was gone. The five of us squeezed in and our new Egyptian friend showed us the perfumes. He would take a drop from a little vial, put it on our arm or wrist, and explain its enticing aroma. We resisted half-heartedly at first, sensing that all this sniffing was going to lead to pressure to buy. He reassured us that he only wanted to educate us about this fascinating aspect of Egyptian culture.

After about fifteen minutes of oohing and aahing, the sales pitch came. We politely but firmly declined and said it was time for us to leave. But now he would not let us depart; he insisted that we buy some perfume. We stood up and left the shop. I regretted that I had gotten us into this awkward situation. The merchant began to yell, denouncing us for all to hear: "You Americans, you come here with your money and your cameras. You act like you own us. You take, take, take. You are disgusting and disgraceful. Why did you come here?" Utterly humiliated, wishing we could be invisible, we slunk away guiltily as his curses rang out. We did a little more exploring, but this disturbing episode left us feeling shaken. We went back to the hotel, had lunch, and went to afternoon classes at the American University in Cairo.

After class, several of us checked our email on the computers at the university library. Drew, one of my students, called me over to his screen. "Hey, look at this. A plane just crashed into the World Trade Tower in New York." Soon we learned the terrible news of what happened on that morning in the United States. The next three weeks in Cairo were very tense and stressful. No one knew how to estimate the danger of our situation or to decide what we should do.

That the incident with the perfumer happened on 9/11 gave it an eerie significance for me, as if it were a tiny metaphor for what was happening in many quarters as Americans asked: "Why do they hate us so much? And who are 'they' anyway?" Compared to what happened in the United States on 9/11 or to the ethical challenges posed by a tsunami, a war in Iraq or Ukraine, or any number of international catastrophes, a tourist encounter in a spice market is not of great significance. Yet the incident in Khan al-Khalili raised certain ethical issues related to intercultural travel that became central to my teaching and writing during the second half of my career. I was involved in several ways with St. Olaf College's International

Family Conscience

Studies programs, including by leading two excursions that each lasted five months: the Global Program (in Egypt, India, Hong Kong, and Korea) and the Term in Asia, which included extended stays in Shanghai, Chiang Mai, and Vietnam. I created an on-campus course, Travel and Ethics, to encourage students to think about past travel experiences and prepare for future ones. I wanted students to think about three ethical aspects of travel, especially to countries substantially less wealthy than our own: the tourist trap of antitourism, guilt trips, and disillusionment. The encounter in Khan al-Khalili makes these issues concrete.

The embarrassing incident in Khan al-Khalili came about partly because I was trying to get away from tourist traps. I wanted an authentic encounter with "the real Egypt," the part that I imagined as not corrupted by commercialization, Western influence, and crowds of gawking tourists in their ultralight, quick-drying clothes, lugging (in those days) their huge cameras and Nalgene water bottles. We all hate tourists, don't we? Unfortunately, this means we hate ourselves. For when we travel, we are usually tourists. Paul Fussell distinguished between exploration, travel, and tourism.[6] Travel is work, as is indicated by its etymological link to travail: it should hurt a little, make us suffer. Travel involves a variety of means of transportation, independent arrangements, and openness to the unpredictable and unplanned. Mass tourism has virtually eliminated independent travel. We book our accommodations before we leave, travel in escorted groups, and want to know in advance exactly what will happen to us. We are almost always tourists when we travel. And yet we long for a different kind of travel.

In a classic anthropological study of tourism, Dean MacCannell analyzed how the phenomenon of antitourism is part of tourism.[7] Antitourism means the ways that we assert our difference from all the other tourists. We hide our cameras, try to go native in dress and eating habits, and are perpetually looking for alternatives to the usual sights. The antitouristic tourist feels an anxious malaise about whether he might really be a tourist after all, rather than an adventurous traveler. He deludes himself in a futile quest for "authentic" experience of another culture if he thinks that "authentic" means not involving tourism. Antitourism is itself a kind of tourist trap. Compulsive efforts to deny that one is a tourist produce an automatic and unthinking response to many situations. If I try to accumulate authentic cultural experiences as if they were my achievement or possession, I may

---

6. Paul Fussell, *Abroad: British Literary Traveling between the Wars* (New York: Oxford University Press, 1980).

7. Dean MacCannell, *The Tourist: A New Theory of the Leisure Class* (Berkeley: University of California Press, 1999).

use the people of other cultures in a subtle form of exploitation. Antitourism leads to some strange encounters with people of other cultures, such as the perfume salesman in Khan al-Khalili. In my quest for authentic, untouristy experience I fell into a trap that was at least partly of my own making.

At the same time, the phenomenon of antitourism reveals something significant about our orientation to travel. We want our journeys to mean more than what tourism usually means. There is often a latent religious dimension in our motivations for travel. Tourists simply want to escape temporarily from their present circumstances, and to consume a packaged entertainment product. When we yearn for something more than this, we wish, like a pilgrim, to be transformed. We want to come back as different persons, and for our travel to influence the rest of our lives. We hunger for more meaning than can be provided by the tourist industry, even as it now sells us "spiritual tours" of sacred places and "authentic" cultural experiences (where no other tourists are visible). Antitourism reveals a hunger for something more than canned experience, shopping for trinkets, and finding a Starbucks café latte abroad. The antitourist resembles a pilgrim, who wants travel to mean more than that and to play a role in spiritual life. I tried to get my students to see themselves as both tourists and that kind of antitourist.

A second topic raised by my Cairo misadventure is guilt trips. Simply by traveling across an ocean, one has disposed of more wealth than most people in the world will earn in a year, and perhaps in a lifetime. An American traveler may feel obscurely guilty for having spent what is by the standards of much of the globe a vast fortune. Being a tourist in many parts of the world means freedom, extravagance, pleasure, fun—and guilt. One inevitably faces situations such as my encounter with the perfume salesman in the market, when someone's need, greed, or desire places a demand on you the traveler. How should one respond to beggars, such as an emaciated child in India who holds out her hand and says, "Please, Uncle, for bread"? Beyond her, down the street, are a dozen other children waiting hopefully: some of these are blind, others are unable to walk, and still others live with a painful skin disease. Our hosts in India told us not to give to beggars. They said that disfigured children are especially prized, and sometimes deliberately injured, because these visible marks pull at the heartstrings and open the wallets of Western tourists. I didn't give much to beggars in India, but I felt guilty. And ashamed: a feeling of wrongness not because of what I had done or not done, but because of who I am, a person with so much wealth in a world with so much suffering.

In January 1984, my class studying liberation theology in Mexico City took a field trip. In our airconditioned bus, we rolled slowly around the outskirts of one of Mexico City's enormous garbage dumps, which sprawl over many acres. Hundreds of scavengers make a living there picking through garbage bags. Children claw through mounds of every kind of trash, looking for cans to recycle or any scrap of edible food. Some of the bags are an orange color. Our guide tells us that these bags are hospital refuse containing body parts and fluids, used razors and hypodermic needles, and excrement. All this deadly material is sifted through by desperate people who scavenge a living in this way. The students and I ride back to our comfortable quarters in stunned silence. We sit in a circle on the lawn and talk about our feelings. Some students cry and ask, "What can I do about this? How can we go on living the way we do?" We feel guilty and ashamed. We want to do penance, live differently, somehow help these people. We want to end world poverty, start a revolution, give up our possessions. But we go back to our relatively luxurious North American existence and I, at least, won't change my life in any way. The memory of this experience stays with me like a scar.

Going to the Mexico City dump was different from a chance contact with a beggar and from my disturbing encounter in Khan al-Khalili. For the "garbage tour," if I may call it that, was a guilt trip. It was a form of organized educational travel that was intended to display a society's problems made vivid in human suffering. A great deal of tourism today is directed to sites of historical injustice and suffering, at places like the Holocaust Museum in Washington, DC; former Nazi concentration camps; and the Cambodian memorial to victims of the Khmer Rouge. Could I go to Israel and ignore the Palestinian people? Can I spend time in India and not learn about the struggles of the Dalit people against caste prejudice? Can I travel through the United States without confronting our history of racism, and of massacres of Native Americans, and the deadly violence in our cities? Most tourists try to avoid the problems. In contrast, a central part of most St. Olaf programs is study and field trips to learn about the disturbing challenges faced by developing nations, or to encounter firsthand our country's problems.

A tourist may wonder whether his activities are helping or harming the culture he visits. From one perspective tourism is a matter of the mobile rich employing the indigenous poor to cater to tourists' self-indulgence and decadence. Tourism injects the wasteful habits of consumer culture into a society marked by desperate human needs. And yet many economies of the world are almost totally dependent on tourism, and without it many people would perish. There is no simple answer to the question of how tourism and travel affect a culture. As a teacher, I wanted students to wrestle with the moral ambiguity of tourism and of our educational program. I hoped they would develop an uneasy conscience and critical self-consciousness about their travels.

Organized "guilt trips," educational programs that we expect will make students aware of moral problems in the world today, often have the effect of making us feel guilty about our privileges and our lackadaisical attempts to respond to human suffering. Such an encounter with human suffering is organized exactly like commercial tourism and can become simply a spectacle, a momentarily bracing or shocking vision from which we return unchanged. An educational program should aspire to something more than tourism offers. Off-campus programs should deepen students' moral sensibility, elicit their compassion, arouse their sense of injustice, sharpen their critical understanding, and motivate their idealistic attempts to do something practical about suffering. A Christian may also discern that God can work in the midst of terrible human suffering.

An educational journey is a "guilt trip" in one sense, for it is a journey that we hope will make us aware of suffering and raise questions about how our society plays a role in creating and perpetuating conditions of oppression. But off-campus travel programs should not be guilt trips that leave us stuck in self-flagellating remorse. We must go beyond guilt to responsibility. We should convert our sense of vague uneasiness and defensiveness into clarity about what we can and should do, individually and as a society, about massive problems that we will not solve or eliminate any time soon.

A third issue that the Cairo market incident epitomizes is disillusionment. It turned out that my Egyptian acquaintance was primarily interested in selling me perfume. Although I half—or three-quarters—expected a sales pitch, it was still a painful moment. Many of the students on the Global Program had similar experiences, so that after a while they became very skeptical, even cynical, about the friendly gestures of those we encountered. Every time you thought you were making a one-on-one connection with another person, there was this third thing: the money. Some of the students lamented the loss of openness and trust that they had felt at the outset of the program. They felt disillusioned.

When we travel to places we have dreamed of, we find ourselves standing in lines to go through security fin an airport that looks like most other airports, eating mediocre food, feeling irritated by our companions or frustrated that we can't seem to connect with the people in a foreign culture even when we are all being polite. My experience on the Global Program was different from study programs involving a more extended stay in one place, especially those involving intensive language training. But even in an immersion program, the experience of disillusionment is frequently part of the process of learning about another culture.

Family Conscience

Do our travel fantasies have anything to do with where we are going? We may be looking for a beach paradise, a utopian society, a lost home and family roots, or the mythic origins of a religious tradition. Whatever we hope to find, whatever the sources of our obscure preconceptions of where we are going, our disillusionment when we don't find it offers an opportunity, if we can grasp it. Disillusionment can be not just a depressing loss, but a liberating loss of illusions. While often painful, it is also an opening into the possibility of a more accurate perception of reality. Perhaps in a Cairo market I might move beyond disillusionment to learn something about a different culture's approach to buying and selling and to the relationship of host and guest. I might come to understand that paying a few dollars for unwanted perfume is a small price for an interesting experience. The end of illusions can make room for a more meaningful life and a deeper joy than one could ever have had from simply having one's fantasies fulfilled, one's illusions unchallenged, or one's journey completed precisely as planned.

I devoted a lot of time and energy to reflecting with students about the ethical dimensions of travel: how it affects both our own character and the places we visit. I hoped that students would develop a conscience about how they travel. I wanted to influence their future journeys and interactions with other cultures. When they said they were transformed by their experiences abroad, I pressed them to explain. They usually struggled to say more than "it was awesome." I can't do much better myself, but I know I should. I tried to get myself and my students to think seriously about what travel taught us, our motivations for travel, and the consequences of our enormous privilege to journey freely through the world.

Chapter 11

A Father's Questions

The family was camping near Lake Superior. We were on a steep hillside with uncertain footing and trees interspersed with areas cleared for campsites. Graham, who was twelve, started tossing around a football with a friend. I told him a few times to be more careful or he would hurt himself. Finally, he responded sarcastically, "Okay, Mr. Safety. I won't kill myself." The name stuck and for several years this was his standard response to my fussy anxiety about whatever mortal danger I saw looming. I was terrified of losing my children, so desperate to protect them from pain that I didn't want them to take risks and learn the hard way.

Now I argue with myself, with my conscience, about how I did. What is the right kind of supervision, caution, and protectiveness, and what is just anxiety? I reproach myself for failing to foresee accidents that hurt my children and also for being too worried and fussy about possible dangers. I shudder to remember incidents when my child was injured or narrowly avoided a horrible accident. In a Rome hotel when he was sixteen months old, Graham nearly toddled into an open elevator shaft. At the age of two, Reed was stung repeatedly by bees as we walked through the woods. As he cried and trembled in terror, I reproached myself bitterly. It was random bad luck, but I lambasted myself: you stupid, blind, idiot! The world appeared full of dangers—lightning, swiftly moving water, biting creatures, or a car swerving into my little bike rider. I wanted to teach my children to be wary but not afraid. It was a challenge to set a good example.

I kayaked with my niece, Alex, near the shore of a warm Wisconsin lake on a calm, peaceful day. I was sure I could teach this strong and fearless girl to do a wet exit: to tip the kayak upside down, and, while under water, tear off the spray skirt that covered the cockpit, eject herself, and swim to the surface. We practiced ripping off the spray skirt on land several times, and then, in the water, tipping over and sliding out of the kayak without the spray skirt in place. I should have stood in shallow water next to Alex and had her practice in that position, where I could easily support her if needed. Instead, I paddled in my own boat into deeper water alongside of her. Alex turned upside down but did not emerge. Bubbles came to the surface. Thrashing around underwater, she moved the kayak out of my reach. I tried frantically to get to her. At last, Alex came up gasping for air, having forced her way out of the cockpit by sheer muscle strength. She could have drowned, and it would have been my fault. I can't just sit back and watch calmly as children sink or swim.

In September 2006, Reed was planning to graduate early from high school and go to Patagonia for three months with an outdoor education program. He would walk on glaciers, kayak down a river into the ocean, and practice survival skills and wilderness first aid. After this, he said, he might go to Alaska to fight forest fires. I admired his adventurous spirit but expressed anxiety about the Alaska plan. Reed said, "Dad, you have to accept that when I'm eighteen next week, I'm an adult. You have to let go."

"Not until you are forty," I joked. He has grown up just fine, I thought, but I can't outgrow habits from an earlier period of fatherhood.

Did I strangle my children as I tried to protect them from pain and myself from loss? The old German legend of the Erlking, which Goethe used in a poem, describes a father trying to gallop with his child away from a malevolent spirit. As the boy thinks he sees and hears the Erlking, the father tries to reassure him, then flees. It may be that the child is only imagining things; the father says that around them are only rustling leaves and fog. Or perhaps the father cannot discern a supernatural being who appears to dying people. In the end, the boy lies dead in his father's arms. Did the Erlking steal the young life, or did the father strangle his child in a desperate attempt to protect him? As a father, I sometimes felt helpless and terrified of death and of my own grief. I clutched my sons closely until they had to pull away from me or be choked. In this generational dance and struggle, a parent must find an embrace that does not strangle the child, and the child must find space to breathe and move without forsaking the parent's protective arms, which the child may still need from time to time. May my sons' eyes be vigilant as they run out into the world, rather than looking back at me.

* * *

I WROTE THE FOLLOWING journal entry in 1988, when Graham was four.

A Father's Questions

I talked with Graham as I was putting him to sleep last night. I sang "Swing Low Sweet Chariot." He asked what it meant when I sang "tell all of my friends I'm coming after you," which led us to heaven, death, God, Jesus, church. What did I believe, he asked, and what things said in church *didn't* I believe? I said that God is the Creator and will always love us. Somehow we will be together even after one of us dies. Graham's spirit is what I will love even if his body dies. Graham said he would always love me, no matter what. Tears came to my eyes. I said the most important thing about Jesus is that he said we should love each other.

"I think so too, Dad."

I said, "One thing I don't believe is when they say he could walk on water." Graham got a skeptical look on his face.

I said God is everything—the sky, the air—and more. In church we are saying thanks to God for everything. Graham: "Like saying thank you, sky, for the sky." He was fascinated by the claim of his friend Willie that there was no Jesus, that it's a made-up story. I said that this is one of the interesting things about religion: people don't agree but have different ideas and nobody knows for sure. "Whatever you decide to believe, Graham, I think it will be right for you, and you will have thought about it a lot."

In spite of my fumbling attempts to put my beliefs into words, I feel like on some level I communicated them to him. There was a wonderful openness and trust and mutual respect between us as we each tried to understand the great mysteries. We shared our doubts and uncertainties as well as what we believed.

* * *

I WAS SO HAPPY to be with my son as he launched himself through the water and realized that his own strokes had propelled him. Standing in the shallow water, I smiled as my eyes misted with tears. I rejoiced for my boy's achievement and felt a wave of sadness. In July 1989, I described seeing Graham's first strokes: "I felt proud of his courage and elated that we will soon be able to play in a new way. Sadness, though, for my own childhood, and not learning to swim until I was ten. I missed out on a lot of fun." My responses to my children are entangled with my own memories, and my emotions carry the weight of many years.

Some parents feel strongly about music lessons, Sunday school, or serving other people's needs. On some scale of ultimate values, these are

Family Conscience

probably more worthwhile activities than sports. Yet a lot of Americans seem to think gymnastics competition or a little league baseball team will influence positively their child's character. For me it was soccer. For nine summers I coached my sons' soccer teams, starting the summer before Graham turned five. A pack of little boys chased the ball around the field like a swarm of bees, while I yelled at them: "Spread out! Pass the ball! Defenders, stay back!" I wanted them to learn skills and they just wanted to have fun. Graham and Reed played on community soccer teams from April to July and on school teams in the autumn.

We parents and coaches rooted for them from the sidelines. Some adults were so intent on winning that they drained the fun out of the game. They were living vicariously through their kids, yearning for the athletic glory that they had or hadn't achieved in their own youth. I heard about hockey dads getting in fights at their sons' games and witnessed a soccer mom ejected when she denounced the referee.

I put a lot of energy into sports and recreation: tennis, racquetball, swimming, hiking, kayaking, cross-country skiing, and biking. I hoped that Graham and Reed would come to enjoy the pleasure of movement, the fun of coordinated teamwork and competition in sports, and the satisfaction of traversing a natural landscape by your own effort. I wanted them to relish the sweet painful joy of exerting muscles, heart, and lungs and a hard-earned sweat.

I was more insistent about these values than church. Going to Sunday school was a fuzzy area; the boys went sometimes, but not regularly. Meg and I insisted that they go to confirmation class, and they both joined the church, though they rarely attended after that. I could have been more actively involved in their religious education and could have shared my own beliefs more freely rather than primarily in response to questions.

We wanted the boys to participate in other activities, too, such as music. Graham sang in a youth choir for a year. When he was in middle school, a large pile of drums gathered dust in his room. Reed played violin and saxophone. After a lot of nagging them to practice, we gave up. "Desire has to come from within" was my philosophy when I tired of being the music police. Meg was much more effective in enticing, cajoling, or badgering the boys to practice.

You want them to want to do it, but most children do not want to practice regularly. Sometimes kids will work for extrinsic rewards, such as a parent's praise, until they experience the intrinsic values and pleasure involved in mastering a skill. One friend paid her children to practice until they were skilled enough to freely choose to do so. But too much parental pressure backfires when a child wants to escape an endeavor loaded with the psychological baggage of expectations from Mom and Dad.

I don't remember that Ian or Deane ever came to watch me wrestle. Deane said that she came once, but "it was a white-knuckle experience, no further repeated." When I think of all the hours I spent as a soccer coach and sideline fan, I don't understand why they weren't more interested. But maybe their detachment freed me to do that sweaty, bruising sport entirely for my own reasons. The desire came from within.

One passion that eventually came from within for my sons was love of outdoor adventures, camping, and the wilderness. When they were young, they were game although not enthusiastic about family excursions to the woods, lakes, or Utah Desert. As teenagers and adults, they became avid outdoorsmen, especially Reed. He participated in a demanding three-month program in Patagonia run by the National Outdoor Leadership School; paddled a canoe with two friends from Minnesota's Lake Itasca to the Gulf of Mexico; discovered a new species of small mammal while on a Fulbright grant in Ecuador; and now works for a state government's Department of Fish and Wildlife. I'm proud of him and treasure our experiences together kayaking, canoeing, hiking, and biking. I admire his savvy and skills, including wilderness cooking, navigation, risk assessment, and calm, confident reliability. I wish I could give some credit to his parents for how he turned out (including to his mother, who photographed the natural world as an artist). Maybe we provided some early experiences that helped him recognize what made him feel alive and joyful. In the context of a family, a person's character emerges neither as a pure "coming from within" nor as the result of external stamping, but rather through a complex interaction between inner traits and outer circumstances, choice and acceptance, parental influence and striving for one's own way of being in the world.

* * *

AS A PARENT I duplicated certain patterns of my parents and did other things differently. Whereas Ian spent relatively little time with his children, I split childcare duties with my spouse. Ian modeled many of the most important aspects of parenting: patience, gentleness, encouragement, expressing affection, and steady, unwavering love. He was not very involved in the daily tasks of child-raising and household chores. Like many men in my generation, I had to find a different way than my father did to balance the demands of work and family.

Gender roles have changed, but certain questions persist. In my men's group, we joke about being "Manly Men." We are critical of traditional macho culture and are trying to become more articulate about what it means for each of us to be a good man. The virtues we admire are not specifically male, but human: patience, courage, compassion, and gentle strength. Yet we wonder, What does it mean to be not only a good person, but a good man? We are serious about this question yet, given our alienation from toxic hypermasculine drivenness, doubtful about any answer. We joke about the topic and our pretended postures of masculine toughness.

The experience of having my own children makes me both more critical and more forgiving of my parents. Raising two sons helped me realize how Ian and Deane made mistakes or could have done better. On the other hand, my own limits and weaknesses show me how difficult it is to be a good parent and help me understand the challenges Ian and Deane faced in bringing up four children. Parents have a lot going on in their lives, and sometimes children suffer because they are not a parent's only responsibility. Evaluating my parents in comparison with myself makes for a complex kind of judgment of both. It looks a lot like not judging, because it is often cautious, qualified, and tentative.[1]

Now Graham is the father of two children. I watch and admire how he sometimes parents differently than I did. In 2020, sitting by a campfire overlooking the Mississippi River after his son went to sleep, I described challenges as I tried to influence the developing conscience of each of my children. Graham's reaction was to say that more important than shaping one's child is to mirror and affirm what he is: it's less like making a sculpture than like cultivating a flower's growth. Each of Graham's children, like him, will imitate, reject, or adapt their father's ways as they find their own way to bloom.

* * *

I HOPED MY GUYS would be autonomous and independent but learn from the wisdom of the ages—that is, me. Often it seemed that a son set his will on something simply because it was the opposite of what Meg and I wanted. Food fights with Reed went on for many years. He adamantly refused to eat most of what we cooked and lived almost entirely on pasta. Also, pizza: cheese pizza, with nothing else on it except a little sauce, but not too much sauce, and no chunks of tomatoes in the sauce. Every meal turned into a battle. When he was six or eight, he would stalk into the kitchen while we were cooking and ask what was for supper. "I don't want that stuff," he would announce, and turn to examine the contents of the refrigerator and

---

1. See John D. Barbour, "Judging and Not Judging Parents," in Paul John Eakin, ed., *The Ethics of Life Writing* (Ithaca: Cornell University Press, 2004), 73–98.

cupboard. After a minute of gloomy inspection, his inevitable conclusion was: "There's nothing to eat." Calmly, rationally, but struggling for self-control, I would tell him that either he could eat what the rest of us were having or I would make him a peanut butter sandwich or something quick and easy. Off he would stomp, disgusted by these revolting choices. I congratulated myself on my matter-of-fact, gentle but firm parenting. Perhaps, I mused, I should write a sunny self-help book for frustrated parents. Half an hour later, as we sat down for dinner, Reed would come into the kitchen like a gunslinger into a saloon, looking for trouble.

"I don't want this crud."

"Okay, fine, I'll cook something for you later. Right now, we are sitting down to eat."

"But I want something right now."

At this point Meg usually volunteered to make something for him. But my blood pressure was rising; some red button in me had been pushed. I was angry with Reed for this manipulative behavior and mad at myself for getting hooked by it. He would be cheerful after supper, while I stayed grumpy for half the evening.

Situations like eating vegetables, reading one more story before bedtime, or watching another TV show sometimes turned into matters of high moral principle for me as a parent: "Here I stand, I can do no other. I only regret that I have but one life to give for my family, for conscience, for the supreme duty to eat one's peas and carrots." An incident of minor importance was a golden opportunity for instruction about courtesy, rules, conflict, and consequences. I reasoned as follows: If I give in on this issue, Reed will surely think he can get away with anything and end up as a person with no Character. He is begging for limits and structure in his life and it's my responsibility to provide that. I must fill his Character with green, leafy vegetables.

Reed just wanted to eat something he liked. Feeling controlled, he pushed back, asserting his independence. He was finding a different way to be himself than his older brother, who devoured everything. When we tried to discipline Reed with time-outs in another room (about the only punishment, or "consequence" as Meg preferred to call it, that we could think of), he simply refused to cooperate. He would howl and run back to the kitchen, demanding attention and making it impossible to eat supper. His vulnerable little body, with stick-thin arms and legs, expressed an iron will. This frustrating and heartbreaking situation happened again and again. A different father would have found a way out through the threat or practice of corporal punishment or by simply letting his child eat whatever he wanted. But I was caught in an impasse, and with me the whole family.

Family Conscience

By the time of high school, Reed liked Thai food, curry, and hot sauce. Why did I need to have all those battles about green vegetables? What noble virtues were symbolically present in peas and broccoli? What were those conflicts really about?

What I thought of as Reed's fussiness expressed a deep-rooted aspect of his character. He has an exacting, discriminating temperament rooted in his aesthetic sensibility. He wants things to be just right, while my usual response to food or anything else that is a matter of taste is, It's good enough for me. Some people feel as strongly about aesthetic matters as I do about issues of conscience. Often control and agency are at stake, not high moral principles. In these battles of will, when should I have relented and when insisted? When did I make some issue a matter of conscience when it was mostly something else?

John, Reed, and Graham. Photo by Meg Ojala.

A difficult decision was where Graham would go to fifth grade. He had gone to an independent school from kindergarten through fourth grade. Prairie Creek School seemed ideal to my spouse and me; it contrasted starkly with what we had experienced in public schools during the 1950s and 60s. The school enrolled only about a hundred students and put a strong emphasis on community. The teachers believed in a "social curriculum" of cooperation and group problem-solving; parents were constantly involved in activities. Students worked at their own pace on interdisciplinary projects and did lots of art and music. The school was located in a beautiful natural setting for environmental education and recreation. It practiced every value that Meg and I believed in, and for several years Graham was happy there. At the end of fourth grade, he decided that he wanted to go to public school. We were horrified and tried to talk him out of this desire: "Why would you want to go to a school that is like a factory, with so many people and rules? You have to get a pass just to go to the bathroom."

But Graham's mind was made up, and he dug in his heels. For two months we agonized about this decision. The principal at Prairie Creek thought that we were too deferential to the whims of a ten-year-old; parents should make this decision, not a child.

In a conversation taped in December 2005, when Graham was twenty-one, I asked him how he looked back on this choice. We were talking about his political radicalism, which he said makes him want to "rage against the machine" and rebel against "the system."

"Graham, you rebelled against one system, Prairie Creek, by going to a more strict and regimented system in the public school. How do you explain that?"

"Prairie Creek was all I had known. I didn't like it anymore. My friend was leaving. More than anything being wrong with Prairie Creek, I wanted something new. I knew that in sixth grade I would have to make the adjustment to public school."

"We really wanted you to stay at Prairie Creek but finally decided to let you do what you were absolutely determined to do. We agonized about that choice more than anything in your childhood. It was a huge test of wills. We let you have your way. We finally decided that you would be very unhappy if we forced you to do something you didn't want to do."

"I remember us writing out the pros and cons and talking about it a lot."

"Some people, including your teachers, would think wow, what weak parents we are, who won't tell their kid what he has to do."

"They were looking after their own interests."

"No," I argued, "they genuinely and honestly believed in the school's mission. And so did we. It was a crucial moment in parenting. It was your first major decision with long-term consequences that went against your parents' wishes."

"I was ready for something else. I knew what would happen at Prairie Creek, and all the hundred people who were there. Public school was a new thing I had to take on. For me it was not traumatic. I thought: This is what I want to do; now I need to convince Mom and Dad."

He did, but I was very unsure if we were doing the right thing. Graham's persuasive skills are considerable, and now he puts them to good use as an immigration attorney.

* * *

WHILE I WAS ENJOYING a lot of time spent with my children, I also craved time alone. In 1995 I started to write a book about solitude as a spiritual experience and ethical issue. It absorbed a huge investment of time and energy at a time when the boys needed my attention and many other demands pressed on me, including chairing the Religion Department. For almost a decade, the solitude book was partly a psychological escape from the pressures of teaching and family life, a wish-fulfilling fantasy about what I thought I needed. I was also questioning and criticizing this impulse. I was dimly aware that my desire to be alone is sometimes running away from other people, and that preoccupation with my own thoughts and states of mind cuts me off. Solitude isn't simply good or bad but needs to be evaluated. Just as I began that scholarly project, when I was forty-three, I wrote a short autobiographical piece that reveals connections between my interest in solitude and my conscience as husband and father.

Solitude and Loneliness

I come out of my office perspiring, my temples constricted, my throat sore from three hours of lecturing. It hurts to talk. As usual I lectured too much, didn't make the students carry the weight of discussion. It is a warm October afternoon. There is no department meeting today, so I can squeeze in a bike ride, one of the last before strong winds, cold, and late-afternoon meetings make this impossible. After a day with students, I long to be outdoors, to move my body, to think my thoughts without having to articulate them or make them coherent to other people.

I race home, change clothes, throw my bike on the back of the car, and flee. It's Meg's day to pick up the boys at the bus stop, and she will be home with them any minute. I would like to see them, but it is hard to just say hi without going into the day, what's happened, and what's for dinner. If I want to return in time to eat supper with them, there is barely enough time to fit in this ride. I leave a note and escape.

A Father's Questions

I drive 15 miles to a bike trail built on an abandoned railroad bed running between Faribault and Mankato. The trail goes past a lake, skirts two depressing villages, and finally veers away from the highway into the "singing hills" of Sakatah State Park, with its prairie, marshlands, and old forest growth overlooking the lake. The sunlight is warm on my skin, but it's too late in the year and the afternoon to get a burn. There won't be many more days like this. I have the trail all to myself for two hours. I pass a teenager and an elderly man going in the other direction. Soon I am sweating, feeling pain and pleasure as tense nerves and muscles relax into the rhythm of the ride.

The bliss of solitude is a state of mind and being that can be realized in a wide variety of activities. What continuity is there in the feelings evoked by music heard in reverie, musings as I putter around doing yardwork, and the serenity and security of the silent house when I look up from working at my desk? In all these experiences solitude is an essential ingredient, but it imparts to each of them a distinct flavor.

After an hour, I stop to stretch, drink some water, and turn around. Now the sun is behind me and I can see much better, my shadow falling far ahead. I go in and out of patches of light and shade. I stop and wander into a little patch of prairie that a conservation group is restoring. A farm lies half a mile away and cars can be heard from the highway beyond the trees, but no human figure can be seen. How seldom do I see a landscape empty of people! I return to my bike.

Halfway back I am seized with the longing to share this day with Meg. But then it would not be this day. The afternoon and the landscape are perfect, and solitude is essential to the experience. In another's company this autumn ride would not have its tang, its tone, its quality. Nonetheless, I want to express my happiness, exclaim at a turtle crossing the path and at a stand of red sumacs, exult in this final day of Indian summer. The only thing that could make this solitary day better would be to enjoy it in Meg's company. My mood shifts as it encompasses this feeling of incompleteness, loneliness, yearning towards her. I am an amateur at solitude, a lover of aloneness in small doses. Someone who had truly cultivated its depths—a Thomas Merton, Thoreau, or Rilke—would not want to spoil or contaminate it with another's presence. I want that which would radically change

Family Conscience

the quality of this experience: companionship as the culmination or fulfillment of time apart from others. Contradictory as this may be, I want it all, and my emotional state becomes less exuberant, more bittersweet, even melancholy. I wouldn't have it otherwise; this mood is part of my character. I have missed it for some time, and now, alone, I return to myself. Solitude and loneliness constantly intertwine in my life as I experience my time alone as pleasurable and as painful, as sweetness to be savored or a burden I would escape.

I am glad to see my family when I get home. Meg is cooking while Graham and Reed play outside. How empty my life would be without them. I belong here. But at supper I get angry when my six-year-old won't eat his broccoli, falling into a maddening pattern we seem unable to avoid. I have and lose the feeling of connectedness with my sons a dozen times this evening, one minute worrying about a spill and then tuning in too late as I realize that Graham has been telling me about a chemistry experiment at school. I missed it, fake a response. I try to pay more attention as he tells me about the Twins game last night. Then he turns to baseball cards; he has six of Kirby Puckett, and one is worth fifty cents. But I don't care about baseball cards or even baseball. I mumble "That's great, Graham" and start to clean up the kitchen, do the dishes.

Later in the evening there is a similar rhythm of engagement and disengagement as I help Reed take a bath. I notice how much better he is at washing himself; he even uses soap without being told. I turn back to my newspaper. "Dad... Dad... Dad!" I look up and Reed shows me a plastic cup. "Do you think this water is hot or cold?"

"I don't know. Lukewarm?"

"No, it's really hot." The faucet is dripping, and he has patiently filled the cup. "Okay, Reed. How about if you finish up so we have time to read a book?" I go back to the paper. A minute later, watching him dry himself with a towel, I remember how I used to cradle him in my lap while I dried him, and he would squiggle down as if into a nest. This precious little creature entrusted to my care.

When the kids go to sleep, Meg and I catch up and talk about the day. Every time we started a conversation earlier, the kids interrupted within one minute. She is concerned about some aspect of the boys' day that I didn't notice. I feel a stab of remorse, reproaching myself for not having paid attention. She goes up to sleep while I stay

A Father's Questions

downstairs and read. Alone, the house quiet, I feel sad. I remember moments when Graham or Reed told me something and I was mentally absent. A sense of missed opportunities, of failure to connect, fills me, and I feel lonely. I wish I could affirm them more and be present in spirit as well as body. I do more than most dads, I argue with myself: I spend lots of time with my kids. But it is not quality time, for I am not all there for them. Maybe I can make it up to them. Tomorrow I pick them up at the bus. We can play soccer together. With this plan for solace, I listen to the stillness of the house. The quality of my aloneness now is mixed with regret at missed opportunities, determination to do better with my children tomorrow, the sense of my apartness from those I love, and awareness of their constant sustaining presence. This bittersweet moment of aloneness, like my earlier loneliness and the blessed solitude of the bike ride, is defined by my relationships with other people.

My legs are pleasantly tired. The air streaming in the cracked window is cold. The wind picks up outside. Time to put on the storm windows. I am alone in my study as my kids and wife sleep peacefully upstairs.

Musing now on this early scrap of memoir, I am struck by how much my desire for solitude reflected my need to escape from family responsibilities and teaching duties. Solitude was a guilty pleasure. When I finally got it, biking or sitting alone in the living room, I was keenly aware of missed opportunities, failed connections with others, or yearning to be with my family. I want to be fully present to them and then fully engaged in whatever fills my solitude. Yet when I'm alone, I think about people and the past, including the ways I've checked out even when I was physically present with my family. My constant concern to justify solitude, my self-criticism for missing opportunities to connect, and my thinking about other people while I am alone may mean that I never fully experience solitude. I am usually too scrupulous or neurotic to know the serenity and bliss of the deepest aloneness, when all this fretting drops away.

Soon after I wrote this story, I gave a sermon about solitude at St. Olaf College. It was basically an in-praise-of-solitude sermon, starting with the prophet Elijah, who heard God in the sound of "sheer silence." I described some of the ways in which solitude can be a spiritual experience. After the sermon a woman came forward to thank me. She said very thoughtfully, "There's a lot of truth in what you say, John. But, you know, the conditions have to be right." She was a woman of about sixty who had just gone through a painful divorce. Her children having grown up and left home, she faced some lonely times. Now I, too, see the dark side of solitude, such as how it can spiral into depression or misanthropy. The conditions for solitude must be right: being alone is only welcome and enjoyable when I can return from it to those I love. Webs of relationship surround my spaces of solitude, and my periods of aloneness are colored by how I evaluate my life with others. How I experience solitude is inextricably linked to my conscience and my feelings about my family.

* * *

IN THE PARABLE OF the prodigal son (Luke 15:11–32), the father waits a long time for his younger son to return home. It was while my sons were living at home during their teenaged years that I felt most distant from them. I told myself to wait and be patient until they return. I tried not to force myself on them, but giving them space turned into feeling disconnected. I felt shut out of their lives and missed being close to them in the old ways.

When Graham and Reed were little, my mother told me that she stood across the street from their day care center to watch them play, unobserved. I wish she had asked me more often to bring her grandchildren to her house to play, or that I had invited her more regularly to our house. Partly because of her experience with Ian's mother, Deane didn't impose on my family and respected our privacy. I appreciated that and tried to do the same thing with my children when they were teenagers. I usually waited for them to take the initiative to talk to me or offer to do something together. When I invited them to go kayaking or biking or to play racquetball, they almost always had other plans with friends. I admired their growing independence and their deepening friendships and activities outside the family. But I was yearning for them, even as I stifled spontaneous expressions of this desire.

In Jesus's parable, the younger son returns at last. "While he was still far off, his father saw him and was filled with compassion; he ran and put his arms around him and kissed him" (Luke 15:20). That father celebrates and rejoices. He didn't just wait; he had to be ready and responsive. I, too, need to respect my sons' journeys, both outward and internal, and sometimes put my own wish for intimacy on the back burner for a while. I respond joyfully when they turn back to me.

* * *

AFTER HE GRADUATED FROM high school, Graham went to India for a year on what's now called the Rotary Youth Exchange program. He lived with an Indian family in the city of Amravati, in the state of Maharashtra. Graham's

A Father's Questions

host father, a doctor, was running for Congress as a member of a right-wing Hindu nationalist party, and they had vigorous discussions of religion and politics. Graham enrolled in a college that trained teachers of yoga. He developed a close relationship with an eighty-year-old teacher, his "Guruji," and practiced postures, breathing, and meditation for many hours daily. He studied Sanskrit and texts of Indian philosophy and engaged in lengthy discussions with his mentor. He went from a typically hedonistic American teenager's life to one of ascetic practice and religious commitment. In August 2003, a month after he started intensive yoga practice, Graham emailed a description of his daily schedule, ending with this reflection:

> At 5:40 a. m. it begins again, and it is the same routine every day. Sometimes I listen to so much Hindi in a day that I think they are trying to teach me about yoga through patience, not by actually teaching me the practice. Either way I'm learning it, and I'm at peace and all my feelings are out in the open. I have become more spiritual than ever before too. When I wake up, I try to be grateful that this day was given to me, and for my health and that I am going to use it to do good things and learn yoga. When I go to bed, I think of the things that I did that were good and that were bad, in terms of discipline, and try to change it the next day. It has helped me a lot. Sometimes I am discouraged, but I think of Koparkar [my teacher] and of how lucky I am and it goes away. A year is a long time but I'm taking it one day at a time and they are passing fast. I love you guys,
> G.

When he returned to the United States in June 2004, Graham was passionate about what he had learned in India and highly critical of many American preoccupations, asserting: "That is not the way." He was glad to see old friends and soon enjoying tobacco, alcohol, and late nights. The next morning, he would do several hours of yoga and try to reframe his perspective. I was deeply moved to see him searching for a way of life that would integrate what he learned in India and his hopes and plans in America; detachment from pleasure and love of friends; and yoga, Christianity, and agnostic doubt.

A year and a half later, when Graham was home from college for Christmas vacation in 2005, I recorded our conversation about family conscience. I was at my desk and Graham sat in a rocking chair. I asked him how he now understood his practice and study of yoga in India: "You said that one day you can be an ascetic yogi and the next day you are Bacchus or

Family Conscience

Dionysus and let it all hang out. One aspect of conscience is self-discipline and self-denial. Where do you think the desire for that comes from?"

"I want to be detached from sensual pleasures and I'm influenced by my practice of yoga. In India I experienced a happiness that was more fulfilling than I'm able to find in a bar. Another thing that influences me to deny myself things I want is political and social consciousness, beliefs about justice, and knowing that some people don't have enough to eat. Also, environmental consciousness. I can feel guilty that I have resources and money. If I think about the money I spend on cigarettes, alcohol, and expensive restaurants, then I think: this isn't right. But I am also pulled toward pleasure. I'm not ready to commit to a yogi lifestyle. I couldn't trust myself to any one philosophy. Maybe I am justifying selfish desires."

"You said that in India you weren't exactly denying yourself; you got a different kind of pleasure from what you were doing."

"Yes, it wasn't a painful denial. I became more self-sufficient. I was happy to just do yoga, go to school, and come home. I didn't go to movies or drink. I hardly listened to music because after I was done, I would still hear it in my mind when I was meditating. Yoga was very enjoyable, but the pleasure didn't come from outside me."

"Now you are back in the United States and involved with friends and drinking and your old lifestyle. What is that like? How do you keep alive the good things from India without being in that culture and the presence of a spiritual leader?"

"At first when I came back, there was no balance. There were two conflicting sides of myself. I would have a crazy weekend and ask myself on Sunday: What am I doing? I would fast half a day and try to get back that spiritual part I had forgotten. I would continue that for a few days and then feel good again. Now, after a year and a half, I'm nowhere near that, but I'm trying to balance both sides of myself every day. I don't want to go overboard either way. Yoga practice has to be integrated into a life of classes, friends, and socializing in a lifestyle that I can sustain. I want to build up my capacity for meditation and concentration, not renounce life. I did a good job all fall semester, but the stress of the final two weeks, with the exams and papers I put off, was too much. I would do yoga to relax but not put energy into it to keep improving as part of a process of self-betterment. Meditation is the hardest thing I've ever tried to do. Practice every day is necessary to improve."

"Do you think that the desire for self-improvement or self-betterment is related to conscience? Or is that not the right word for that part of you?"

"I would call it consciousness. But conscience is part of consciousness. It depends on how you define these things. I feel that I have a potential, like every person. We can do anything we want. I can walk into a room and influence people. Meditation gives me hope that I can realize my potential, and conscience comes into it in the hope that I would use my potential for good things. Yoga gives me hope. Regardless of whatever else is going on in my life, if I'm meditating, I'm improving myself."

"So conscience is about what you do with the consciousness that develops," I ventured. "Do you think that what you learned in India builds on what was already there in your life, such as Christian, American, or democratic values? Or is your spiritual path after India completely different from what led up to it? Did you have a conversion or a building on?"

"It wasn't a conversion at all. Beyond the physical yoga, such as postures and breathing, a large part of my immersion was the philosophy of yoga. We read sutras and I had one-on-one teaching with a guru who talked about each text. We spent many hours talking about what just one word means, like karma. It means work or action but also the cycle of life and death. When he was teaching me this philosophy it made so much sense. He was putting into words what I already believed, in a way that I never experienced in church. Maybe I could have if a pastor had explained each verse. It went beyond God. The yogic sutras talked first about the human mind and our desires and pains. That was the first part, explaining why you should practice yoga. If something brings you pleasure, you become attached to it. If something brings you pain, you hate it. I started to realize why I had the emotions I did, and that this is something I can control. Most people are at the mercy of their desires. But through ardent practice you can control your mind and know a higher soul that is universal. I have had experiences that lead me to believe I'm on the right track."

"Do you think of yourself as a Christian?"

"My yoga teacher said: 'You will always be a Christian.' Before India I loved Jack Kerouac, who was a Buddhist. *The Dharma Bums* was one of my favorite books. But the book Kerouac wrote when he was dying of alcoholism, *The Big Sur*, has a dying vision of the cross. Even though he had renounced Christianity, the church and Christ had power for him. I would say the same thing, because I was raised that way. The more I learn about Christianity, like in the New Testament class I took last semester, the more I realize this. I don't believe that Jesus died for my sins, or in the resurrection. But the message of Jesus is very important, and I see it in a positive way."

"What about our local United Church of Christ church?"

"The UCC had a positive role for me. There was a point when I said religion is an opiate for the masses. When I was about sixteen, I decided that it was complete bullshit. I knew people who said that if I don't believe in this or that I'm going to hell. I saw they didn't know what they were talking about. Most adults have no experience of God, in my opinion. They are feeding others a God that's been fed to them. In my confirmation class, pastor Sandy asked: 'What God is it that you don't believe in? That isn't God.' She opened my eyes. I knew the God I didn't believe in, but I didn't see an alternative until I was in India. My understanding of God is the same as that of Jesus, I think, or St. Francis of Assisi. God is everything. It's not like there is a divine being apart from everything; that's like Santa Claus to me."

"That sounds like pantheism," I suggested. "God is everything in the world but does not transcend the world."

"God transcends the world in ways we don't understand. After someone dies, his spirit lives on and becomes part of God. Everything that is, is a part of God, whether we know it or not. Before I couldn't pray because I didn't believe there was a God that would help me or that I could be thankful to. Now I feel grateful to be here, and I can say 'Thank you God,' which is powerful because I was raised in a church."

"What about evil and sin?"

"Everything happened just right for us to be here right now. Maybe the whole universe will end, and there will be another. In a bigger picture, it's okay."

"What about guilt, remorse, and regret, and the destructive side of these attitudes? Part of conscience is the sting of being hard on yourself. It sounds as if you would not want people to have that capacity."

"When I have been at a spiritually high place, I would like to think I would not hurt another person to benefit myself. I also understand that there is no way to hold myself up to that. Even the products we buy have negative effects. Two nights before I left school, I was at a party talking to my friend, and he attacked me for not being a good friend. I can hurt people sometimes by not even doing anything. In Northfield there are a lot of people who want to see me. I don't have the energy for every person. I'm not saying I don't care about them. People's expectations of you hurt them. Sometimes I act impulsively, and then guilt is valuable because I can learn from it. If I act out of selfishness, I should regret it. Let's say I betrayed someone for pleasure. I would feel bad and learn something if I listen to my heart."

"Do you find yourself feeling badly when it's not useful? It sounds as if you don't feel a lot of neurotic guilt. For me, feeling bad about things is sometimes an issue; I can't tell if I'm crazy or taking things seriously."

"I experience that, but not in a big way. It is what it is. I am what I am. What happens, happens. Make the most of it."

I admire and envy Graham's apparent freedom from useless regret. It's not that he does not have strong moral convictions, but he seems to have

A Father's Questions

largely escaped lingering self-doubt and pointless lamentation. Maybe he just has a lot of serotonin or maybe he has a different kind of conscience than I do. I told him that I was writing about my feeling that I had neglected or abandoned my sister and asked whether he ever felt that way about Reed.

"Not really. Big brothers just aren't very interested in their younger siblings. You were into something else then. If you had been with your sister you wouldn't have been able to do whatever was important to you then. Now I have friends I love, but I don't always send them a birthday card, and sometimes I don't have time for someone. There is no good or bad about this. It's just the way it is."

"I've been thinking lately about how my uncle Hugh was sometimes paralyzed by making decisions. I think that's a Barbour family tendency, at least in me and my siblings."

"I think we're all crazy to be so focused on ourselves. Why is it so hard to make decisions? It's a kind of egotism to think so much depends on your choice. We can fight this. In India, my teacher told me that anything that pleases you takes you farther away from peace of mind. This is at the heart of yoga: the mind is running wild. Everyone suffers because we all want something for ourselves."

"That sounds very Buddhist."

"It is Buddhist and also the essence of yoga. Love is usually selfish, but we have the potential to love purely and to control the mind: to be perfect, like Jesus, enlightened. There is unconditional love that does not expect anything back. I'm striving not to be attached. I suffer less than most people I know because of the way I see the world."

"What about the suffering of conscience? What is that from the perspective of a yogi?"

"Many of the things you see as family conscience are the human condition. But I deal with them differently because of the way I look at the world."

The wisdom Graham came to in India provides an alternative perspective on Christian and Western conscience, yet there is a similarity. He suggests that my remorse, regret, and guilt show my attachment to an image of myself as morally perfect. I see analogies between this viewpoint, my understanding of Buddhism, and a crucial Christian insight that humans are constantly trying to justify themselves and give their life a value that can only come from God. From all these perspectives, the scab-picking, self-flagellating routines of conscience are egotistical. Mind is running wild.

* * *

Family Conscience

ONE MORNING IN MARCH 2004, I woke up early in Hong Kong and packed my bag. I had thought carefully, perhaps obsessively, about exactly what to bring. India would be hot, so I carried a pint of water with my book bag and a quart in my backpack. You can't plan for the worst-case scenario. But I prepared for being separated from my checked baggage by carrying a change of clothes and a few necessities, as well as enough reading matter to occupy me for weeks on a desert island. I arrived at the airport more than two hours early. When I saw the long line ahead of me, I congratulated myself on my foresight and efficiency. I was ready for anything.

I had been in Hong Kong for an academic conference for five days, presenting a paper on Thomas Merton's final journey to Asia, a two-month trip in 1968 to India, Nepal, Sri Lanka, and Thailand. Now a more personal journey would begin. I would travel to India to meet Graham. He had been in Amravati for eight months, living with his host family and studying yoga, Hindi, and Sanskrit. After a sometimes-tense relationship during his high school years, I longed to see him and fantasized about our reunion. Seeing him off at the airport the previous July, I could not hold back my tears. On this day Graham was taking the fourteen-hour train ride to Mumbai, where we would meet at a hotel. We would take the overnight train back to Amravati, meet his family, spiritual mentor, and friends, and return to Mumbai together. We would bond and any hurts from the past would be healed. I wanted the parable of the prodigal son to happen in my life; I yearned for the father and son reunion. But I was the one traveling from afar, and he the one welcoming with open arms.

I moved through the long line to the check-in counter for the airline that would take me from Hong Kong to Mumbai. The agent went through my documents. "Where is your visa?"

"Visa? What visa?"

"You have to have a visa to go to India."

"I didn't know. No one told me. Can't we work this out when I get to Mumbai?"

"No. You cannot get on the plane without a visa."

I was utterly overcome with feelings of stupidity and humiliation. My face flushed, my eyes burned, my heart pounded. How could this have happened? I had been to India before, for six weeks in 2001 with students on the St. Olaf Global Program. The International Studies office handled all the visa and documentation procedures, and I hadn't paid much attention. But only a year earlier I had sent Graham's passport to the Indian consulate in Chicago to get his visa before he left. How could I have forgotten that I needed to do the same thing myself? I triple-checked countless details and

A Father's Questions

fussed over how many pairs of socks to bring, but I didn't fulfill the one essential condition for entering India.

Standing at the counter, I desperately begged the check-in agent: "Please let me on the plane. I'll pay anything. We can sort it out in Mumbai. I can't leave my child alone there. I'm supposed to meet him. I have to be there."

The agent was polite but firm. She called the Indian consulate. No answer. It was Saturday afternoon. She finally got through to someone who said that the consulate was closed for the weekend. If I would come first thing Monday morning, I might be able to get a visa in four days. Maybe.

I recognized that "maybe." I had encountered it before in India, when someone did not want to disappoint a Western visitor. If everything worked out perfectly, I could get to Mumbai very late on Thursday. My plane was to return to Hong Kong at five o'clock on Friday morning. I had already missed several days of teaching responsibilities and couldn't prolong my trip. I couldn't go to India. I felt nauseous, braced myself against the ticket counter, and staggered away.

I spent the rest of that day frantically running between telephones, email outlets, and airline and hotel counters. I couldn't get my prepaid phone cards to work; my fingers trembled as I tried to get through the long series of digits to activate the card and dial an international number. I called the Indian consulate, Meg in Minnesota, the hotel where Graham was staying in Mumbai, a hotel in Hong Kong, the airline that would have taken me to India and one that could take me back to the United States if they found a seat. At last, I arranged a flight back to the United States the next day and decided to stay in an airport hotel that night in Hong Kong.

My phone call woke up my spouse. I broke down in tears, sobbing in the airport lobby. "How could I do this? How could I be so stupid? I am so ashamed. I can't stand it." Meg was consoling, reassuring. She was relieved that I was safe; a midnight call might have brought much worse news. It helped a little to share my grief with her.

In the midst of this distress, I had the feeling that someone was trying to tell me something. I am skeptical of Christians who interpret every event in their lives as a direct message from God. I don't think that every accident or piece of good fortune is a divine punishment or reward. Although Jesus said that God knows even the fall of a sparrow, I don't see myself as the focal point of God's constant attention. Yet in the depths of anguish, I felt that there must be a crucial meaning in this experience. Something about my own nature was revealed, as well as the possibility of a self-transformation just beyond my reach. The missed travel connection to Graham seemed to symbolize what was wrong with my life, but I couldn't quite grasp it. Was

Family Conscience

the hidden lesson that I should be more vigilant and organized, or was it to be more resilient when a bad trip happens? Do I need to be more careful about details, more alert and decisive? Or is it that life isn't organized according to my desires, and emotional connection can't be scheduled? Was my searching for deep meaning in this mishap and taking it as a judgment on my character the sign of a grandiose, overwrought conscience?

In the evening, totally depleted, my hopes revived. Graham sent me this email:

> Subject: Singapore? Tokyo? Hongkong?
>
> Dad, I can't believe it and I'm disappointed too but hey it's not the end of the world. In fact there's flights leaving today to all over Asia from Bombay and I DO have my passport with me. So if you want to shell out the bucks you can still see your firstborn son in Asia. I'd like to talk to you. I'll be checking my email and calling mom so give a # where I can reach you, or you can call my hotel if you can get through. I could fly to Hong Kong tonight. Or I've never been to Singapore—maybe it'd be cool. Let me know whether to give up and go home or if we should work something out. No worries y'all. I love you, Graham.

How resilient and resourceful he is! After many busy signals, wrong numbers, and sudden disconnections, at last we talked on the telephone.

"Dad, this isn't like you!"

"I know, Graham, I screwed up big-time. I'm so sorry, brokenhearted." We tried to figure out a way to meet, then realized that Graham had a single-entry visa that allowed him to enter India but not to leave and return. We couldn't meet in Hong Kong or anywhere else. Although disappointed, he was generous, resilient, and affectionate. My children are my best teachers.

I went to the hotel exercise room and punished myself until I was too tired to move. I tried to stop thinking. Every time I imagined being with Graham, my head and chest felt unbearably hot and tight, like my skin was sewed on too tightly. I thought of him alone in Mumbai, then pictured the two of us walking together through chaotic Indian streets. You can't lose what you never had, I told myself, but it didn't make me feel any better. I had lost something precious that I had fantasized about for a long time.

Graham spent that night alone in Mumbai. He explored the city the next day and took the night train back to Amravati. He explained to his host family and friends that his father wasn't coming to India after all.

I wandered around the airport hotel, gazing in wonder at all the people who were not my son. This was the kind of place I had always despised, a no-place that looked like any slick international corporate headquarters.

A Father's Questions

The check-in clerk was sweet. At first, she said that the hotel was full. As I told her my sob story, my tears welled up, and she immediately found a room. She gave me a Kleenex and said: "You will see your son again. Be happy." Later, in the exercise room, a Thai businessman, who was in Hong Kong for two months to learn a computer system, showed me how to set the program for a bicycle machine. I was immensely grateful, as if he had given me a visa for India.

The hotel bustled with pink, chubby American tourists in shorts and baseball caps, dapper Asian businessmen, multigenerational Indian families, young German and Scandinavian couples, and teams of flight attendants and pilots from every nation. The hotel had Cantonese and Mandarin restaurants, a Japanese sushi bar, and an American sports grill. I went to the Japanese restaurant for a beer and tempura, feeling at once very lonely and strangely companionable with the other travelers eating at their tables. Some of them were alone like me, missing those they loved, trying to make the best of the situation. I mused sadly: "Here we all are, together in our cozy airport hotel. I wish Graham was here, too." The next day I flew home.

For the next few weeks, I tried to talk myself out of my feelings. I told myself that things could have been much worse. No damage was done; I simply missed out on an experience I wanted to have. I had a great deal to be grateful for, and Graham would come home in a few months. I tried to minimize the pain I felt by putting the miniscule capsule of my disappointment on the vast scale that weighs human suffering. I framed the incident in a broader perspective, trying to view my overwrought emotional reaction from another place, from outer space, from nowhere. Still, I bitterly condemned myself.

Meg gently suggested that perhaps this experience might give me more compassion when other people make mistakes. After my humiliation in the airport, I felt new sympathy for people who for whatever reason lose control or make a bad judgment. My father-in-law was struggling with memory loss: giving up driving, not remembering how to cook, and forgetting what day of the week it was. I thought about several individuals whose disorganization irritates me. I am nearly always punctual and efficient, and I don't understand people who can't seem to arrive at a meeting on time or make a deadline. A sister loses her keys; a friend is unpredictable. I thought that such absentmindedness or carelessness could never happen to me. I had been proud of my competence as a world traveler. Now I felt ashamed not only of my stupid mistake but also of the way I judged people for mistakes.

This experience of failure shattered my self-image, at least for a few days. I saw the fragility of my sense of myself as capable, organized, and in control. I wish I could have just laughed, but the shock when my idealized self-conception disintegrated felt like a breakdown or collapse, and my shame was overwhelming.

Then something shifted. I felt humiliated but also alert to a new reality. I had a moment of self-recognition: this is who you are, so proud of being in control. This is a wakeup call. Someone is trying to tell you something about yourself. I vowed to remember the details of the incident, to burn them into memory's folds. I wanted this shame to engrave my character forever, so that what I learned would stay with me. I wanted pain to purify me of egotism and perfectionism.

Sometimes conscience revisits and revises earlier judgments. In this ordeal of self-judgment, as I considered my immediate reaction, the shame faded, partly displaced by a more deliberate reflection and new intention. I vowed to create a different kind of future: there will be other opportunities to be with my sons and others, and I resolve to seize them. I'm not the perfect model of a world traveler or grace under pressure, but maybe I can learn something from my mistakes. I did not have the mythic reunion I envisioned, the prodigal father's return to his son's embrace. Yet the surge of love and longing that I felt for Graham across the vast distance was a deep form of connectedness, a movement of heart and soul, and what I hoped to find in India.

* * *

Drugs and alcohol are so deeply entrenched in American culture that it seemed to me impossible for my teenaged sons to avoid them. I accepted that they would experiment and hoped that they would emerge from adolescence without a terrible accident or creeping dependency. Meg and I were anxious and worried about addiction, since we both have ancestors who were alcoholics. I would do anything to save my sons from that fate, but what I should do at a particular time was often not clear to me.

I could have investigated more diligently and searched their rooms regularly. I snooped around a few times, but not often. I could have stayed up until midnight every night they were out and smelled their breath for liquor and their clothes for smoke. I played the role of traffic cop more than detective, responding to blatant violations of the rules. I've known several teenagers in my own and my sons' generations who were totally alienated by parental surveillance and became more devious and determined users. Better to have them indulge in moderation and keep the lines of communication open, I told myself. This was wishful thinking; they didn't want to communicate with me about drugs and alcohol.

A Father's Questions

We stand in the kitchen. One of my sons has come home with a glazed look in his eyes and seems more animated and talkative than usual. His mother asks him whether he has been smoking pot. He says no. We ask other questions: Where have you been? Who were you with? What did you do? The answers are sketchy and evasive. There is something upsetting, even sickening, about interrogating my child. I want to believe him but suspect that he is lying. Or rather, he is trying his hardest not to lie by not saying anything at all. By pressing so hard, are we forcing him to deceive us? I think we get a portion of the truth, carefully edited. But usually our fifteen-year-old stonewalls us, shutting down. I can see his smoldering resentment and anger. To persist in this investigation seems futile. It will not reveal anything and may only make him better practiced at withholding the truth and fabricating misleading stories.

I tell myself I'm a wimp. You have to get tough, you spineless, liberal, psychobabbling, intellectualizing coward! You should make your kid uncomfortable, and if he chooses to lie that's his choice. Let him live with a guilty conscience; let him squirm.

He tenses, fidgets, and moves across the kitchen to relieve his agitation. Sometimes his eyes dart around and at other moments he stares back defiantly. As Meg bores in, relentlessly probing for the truth, he wrings his hands and says, "Mom . . . Mom . . . Don't *do* this!" The conversation may end in sullen silence or in an explosion when he slams the door and stomps off to his room.

The bond between parent and child that was so tight has become a chain that he wants to break. He's not going to tell us about this huge part of his life. He wants to find out what other states of consciousness are possible. He craves another reality than a secure childhood home. He will seek good times with his buddies even if he becomes estranged from his mother and father.

Late one night we get a telephone call from the police. In the trunk of my son's car they found two cases of beer, two bottles of rum, and two large bongs. Where did he get all this stuff? He was only transporting it for other people, he claims—my son, the professed public servant. He has tested negative for alcohol, so at least he wasn't driving under the influence.

The so-called consequences for this behavior were that he had to pay sixty dollars for the tow truck that the police called to break into the car. He had to do twenty hours of community service, including writing a paper on the effects of drugs and alcohol on the development of a teenager's brain, and he had to spend several mornings laying down white lines on soccer fields. We grounded him in a half-assed way: for a month he could use the car only to go to work or soccer practice. There were lots of fuzzy areas and exceptions.

Two days after the police incident, my spouse and I wrestled with a difficult decision. Our son was supposed to drive with friends to Bonnaroo, a huge outdoor rock festival in Tennessee. He had looked forward to this festival for almost a year and invested several hundred dollars and a lot of planning in it. Now he pulled out all the stops, asserting: "My world will crash if I can't go. This is what I've been living for." Without him to drive, his friends would not be able to go. Meg and I sat on the porch for two hours, agonizing about whether to let our son go to his generation's Woodstock, while he waited in the kitchen with a friend. Twenty times one of us said: "If we let him go, we are caving in." The next moment the other one said that not letting him go would only embitter him. One of us would wonder aloud: Are we just chickenshit, afraid of his anger? In the end, we let him go. I don't defend this decision; I would advise another parent to practice tough love.

You do the best you can as a parent and hope it is enough. You love your kid more than you can stand and watch as he drives off with a carload of friends looking for a good time. Maybe you pray: Lord, protect my child.

When one of our boys was about two, my mother gave me a photograph of him learning to walk. The photo, taken from behind, shows the toddler walking away, a little unsteady but determined. Under this picture, Deane printed out this ancient Irish "Prayer for a Little Child":

> God keep my jewel this day from danger;
> from tinker and pooka and black hearted stranger,
> from harm of the water, and hurt of the fire,
> from the horns of the cow going home to the byre,
> from teasing the ass when he's tied to the manger;
> from stones that would bruise and from thorns of the briar,
> from evil red berries that waken desire,
> from hunting the gander and vexing the goat,
> from the depths o' sea water by Danny's old boat,
> from cut and from tumble, from sickness and weeping;
> May God have my jewel this day in his keeping.

When they were children, I worried most about the dangers of fire or water; only when they became teenagers did I notice the verse about "evil red berries that waken desire."

It was different for me when I was a teenager. Deane admitted that she and Ian were "hopelessly naïve" about drugs and were not suspicious. I tried alcohol in high school a few times but never got seriously drunk and only smoked marijuana once before college. At Oberlin during my first year, I took mescaline twice. Experimenting with drugs was somehow as necessary to becoming an adult in the spring of 1970 as participating in antiwar demonstrations. I enthusiastically described the mescaline experiences to my mother. She listened with interest and surprisingly little alarm. My alcohol and drug use were not entangled with my relationship to my parents, and that made everything easier than the painful struggle I was now in with my sons.

Having used drugs and now drinking wine or beer regularly with dinner, I couldn't honestly tell my teenaged sons that these are evil things. Alcohol can be good in the right context for an adult. But you don't become an adult overnight when you turn twenty-one. A teenager is a tadpole, in between the larvae and the frog stage, and as he matures he thrashes his tail spasmodically.

Our conflict about drugs and alcohol was inextricably entangled with my sons' friendships. Their friends were other boys, and then girls, who were also users. They were good kids, although overly confident about their invulnerability. Friendships among high school boys are the most important thing in their lives. They will not reveal information about each other, knowing that parents talk to each other and compare notes. They cover for each other and provide alibis. Their highest principle is, "Don't squeal on your buddy." A parent's greatest concern is, "I must protect my precious jewel. My innocent babe is being corrupted by other kids."

I wanted my son to be able to say No to peer pressure. He should have a conscience that can resist the urgings of his friends and the inner craving for approval. I wanted him to have a source of self-esteem that did not depend on doing whatever his gang was into this week. He should be an immovable rock when everything around him is slipping and eroding away. I wished his integrity was what mine has never been. Was I any different from the sports-crazy father going ballistic on the sidelines, living out his own athletic fantasies through his child on the field? In the family drug wars I was trying to be a responsible parent. I was also trying to shape each son's conscience so that he would live out my own myth of soul-making.

* * *

IN JULY 2005 MY relationship with Reed was rocky. He was sixteen and seemed to want nothing to do with me. He was morose and withdrawn when he was around me and happy and sociable with his friends. One sunny afternoon he decided to go canoeing with some buddies. Six of them set forth in two canoes, intending to paddle ten miles from Faribault to the landing in the Dundas City Park, a quarter mile from our house. It turned

Family Conscience

out to be a longer voyage than they had bargained for. They finally came home just before 10 p.m., when it had turned dark and chilly. The three girls, wearing only bikinis, were shivering. I loaned them three jackets for their ride home.

The next day I asked Reed to retrieve the jackets. He said that he would do so soon. I asked him again the following day and he said, "I'll get around to it." This script was repeated for several days. I became increasingly irritated but tried to suppress it. Finally, I got angry and said that I really want those jackets, because they are valuable and we need them for a kayak expedition we will be taking in a week, while Reed goes on a backpacking trip. A day or two later, two of the coats came back, but the third coat was still missing. It was a thick, warm purple fleece jacket that zips up tight around my neck. I had used this coat for a decade for camping trips and to smoke cigars outside when it's cool. It was not valuable in monetary terms but it served me well. The purple coat became the center of a power struggle with Reed, a conflict I was powerless either to resolve or to turn away from. He never explained why it was so difficult to get the coat back but continued to assert that he would bring it home eventually and I should back off.

For several more days I kept asking. I patiently explained again why I needed it and asked what the problem was. Still he procrastinated, and still I could hardly get a word out of him. Finally, two days before we were to leave on our camping trips, I exploded. He was lying in bed at about eleven o'clock, sleeping late as usual that summer before his afternoon job, and I wanted to check in with him before I went to my office. When he said he still hadn't retrieved the coat, I yelled at him: "I can't believe it! What is this passive aggressive behavior? Why are you doing this? I can't stand it when you and Graham don't take care of other people's stuff. If you don't bring me that coat before I leave for my trip, I'm going to buy a new one and you can pay for it." Reed groaned and covered his head with his pillow. I stormed out, infuriated and cursing, as angry with myself as I was at Reed. It was crazy to act this way, but I couldn't help myself or find a way out of this situation.

Taking care of other people's property has always been an issue for me. It's one thing to not take care of one's own things, although I'm all for good stewardship. It's another thing not to care about other people's stuff, and a sign of a spoiled rich kid. I don't want my sons to be irresponsible about material things, to say "It doesn't matter, what's the big deal?" when it does matter to someone else. There was a moral principle at stake in my outburst. I wanted Reed to have a conscience about taking care of other people's property. If I don't teach him this, who will?

But it's more complicated than this. Meg pointed out that I've always been touchy about sharing my possessions. I don't like it when a book or an

A Father's Questions

article of clothing I want is gone and someone has taken it without asking. Okay, call me a clutching, ungenerous person. Graham and Reed must have seen me as obsessed with trivial things when I got angry that headphones, CDs, clothes, or camping gear were damaged or lost. Other people who have a lot less than me are far more generous with their stuff. Where does my possessive impulse come from? Is it stinginess or Scottish thrift? Ben Franklin's responsible accounting or Scrooge's grasping, hoarding sense of ownership? A Christian sense of stewardship or a materialistic fixation on things at the expense of human relationships? Would dropping the whole matter, forgetting about the purple coat, be good or bad parenting?

Meg asked: "Why are you letting your entire relationship with Reed revolve around your ratty old coat? This is all that you have in common with him now." She pointed to a newspaper story on crumbling yellow newspaper that had been tacked to the kitchen bulletin board for about a decade:

> Dad Mows Son's Room after Teen Refuses to Cut Grass
>
> Belton, Mo.—A boy who wanted to sleep rather than mow the lawn received a rude awakening when his father started up the mower in his bedroom.
>
> Rickey W[---] woke up his son Michael at 6 a. m. Saturday to mow the lawn, but the 17-year-old told him to go away, saying it was too early.
>
> His father returned, this time with the mower. He pushed it through the door and started it up, cutting clumps from the bedroom carpet, said police Sgt. Randy Scott.
>
> Michael threw a fan at the mower, and his father left. The boy called police, who arrested W[---] and charged him with assault. No one was injured.

This absurd story suddenly seemed significant. A father was so intent on forming his son's moral character—and asserting his authority—that the two of them became completely alienated.

By this time I was weary, disgusted with the whole situation, and resigned to somehow making Reed pay for a new coat. The night before we left home for our camping trips, he brought back the purple coat. It had taken him a while to locate it, he said. Graham's perspective on this incident, two weeks later, was that girls like to have boys' clothes, and it may have required delicate negotiation to get the jacket back.

Today my reactions in this situation seem like a fit of insanity. The coat must have had a symbolic value or unconscious meaning for me that explains the depths of my anger. Or maybe it is quite simple: I wanted Reed to care not only about other people's stuff, but also about me. He was ignoring my wishes and withdrawing silently into a shell to get away from my increasingly lunatic outrage.

Three weeks later, after we all came back from our camping trips, I had a sandwich with Reed in a local restaurant. This would help us stay in conversation for a few minutes, I hoped, at least until his cell phone rang. I asked him how he now saw the Battle of the Purple Coat. I said that I was writing a story about it and wanted to show his point of view as well as my own frustration. He said: "The coats were in various locations. I didn't know who had which one. I told Kaycee to bring it and she didn't. I'll think about it more. I gotta go now." He had seen a friend passing, and he got up and left me still eating, still chewing over the conflict.

A week later Reed was sitting in the kitchen eating a waffle. I gave him a first draft of this story and asked what he thought of it. He read it and said: "You are kind of harsh. And it's sensationalized. It wasn't that big a deal to make a story of."

"What is it like to have a father who acts this way?"

"You toned down your anger about tenfold. You were yelling and screaming at me while I was asleep. You overreacted even more than your story shows."

"What about Graham's explanation of why you didn't get the jacket?"

"No, that wasn't it at all. It wasn't a cool jacket. It probably smelled like you. I just didn't get around to it for a while. Do a lot of people write this kind of thing? Is this for your book about the family?"

"Maybe. A lot of people write stuff, but it's hard to publish a true story about your children because they might be embarrassed. I haven't figured out that part yet."

Reed smiled. "I'm not too worried about its becoming a best seller. I'm cool with it."

* * *

IN MAY 2007, WHEN he was eighteen, Reed returned from his first extended adventure away from home, a three-month wilderness expedition in Patagonia. He had graduated from high school a semester early so he could kayak and climb mountains in that remote area. I told him I wanted to record his unique voice so it would come through clearly in my family memoir. As we sat in the living room together, he responded to my questions with pithy, matter-of-fact statements, as is his wont. He gets to the point.

I asked: "What does the word 'conscience' mean to you?"

"The little voice inside your head."

"How would you describe yourself in terms of religion?"

"Agnostic. I'm glad I went to church; it's a good experience to have had. But I didn't fall for it."

"How would you describe yourself politically?"

"Green. Progressive. I think we need to save the earth and people from destruction."

"How important is work to you? Do you have a work ethic?"

"It's kind of important. My attitude keeps changing. You have to work for money. For the system. Sometimes you work to keep yourself happy. There are times when I could leave it."

"What would you say about our parenting style?"

"You could have had more tolerance for food issues. There was a pretty good balance of control and not."

"What do you mean, 'not'? What's the opposite of control?"

"Revolution!"

"What would you do differently if you were a parent?"

"Improvise."

"What do you mean?"

"Not have it all figured out beforehand. You tried to prevent me from making mistakes, but kids need to learn from experience."

"How do parents control kids? We don't hold a gun to your head."

"You show your disapproval and hope our conscience stops us."

"But Reed, what about a parent's fear that his child will be permanently harmed? Like in an accident or by becoming addicted? I can't just stand by and watch that happen."

"You can't stop it. That has to come from the person."

"Would it be conscience that stops a kid from drugs? Somehow that doesn't seem likely."

"Common sense. You have to see from the outside what drugs can do."

"Why are drugs and addiction such a problem in our culture?"

"Opportunity. And there is an emptiness inside that kids try to fill."

"I don't think you are going to get addicted to anything. You don't believe in God or have religious faith. So, what fills your emptiness?"

"Human connections, especially friends. And the woods."

"What do you think about the way sex was presented to you by me and Meg? I didn't really say or teach you much about it explicitly. That probably wasn't good parenting."

"It can be more easily overdone than underdone."

"You really prefer a hands-off style of parenting, don't you? And that's also been true of your attitude to coaches, teachers, and other leaders."

"That's right. In South America, families are different; they are together more. Students going to university live at home. But I don't want that; family structure here is different."

"You were in wilderness conditions in Chile for three months with a completely new group of people, and it was your first time as an adult away from home. What was your role in the group?"

"It was great to be free and independent. In Spanish I was *buena onda* [literally, a good wave]. I try to bring good vibes, smile, make things lighter, bring some fun. There are enough negative and sarcastic people already. I try to have a positive attitude."

"How do you see this whole memoir thing I'm doing? I want to get your perspective in it."

"You really can't show a full picture of me. You are the one selecting what I say, what bits of me are in there. It's not a family textbook, but a family memoir."

"That story about the purple coat describes my feelings when you were younger, and there was a lot of estrangement and alienation I couldn't overcome. How do you see that time now?"

"There were growing pains. Being a teenager is not like the *Barney* [a pink dinosaur] show we watched as kids. It's sometimes more like *The Sopranos*. For me it's about finding a balance between pulling away and being crowded. Growing up is finding the right distance."

Reed, too, sorts through a moral inheritance as he finds the right distance and chooses his own values. I love it that he sees himself as *buena onda*. I could use some more of that. His process of sifting and choosing goes on, as does mine, partly because of what he teaches me.

CHAPTER 12

When the Memoired Protest

My Story and Their Privacy

Writing this memoir raised many questions of conscience for me. What version of my story can I publish when family members object? Even when a relative has died or given permission, I feel ethical constraints on what I can write about others. This final chapter, the story of the story, explores one of the most troubling and ambiguous ethical quandaries with which I've struggled.

I started this project in 2003 by trying to understand my grandfather's suicide and its impact. Over the next several years, I wrote chapter-length interpretations of other family members. Along the way, I compared my experience to theirs. In addition to relying on memories and documents, I tape-recorded and transcribed interviews with each family member. I gave each person a draft of the chapter about them and responded to their reactions. Finally, in August 2007, I gave everyone a copy of the whole manuscript, 406 pages bound with a spiral wire, and asked for feedback. My motivation for this biographical structure and collaborative method was to portray diversity within the family and challenges to my views. I wanted to show alternative perspectives on and disagreements about what happened in the past, specific moral issues, and understandings of conscience. I quoted other people copiously, drawing from letters, taped interviews, and conversations that I wrote down immediately after they happened. I wanted family members to speak for themselves rather than always being filtered through my interpretations.

Despite this attempt to be fair to other points of view, most people felt that I had taken away or distorted their voice. I had reduced, used, or exploited them. Family members raised several crucial issues of conscience for me, including that there are certain issues in my own life that I don't discuss. They questioned choices I made as to which events or issues to discuss and which to omit. Why take one random conversation or incident as revealing a person's conscience, while leaving out so many other things? One sibling pressed me about this at a time when I was teaching Augustine's *Confessions*. Although his relationships with other people are crucial, Augustine is highly selective in what he reveals about them. He describes his mother, Monica, more than anyone else, yet only in relationship to his journey to Christian faith. We catch only glimpses of his best friend, Alypius, and of the unnamed mistress with whom Augustine lived for many years and had a son. We learn about this son only when Augustine tells us that, at fifteen, the boy died. Brief anecdotes about these individuals, vital presences in his life, describe only how they influenced his religious development. I looked to Augustine to justify my memoir focused on a single theme.

One of my wife's chief concerns about this memoir was its effect on our sons' memories. As a teacher of photography, Meg said that representations of the past change our relationship to it: "I'm very concerned about how this memoir may narrow Graham's and Reed's perceptions of their early lives and their roles in our family. It might reduce their sense of the richness of the past. Just like I don't want a photograph to be all that we have to remember the past by. Sometimes, too, a photo of a happy family doesn't fit with your memories, so you wonder what is reality. If your memoir becomes the way the boys think of the past, it leaves out so much. I don't want it to replace or reduce their memories, which are rich and layered." A memoir's selective focus on certain events can affect a person's view of the past and sense of identity.

Another challenge was the accusation that I hurt vulnerable people when I reveal painful incidents from their pasts. One day in September 2004, I drove Blair from Northfield to the Minneapolis airport. She had just spent several days visiting our parents at a very hard time in her life. She told me that Deane was upset about my depiction of her mother: "There is a big rift in your relationship, the biggest ever, and you should talk to Mom as soon as possible."

"Okay," I said, "I'll talk to her. What is the issue?"

"What you have written is simplistic and thin. You show just one dimension of very complicated people. You speculate about matters you know nothing about. You only discuss one reason for Deane's depression: her father's suicide. What about genetic factors? And her having to raise four children, much of the time by herself?"

"This isn't a study of depression or an explanation of all its sources. I'm writing about conscience in our family. I think a harsh conscience is sometimes related to depression."

"I think you should throw away everything you have written and start over. You should get into therapy and go a lot deeper. If you write, do it about yourself and not others."

"But," I protested, "I can't tell my story without telling that of others."

"Can't you discuss the issues without telling others' stories?"

"Yes, but that would be a purely theoretical argument. Or an academic study of books like all the other things I've written. This is different."

"Why not make it fiction?"

"It wouldn't be the same. There is a truth of fiction, but I want the truth of memoir."

"Well," Blair challenged me, "it sounds like you are claiming to have *the* truth about the family."

"Just my truth."

I was quite disturbed by this conversation, which came at a time when I was sleep-deprived and reeling from other family drama. The night before, Anne-Sophie, our French exchange student, hadn't returned home until 2 a.m., two hours late. I was already anxious about my parents' reaction to the manuscript. I wanted to be supportive of Blair at this difficult time for her, not to argue. I felt overwhelmed and irritable. I screamed inside my head, "I don't have time to take care of everyone else's feelings about my work. They can write their own damn books!" The hell with them all, I thought, and tried to concentrate on driving.

Blair started again: "And another thing. There is a huge generational factor that you aren't acknowledging. We are from the generation of Oprah, where people spill their guts in public. Mom has a strong sense of boundaries and a belief in the importance of privacy. This stuff just isn't other people's business. How would you feel if Graham or Reed were to tell your secrets to the world?"

"I don't know," I said uneasily, and we rode for a few minutes in silence. Then Blair quoted to me something that Deane remembered her mother, Dolly, as saying: "Fools' names and fools' faces are often seen in public places." (Later Deane told me that Dolly was quoting her venerable great-aunt "both humorously and wryly." With whatever degree of accompanying irony, that saying has been passed on through five generations, and now I pass it on again.) Blair has a strong desire to guard her family's privacy and protect vulnerable loved ones. In addition, she spoke from the perspective of a therapist and viewed my writing as a possible violation of boundaries. I thought that she saw only the potential for harm that could come from portraying our family's experience, not whatever good might emerge. But just what kind of good would override the objections of people I love?

Blair asserted that I have no psychological training to indulge in interpretations of other people's motivations and internal conflicts. I responded: "Neither did Shakespeare. You don't need an academic degree or professional certification to be fascinated by tangled webs of insight and self-deception." Shakespeare! Augustine! I am in good company!

I gradually admitted that Blair's objections raise crucial ethical issues. She spoke her concerns as a therapist, a daughter, and a sister. My defensiveness eased a bit, although I remained in a fragile state. If I can represent Blair's criticisms accurately, I decided, they will become part of the truth of the memoir, revealing another side of the family conscience. Her intervention expressed her scruples, her concern for Deane and me, and a contrasting perspective on the moral issues involved in writing about a family.

Some months later, in April 2005, Blair and I were sitting in a coffee shop in Chicago. She told me how disappointed she was that a friend was being narcissistic and demanding when Blair was going through emotional turmoil. She said that the friend was not very conscientious. I perked up at this word, so close to "conscience" but with a different shade of meaning. "What does it mean to be conscientious? I think it means being reliable, following through, keeping your word, and being consistent."

"To me," Blair responded, "'conscientious' means thinking of others' needs. It involves going beyond your own preferences and desires to do something for others."

She interpreted conscientiousness as being responsible for other people, whereas I focused on consistency between a person's words and deeds and between intentions and actions. Blair's view resembles the "ethic of care" that Carol Gilligan proposes is the usual moral framework that women develop.[1] In contrast, my view sounds like a typical male perspective that emphasizes acting according to principle, observing rules, and being able to justify one's actions. I saw a gender-based contrast in the ways we interpreted this key moral term. Blair's interpretation of conscientiousness reveals a more altruistic or other-regarding ethics than does my own take on the meaning of this virtue, which could lead to rigid, perfectionistic consistency or legalistic adherence to rules. My blind spot would be how my actions, however consistent or well-reasoned, affect other people. If being conscientious means adhering to strict dutifulness and consistency, then moral emotions such as generosity, compassion, and gratitude may

---

1. Carol Gilligan, *In Another Voice: Psychological Theory and Women's Development* (Cambridge: Harvard University Press, 1993).

remain underdeveloped. Exhibit A of such underdevelopment may well be this conversation I had with Blair, if I failed to be present emotionally when my sister was at a difficult time. What a strange response I made, when in the presence of Blair's emotional pain, I analyzed the meaning of conscientiousness!

I realized that my understanding of conscientiousness was deficient in comparison to Blair's more other-regarding orientation. It seems a paradox: how could I come to see my sister's way of being moral as better than my own if I hadn't already adopted her perspective? Yet something shifted. Talking with others about ethical questions often disclosed this dimension of conscience: the way it continues to evolve and reconsider its earlier judgments and standards. Conscience assesses not only actions and failures to act, but also its own past verdicts, in a never-ending process of scrutiny and revision.

A few months later I showed Blair a written version of our conversation. Her views, too, had developed: "I don't think I still see it that way. I think I understand conscientiousness the same way as you. It means remembering your priorities and acting on them. A priority for me would be caring for other people. But there are other ones, like being true to myself. Everything you say freezes me in a particular moment in the past. But people change. I need to be careful about this as a therapist. I try to say not what people are, but rather how I experience a client in the present moment."

Blair raised another question: "The issue your project raises is not simply about privacy but control over information. This is not like a therapist's office where you can trust it's not going to go further. We are entrusting you with our personal stories and feelings."

"Do you think our family has a greater need than others to control information? How did we get the message in our family about the need for privacy? And about the danger of losing control of information or secrets? How did you learn that lesson?"

"I have only a vague memory of something. In our first house in Northfield, Dad built us little offices. They had wooden walls and we each had our own space where we could arrange our things. We had rugs or mats."

"They were little compartments like boxes," I said. "We each had our own play space. And solitude. That's an interesting spatial message. Did we communicate with each other? They sound like cages, but I don't remember not liking them. There was also a common space in the middle."

"The youngest, David, would be getting into everyone's stuff. The middle child would be trying to keep the peace." We laughed.

Family Conscience

"That would be you! Was the message to play in your own space and not interact with others?"

"It taught us about boundaries," she said.

"I'm trying to connect all this with the issue of privacy and control of information. Why did you think of the offices? I've suddenly thought of something else. You told me once about a time when you were getting married and there was a question about when to tell your friends. Mom didn't want you to do that at a certain point."

Blair recalled this incident: "It was on Christmas Eve and Randy and I had just told the family we were getting married. We were excited and happy and I asked, 'What about making an announcement at our friends' Christmas party?' Mom's response was to think about others' feelings, especially people who are single and don't want to be. She knew that about someone. Maybe, too, she just wanted some time to absorb the information herself before everyone congratulated her. But at the time, my interpretation was that it felt like a damper. As if I had had a shameful thought. It felt like she had interrupted my bragging, though I hadn't seen it as bragging. The positive value at stake for her was humility."

"When does this concern not to hurt other people's feelings, which is a legitimate moral concern, lead to walking on eggshells, tentativeness, or stifling even your feelings of happiness because others aren't happy? Why does this situation develop? It has something to do with conscience. The emphasis on humility makes us very cautious about sharing things, even joyful things like 'I'm getting married.' I often feel confused about what I can say about challenges people have wrestled with. For instance, many years ago I revealed things to Hugh and Sirkka about David that Mom and Dad hadn't told them. It was a painful experience for Mom. I wasn't really thinking about who knew what. When I have to analyze what I should say or not say, I get paralyzed. I hate that, so my impulse is to say the hell with thinking about it. Everything should be public! No more secrets! I wonder if this influences what I'm doing in this memoir."

"It's a good thing to be aware of," she suggested. "Not that it's your only motivation. Part of you is enjoying having control of information. That can be for destructive reasons. I don't think it's a huge part of you, though."

"As a psychologist, do you see other things that would explain why I'm writing a family memoir? You were the most skeptical and critical of this project, at least a couple of years ago."

"Yes, and I still am."

"Because of the danger of hurting people?"

"Not just that. The whole Oprah, Jerry Springer thing. Going on stage to reveal dark secrets. That part of American culture is trashy."

When the Memoired Protest

I mused: "Am I feeding it and buying into it if I do this? Is memoir any different than so-called reality television?"

"Here's another memory," Blair offered. "When I first moved to Chicago, I had issues about wanting to get at the truth. I felt that Christmas letters offer a certain self-presentation that's very controlled. Yet I'm sure you wouldn't broadcast it if your child had a drug problem. About ten years ago Mom and Dad gave me that oval-shaped coffee table that used to be in the living room. It had a thick coat of varnish on it. I wanted to take it off and make it beautiful and see what was underneath. It ended up being a mistake because you had to treat the wood. I thought it had to be done right away and started, but it involved several more steps. It was all tied in with secrets and wanting to get at what was authentic."

"So cleaning the table stood for something?"

"Yes," she said, "for what I was doing in therapy, debunking the myths. The table stood around for a long time. Finally one Christmas, Randy and Alex put some finish on it and wrapped it up with a bow. It was very nice. He finished the job for me without even telling me. I couldn't do it myself. I couldn't get my act together."

"That story makes me wonder if I can do this. Do I need somebody else to take off the varnish? Perhaps a therapist. But then maybe I wouldn't need to write this. My interviewing family members is asking for help. Meg asked: 'Why are you writing about Blair, David, Uncle Hugh? Just say it yourself.' I'm getting there, to saying it myself, but I can't do it alone. I discover myself in my family. The table is a metaphor for that."

"How so?"

"First removing the veneer was important. That's what I'm doing to the family. Not because I don't love them. I love the wood, not the veneer."

"What's the veneer for you?"

"The sense that some things haven't been talked about. I don't want to blame this on anyone else. I haven't been able to talk about or even understand attitudes to money, sex, religion, values, other important stuff. To do that, I have to remove veneer. But I can't do it by myself. When you bring up the offices we played in, for example, that suddenly seems significant. I remember them, but until you said that I didn't see their significance in teaching us to respect boundaries. Self-knowledge is indirect, like therapy. You can't do the work alone."

"You need to be witnessed."

"This isn't the same as therapy, but it, too is a quest for self-knowledge that depends on the perspective of others. It involves self-recognition in the memories of others. There is a lot of theory behind this—ideas about ethics and autobiography—but what is important is the images, like the coffee table or those offices. That's how the mind works, with images that seem inexplicably significant."

"As long as you don't become too rigid in your interpretation of the images. It's not the truth, but the truth for you."

Christmas, 2009. Front row: Heather, Ian, Deane.
Back row: Tom, Alex, Reed, Meg, David, John, Graham, Blair

* * *

IN HER ART STUDIO in Atlanta in November 2003, Heather was showing me her work. When I told her I wanted to write a family memoir, she, too, asked: "Why don't you just write a novel?" She expressed her concern about vulnerable loved ones in a different way. She told me about a relative who made a video about his family that was very upsetting to them. "What was the issue," I asked, "the privacy of the family's struggles and conflicts?"

"More than that," she replied, "the right of people to speak for themselves."

Heather is very cautious about speaking of other people. When we were talking about how family members have experienced depression, at several points Heather abruptly cut the conversation off, saying: "I can't speak about someone else's experience." It wasn't just a matter of her not knowing, but a strong moral scruple about claiming to understand and describe another person.

When the Memoired Protest

With Heather's permission, I read all the letters that she wrote to Ian and Deane. I compared my own memories of her with those of Ian, Deane, Blair, and David. Everyone was very cautious to "avoid speaking for Heather"; they were so guarded that they almost wouldn't talk about her. In trying to respect one another's privacy, my family erects walls when other families would freely share information or speculate about each other. Sometimes I think we have too many barriers; at other times I think we are so cautious because we have no psychic boundaries at all and our identities are interfused.

My family understands and often practices a shared scruple about speaking of others. Deane often said that she would prefer that one of my siblings tell me something "in her own way." We don't gossip or speculate about each other much; we are usually vigilant about how words may misinterpret or harm other people. Yet I want to be able to share news or insights or concerns about family members, so I often feel uncertain and uneasy. No simple rules tell me what I can say or not say. Concern, anxiety, and confusion about this issue, more than any clear principle or rule, rule my conscience.

Heather and I discussed the secrecy connected with suicide. It was on a driving trip to Yellowstone Park when she was a teenager that Ian told Heather about her grandfather's suicide. Much later, in 2000, Heather was disturbed by the apparent suicide that year of a cousin whom I shall call Francis. She said to me: "Francis's alcoholism and depression was a secret. I met him only once, so I didn't really know him. There were many opportunities for a relative to tell me what he was struggling with. I don't understand why that was a secret, especially in our generation when people talk openly about depression and suicide. I thought our generation was going to be free of suicides. There are great possibilities to get help now. Francis's suicide was a rude awakening."

It's complicated and confusing: we want privacy for ourselves and to know about challenges family members are struggling with. Secrecy surrounding depression and attempted suicide isolates those who suffer these things and increases their misery. Yet the best alternative isn't to disclose someone's story. A person who has been through such an ordeal needs to be ready and willing to reveal this to others in their own way. Even if I sympathetically believe that some act or condition—for instance, sexual orientation, racial background, a medical problem, or suicide—is "nothing to be ashamed of," that does not give me the right to make this information public, to "out" a person against her will. The ideal of more open and honest acknowledgment of what society represses must be balanced against the right to privacy. This constraint limits my ability to describe how my

Family Conscience

grandfather's story and the afterlife of his suicide continues to reverberate in my family's history.

At what point does respecting a family member's privacy become harmful secrecy or denial of the truth? Secrets are usually seen as bad or questionable unless they are trivial or temporary, like a surprise party. In contrast, the right to privacy is essential to human dignity: we need to be free of intrusions and unwanted disclosures by others. I sometimes can't tell the difference between privacy and secrecy, and between justifiable and harmful instances of each. Yet when I make a mistake, conscience reproaches me: "You should have known better."

* * *

"Conscience" is a shorthand term that lumps together many kinds of self-scrutiny. As David and I talked in his apartment in Minneapolis in 2005, he emphasized not the guilty conscience but conscience at the moment of choosing: "How can I be the best person I can be right now? What's the best thing I can do now? What can I do now that I'll look back on in the future and think, I'm proud of that; I did some good. The power is all yours in the present, to either be the person you aspire to be or not." He linked this capacity to a Robert Burns poem, reading me these lines from "To a Louse":

> O wad some Pow'r the giftie gie us
> To see oursels as others see us
> It wad frae monie a blunder free us.

David asserted that conscience is a matter of intuitive certainty and self-confidence, yet he also wanted to be able to see himself as others see him so as to correct mistaken views. These ideas seem inconsistent, or at least in tension, but I agree. Although my conscience sometimes speaks with certainty, it is not infallible, and I need to be open to the challenges of others. When I think I'm doing the right thing, I might be mistaken. So being open to criticism and having the capacity to doubt one's convictions are as important as acting with confidence.

For David, "To a Louse" describes how the present moment offers the possibility of becoming the person you want to be. I resonated with Burns's poem for a different reason: "This is what I'm trying to do with this interview format and dialogue. I'm not just writing my memories of you; I'm trying to understand how you see things. And to see myself as others see me. Conscience can't be just my intuitive sense of what's right, or I'm in danger of being isolated, trapped in self-deception."

When the Memoired Protest

"Tape-recording a conversation raises other problems," he went on. "It falsifies a person's views by making appear dogmatic what are tentative attempts to interpret what one thinks. The problem with an interview like this is that it makes permanent things that were temporary. I might have changed my mind since the other day. But there it is in print: 'you said blah blah blah.' 'Well, I don't think that anymore.' 'Well, you said it.'"

I agreed: "I don't want my every word to be out there in stone forever. I know I try out ideas and think out loud. I may say something that expresses my mood at a moment, but I might not want to be held to that forever as my philosophy of life."

"Words take on a life of their own," he said. "A novelist writes a book and it's written. But I don't want to be represented by what I was in the past."

I can only honor that desire of David's by acknowledging it. I've represented his past at certain moments when what happened to David happened also to me, and his words when they suggest a truth more complex than I can state alone.

There is a striking parallel between David's concerns about this memoir and those of my parents. David cared most about how his spiritual guide is presented. He wanted to be sure that I describe him respectfully, fairly, and accurately. (I do not identify him or his movement.) My father's criticisms, when that same month I showed him drafts of several chapters of the manuscript, focused on how Deane was portrayed. My mother, in turn, was concerned about what she saw as misrepresentation of her parents. In each case, a family member expressed apprehension about my portrayal of someone else. It seemed like what I said about anybody upset someone else.

There isn't a clear line between characterizing an individual and depicting what he or she cares most about. Personal identity is not discrete, but extends to what one loves: those precious others with whom one's life is bound up and ideals such as honor, religious faith, and family loyalty. At one point my brother said to me: "You are describing my relationship to God." If this memoir is unfair to a person or to an ideal that David, Deane, or Ian cared about deeply, does it hurt them? It seems to me almost unavoidable that a person will object when I describe in my terms what they value most.

When we think about what is most intimate and makes us vulnerable, we think immediately of sex. Memoir writers and scholars of life writing, as much as the larger culture, have fixated on sexuality as the dark secret that must be exposed in autobiography. Yet many other private matters may make a person feel vulnerable if they are disclosed. What is more important and precious than what one believes is holy and ultimate, or the moral ideals one strives for? Yet for someone else to describe these in print risks oversimplification, even caricature.

Family Conscience

* * *

ONE FAMILY MEMBER QUESTIONED whether it misrepresents people today to characterize them by what they felt at some moment in the past, especially as revealed in an old document. She challenged my using an application to college: "This is a very specific kind of writing for a particular purpose. It can't be taken as indicative of who they are." I countered: "A college application is a self-representation for a certain audience. It's revealing."

"In how many families would this kind of document be very important?"

"I don't know," I said, "but the fact that I take them as significant shows something about my family and about me. How many families even bother to save these application essays for posterity?"

"I hope you won't use my college application in my funeral eulogy."

"I don't plan on it. I won't. But I wish I could see it. Do you still have it?"

She didn't.

She suggested alternative titles for this book: *Conscience Schmonscience*, *The Bleaker the Better*, and *Fuzzy Boundaries*.

I said I would try to incorporate her point of view into the manuscript, as I've often done when confronted by other criticisms. Contrasting points of view on the ethical issues in writing memoir will enrich the total narrative, I asserted. But she challenged this strategy, too:

"You use people's responses to your drafts as additional material. They don't know that you are going to show their objections to what you wrote as indications of their character. For you, everything is fair game; it all becomes grist for your mill."

"Why is that unfair? It shows something about that person's conscience and about mine."

"It makes people look like they are most concerned about how they come off to others. I also think it's deceptive for you to tell people at the outset that you are going to fix the manuscript so that everyone is happy. You imply that they have veto power to reassure them at the interview stage. But you may or may not use their suggestions and reactions."

"I have final control; I can't give that up and still put this damn thing together. Maybe I should give everyone the chance to respond in writing to the final manuscript and include that as an appendix. How about if you write an afterword?"

She laughed. "It's like a trained boxer inviting someone into the ring and saying: 'This is your chance for a fair fight.' It's all finally on your terms, under your conditions, but it isn't clear to others what the rules are. You didn't know what you were doing when you started, and you are still figuring it out. But as the writer you always appear in control. You will always have the last word."

* * *

IN THE SUMMER OF 2004, I showed Ian and Deane the first drafts of chapters about them and their parents. Deane's initial response was highly critical, on several grounds:

> I'm most disturbed about how you present my mother. This isn't my Mom. When you described the incidents when she called me Honor, and when she was so careful about what people say in print, you made her sound cold and manipulative. She was warm and generous. You would need to read her letters to understand her better.
> I don't want our family to be the doomed House of Atreus.
> I don't think this writing is as good as your scholarly work. You have fictionalized and made more dramatic certain incidents. You need to be very careful when you use quotation marks. Dorothy Barbour misrepresented what people had said to try to influence others. The criteria of scholarly writing are relevant. It is important to labor over the exact word.
> I'm concerned about your publishing some of this material. Some of the things I told you I haven't discussed with even my sister or brother. This will be a strange way for them to find out. Can you explore these issues in other ways, for instance psychotherapy or prayer? Writing is so public.
> I ache to think of the pain my 'grayness' brought to others and to you. For instance, that time when you run through the room while I am crying, and you learn that you have to be cautious. No apology from me can make up for that. Someone once said a mother's first duty is to be happy. I don't know. I wonder if when my children were young, I should have said: Some people are so unhappy that they don't want to be in the world anymore. Your grandfather was like that. And sometimes it makes me sad.

That was a painful time for both of us. Deane reached out to me, we talked more, and she affirmed the memoir's value, at least for me. I think she saw it as self-therapy, not a book.

Ian objected to the way the first draft characterized Deane: "You show her as traumatized by her father's suicide. That's important but it's not the whole story, or even what's most important. You show her as a child more

Family Conscience

than an adult. You might read the letters she wrote from our work camp in Germany in 1948. Deane was from the South, yet she criticized the racial values she grew up with. She moved out of a co-op in Philadelphia to live with a woman who had been kicked out. Deane's conscience has always been expressed in her concern for individuals rather than in political causes."

My father thought that in reacting to family secrets, I went too far and did not acknowledge the legitimate need for privacy. In 2004, he questioned whether my writing should be showed beyond the immediate family:

> "Family secrets" and reluctance to discuss some events in the past have indeed been a destructive influence in our lives. But I believe there is a legitimate place for *privacy* when a person might be hurt by a written record even when it is read only within the family. You yourself evidently did not want to give any details of your depression and thoughts of suicide in 1989, and you are reluctant to write about your own children. David has told me many things about his life which I have kept in confidence (even from Deane, in some instances); he can of course tell you whatever he wishes in an interview. I can see risks even in what you have already written, since it seems to portray our lives as a protracted response to suicide. Is this the picture we want to convey to other family members? The risks seem to me greater when you start writing about your siblings.
>
> My own tentative conclusion is that the benefits outweigh the risks for *family circulation* of a (revised) version of the chapters written so far, and perhaps of chapters on your siblings (especially if they could each review the sections on themselves before circulation to others). But I am dubious, as I think you are, about sharing with the family your understanding of your boys and the role of conscience in their lives. Revision for *publication* at a later date raises more difficult ethical dilemmas. The *risks* would be greater than those above because all our foibles would be displayed before a wider public. The *benefits* would also be greater because other people could learn from your insights.

After I revised and expanded the chapter on Deane, Ian said he thought the portrait was fair. He wrote in January 2005: "I can begin to think of myself as a character in a book! I am less worried about invasions of privacy because you are making revisions after showing drafts to each of the people involved, and you have specifically discussed the privacy issue at several points."

Ian had a fairly thick skin and wanted to be supportive. Although he was very concerned about others, he didn't seem to feel any need to keep his own life private. I worried less about hurting him than anyone in my family. When I asked whether I could publish everything he had said in our recorded interview, he responded: "Yes. I don't mind being portrayed as not a very good model." That remark, showing his humility and openness to criticism, shows one reason why for me, he is a very good model.

* * *

THE FIRST TIME I presented this material outside the family was at Indiana University in March 2005. I procrastinated on asking Deane, then called her the night before I left to say that I would be reading from the chapter about her. "I guess I'm sort of asking permission," I said, but it was ambiguous whether I was requesting that or announcing what I would do. This was months after I had accepted the invitation.

Deane responded: "I trust you. I trust what you will do with what I told you." Does that statement give me the right to do whatever I want with her oral and written stories? She did not reveal how difficult it was for her to have her story made public. I took for granted that she would make any sacrifice for me.

In "Other People's Secrets," Patricia Hampl describes how her poetry revealed her mother's epilepsy, which had been a family secret for many years.[2] In Hampl's mind, she was setting her mother free, liberating her from a prison of silence. Much later, she realized that her mother had given a reluctant and half-hearted permission to publish because she loved her daughter. Similarly, my mother's permission or acquiescence was based on her wish to be supportive of a project she knew was important to me. Did I exploit her capacity for self-sacrifice? Was a hard-won, uneasy permission really a protest? How articulate and assertive does an objection have to be for me to revise my writing—or not publish it?

Writers of memoir often acknowledge that their family is not entirely pleased with the ways in which they are represented. In *Dreams from My Father*, Barak Obama writes of his family that "without their willingness to let me sing their song and their toleration of the occasional wrong note, I could never have hoped to finish."[3] Mary Karr thanks her mother for support in writing *The Liars' Club*: "She has been unreserved in her

---

2. Patricia Hampl, "Other People's Secrets," in *I Could Tell You Stories: Sojourns in the Land of Memory* (New York: Norton, 2000), 208–30.

3. Barak Obama, *Dreams from My Father* (New York: Three Rivers, 1995), xvii.

Family Conscience

encouragement of this work, though much in the story pains her."[4] Mothers especially are recognized as having sacrificed so that their ambitious offspring may publish a book.

Many outstanding autobiographical works would not have seen the light if the writers were as scrupulous or reserved as their families would prefer. Maxine Hong Kingston's *The Woman Warrior*, the book that drew me into the study of family memoirs, begins with her mother telling her: "You must not tell anyone what I am about to tell you. In China your father had a sister who killed herself. She jumped into the family well."[5] Kingston's story begins with, indeed seems impelled by, a prohibition of discussing a family suicide. In my case, it was a conspiracy of silence about Everett's death that drew me into family history. If writers heeded their families' injunctions to silence, there would be few autobiographies that courageously explore life's difficulties and problems, which is the main reason I admire and want to read this kind of writing. I'm grateful for writers who share their experience even when it may threaten or hurt members of their family. They witness to truths about their lives that help me understand mine or enrich my perspective.

I resolved my doubts by deciding that including my mother's reactions would reveal a lot about my family, myself, and the moral issues at stake in family memoir.

* * *

UNCLE CHARLES WAS MY mother's brother. He was a large-hearted, kind, and generous person with a wide-ranging intellect and keen interests in other people and the history of our family and country. He took me to a Joni Mitchell concert in a tiny nightclub when I was sixteen. Twice he put me up when I went to antiwar demonstrations in Washington, DC.

I sent Charlie the chapters on Deane and her parents in 2005. He did not respond. A year later, guessing that the manuscript must have been upsetting, I went to see him. As we sat together in his basement lair, Charlie said about many passages: "You have no evidence about this. There's no paper trail. It's all speculation." He dismissed many things that were either plausible interpretations or incontrovertible facts, including the newspaper stories about Everett's suicide. I asked him: "Well, why do you think Everett died?"

"I have no idea. I'm not interested in the past but in my family now."

---

4. Mary Karr, *The Liars' Club* (New York: Penguin, 1995), xx.

5. Maxine Hong Kingston, *The Woman Warrior: Memories of a Girlhood among Ghosts* (New York: Knopf, 1976), 3.

"I can't help being interested. He was my grandfather. How can I not try to understand, even if that means speculating? But maybe my interpretation is wrong. I would really like to have my perspective balanced by yours."

"I want nothing to do with your project," said Charlie. "Take my name out of it."

"I'm sorry I can't describe your angle on the family, which shows another view and another kind of response to the past."

"Why are you so obsessed with the past? I sense only hostility to your grandfather, not forgiveness. Why are you writing, anyway? Is this for yourself?"

"Absolutely. I need to understand my family to understand myself."

"Well, it's self-serving. And now you have become a radioactive property to your family."

I left, amazed and shaken, but confirmed in my belief that our family's story matters. Or rather, our conflicting family stories. Charlie came to terms with Everett's death in a very different way than I did and saw my writing as dishonoring my grandparents. I believe that I honor them by understanding and portraying their struggles. I changed some things in the manuscript to respect Charlie's wish for privacy. I describe this much of his reaction to show his very different view of family history and our moral obligations to the dead and the living. Our conflicting beliefs led to a painful estrangement.

Now, too late to express it to him, I feel compassion for my uncle, who was three when his father took his own life. His way of honoring and loving Everett was to idealize him and preserve that image. Charlie became a sort of curator of his mother's home and furnishings after her sudden death, and this led to painful feelings and conflicts with his two sisters. One of Charlie's children, my cousin, expressed a keen insight in an email: "I am sorry that he was not more generous in the 1960s–80s (and beyond?) in sharing lovingly and equitably sentimental items that meant a lot to Deane and Winn, including a childhood bed. I suspect, but can't be sure, that his own grief led him to build an untouchable sanctuary frozen in time, with things exactly as his mom had left them." Charlie also hoarded the written record, refusing to share even copies of letters his parents had written. His way of honoring his parents led to denial of the truth and possessive ownership not only of things, but of family history.

At a memorial service on the Zoom platform in 2021, many people spoke of Charlie's impish humor, warm and gracious hospitality, empathetic interest in other people and cultures, and love of family. I feel very sad that we were never reconciled. When neither of us could compromise values that were crucial to our sense of integrity and identity, our differing versions of family conscience created a painful estrangement.

* * *

THERE ARE MANY STEPS in between complete privacy and book publication, such as sharing a manuscript with family members, friends, academic colleagues, other writers, or editors. I can discuss a work in progress, read part of it out loud, or send it as a text not to be quoted. Sometimes I didn't ask permission from everyone in the family when I sent out a manuscript. One person gave permission for me to share the manuscript with anyone but later revoked that permission after I sent it to Hugh and his family. I recalled the manuscript. Imagining specific individuals reading about one's life can be harder than conjuring up a vague general audience. There are many layers of privacy and secrecy within a family, creating uncertainties about who does or should know what.

As I weighed my scruples about harming family members, I could find no clear way forward. I decided to seek other writers' wisdom by sending them manuscripts while I remained undecided about publication. The reactions from people outside the family were very different from those within it. In July of 2006 and 2007, I went to workshops for creative writers at the Collegeville Institute at St. John's University in Minnesota. Poets and prose writers discussed each other's manuscripts with an inspiring teacher, Michael Dennis Browne. Along with positive feedback, they also made me doubt what I am doing, but for different reasons than my worries about family privacy. Michael's first statement to the class: "Most writing is done for the approval of others, not to get at the truth."

This group was impatient with my worrying in print about the ethics of memoir. They shared these criticisms: "You care too much about your family's reaction. You are too cautious; you have to let go, follow your imagination."

"The writing is so self-conscious that I don't ever find out who your sister is."

"I'm more interested in you, the writer, than in your family, but I'm interested in your heart, not your integrity or virtue."

"I don't need to read about your reservations. If you always tell us what you don't know or won't discuss, the reader won't trust you. Quit apologizing and get on with the story."

"A memoir is a work of art, not oral history. Conversations need more shaping and editing."

When the Memoired Protest

"Does a memoir have an obligation to be fair? Does a poem? Does a symphony? What does it mean to be fair to the demands of the work?"

These creative writers emphasized that a memoir has a different kind of truth than can be checked or confirmed by others. They said I should just write my story and decide later about the ethics of publishing. More than this: they implied that my concern with the ethics of memoir was operating as a censor or superego that stifled the impulse to write freely, go deep, and express difficult truths. They urged me to forget about conscience.

Several authors of memoirs advised me: "Don't ask for permission; ask forgiveness later, if necessary." Another counseled: "It's your story, after all. They can write their own memoirs if they wish." My practice of submitting drafts to family members for approval seemed to these writers to be wrongheaded and crippling because it inhibits the kind of courageous truth-telling that is indispensable in memoir. Several people predicted: "They'll get over it. Write what you have to write."

By this point, the process of writing a memoir had become not only a troubling issue for my conscience, but the central story of my life. Describing it threatened to displace any narrative that most readers could be expected to care about. Where's the sex? Where's the violence? Who wants to read a book about a guy trying to write a book?

Academic readers had different questions. In Hawaii in 2005 I presented some of my writing about my brother to fellow scholars of autobiography. John Eakin asked: "Is this a life writing project or a religious studies project? Can you do both at once?"

Roger Porter said: "Your parents don't drive you crazy enough! There is emotional blackmail going on in your family, and you identify with your brother because you resent the ways conscience controls you."

Craig Howes noticed that the early version of the memoir had the same structure as my scholarly works: each chapter analyzed one family member in terms of a central theme. "But what happens when you read your family members as texts illustrating an idea?"

Margaretta Jolly understood that an eldest child who follows in parental footsteps has complicated relationships with siblings. She advised: "You need a story as well as analysis. Show, don't tell. Your brother has a story in his early life: conversion. What is your story? Is being a witness of others an action?"

Tom Couser affirmed that an academic's life can be interesting to academics, but wondered: "Is it also interesting to others?"

Tom's writing about "vulnerable subjects" explores how life writing exposes others to harm or hurt that may or may not be ethically defensible. In discussing how obligations to deceased family members are different from those to the living, he asserts that death "entails maximum vulnerability to posthumous misrepresentation because it precludes self-defense."[6] Another scholar challenged that claim: "The idea of posthumous harm does not make sense. The dead belong to the living."

What good can come from exposing living family members to possible violations of privacy? There may be potential benefits for me in the form of self-expression and recognition beyond my family. I may find healing in coming to terms with old wounds. I want to record the history of my family for truth's sake, and because I love, honor, and value these individuals in their precious singularity. I need not portray them as flawless saints; their lives are more complex and interesting than that. Some readers may recognize that my family's story illuminates how conscience shapes their own story. Readers may feel connection, companionship, or solidarity with an author whose life involves similar challenges, uncertainties, and consolations. These possible beneficial outcomes must be weighed against the dangers of exploiting vulnerable family members. "First of all, do no harm" is one moral guideline for memoir writing. How to weigh that principle in the balance with other values at stake in writing a family memoir has preoccupied, distressed, and fascinated me.

* * *

DISCOURAGED BY THE OBJECTIONS of my siblings and spouse, I set the manuscript aside in September 2007. I tried to forget about it, but it wouldn't go away. I felt increasingly depressed. Two years later, I started revising it, trying to make the narrative more autobiographical and less biographical. The thought of publishing this memoir filled me with anxiety about hurting family members, but to abandon it brought frustration and gloom. I felt caught in an enormous spider web, held in bondage by invisible fragments.

I sought psychotherapy. Peter, the therapist, had a bookcase displaying the collected works of Freud and no other books. He asked: "Why have you placed yourself in the position of needing to get the permission of others? You have put yourself and your family in a torture chamber." His diagnosis: not depression but anxiety. I'm afraid to lose the love of my family, and that paralyzes me.

---

6. G. Thomas Couser, *Vulnerable Subjects: Ethics and Life Writing* (Ithaca: Cornell University Press, 2003), 16. Other scholarly works that influence my thinking about the ethics of memoir include Paul John Eakin, ed., *The Ethics of Life Writing* (Ithaca: Cornell University Press, 2004); David Parker, *The Self in Moral Space: Life Narrative and the Good* (Ithaca: Cornell University Press, 2007); and Helena de Bres, *Artful Truths: The Philosophy of Memoir* (Chicago: University of Chicago Press, 2021).

When the Memoired Protest

He was keen to get me to acknowledge "murderous rage" at my family. "Hmm," I fumbled. "Um, that seems a bit strong. I'm frustrated, maybe a little bit angry with them. But I'm more the suicidal type than a murderer."

"Suicide is a form of revenge," Peter countered. "You imagine them finding your body. Maybe this whole memoir project is a way of expressing anger or getting power over your family."

I can't know my unconscious motivations, but I've considered what they might be. I may be trying to compete with my father by writing a book that he would never write. I may have been trying to make my mother choose to support me in a conflict with my siblings. Perhaps I was unconsciously trying to destroy my marriage. Maybe, may be, maybe. Speculation about unknowable motives is interesting, but a black hole, and it doesn't help me decide what to do. For that, conscious intentions are more important, as well as trying to foresee the consequences of my actions.

My intentions reflect two conflicting values. I want to protect vulnerable loved ones and to portray a moral inheritance that I believe is significant in and beyond my family. I feel a moral obligation not to harm family members and also a desire to make something of my experience: to learn from it, express myself, and share things that might help someone else make sense of their life.

* * *

AFTER I SUBMITTED MY manuscript to an editor interested in it, other people raised objections I hadn't considered. One issue concerns the dangers of publication in the age of search engines. "F" had "parked" a personal journal in an online storage space that was indexed by Google. According to F, any document that is not explicitly hidden is fair game for Google's web-crawling search engines, which are programmed to seek out every item not walled off. F received an email from a friend, saying that when anyone googled her name, a link to F's journal came up. The journal entries were not flattering, and the friend was understandably upset. After considerable effort, F persuaded Google to delete the page from its index. This incident permanently damaged F's relationship with the friend.

A memoir may become evidence used against anyone working for a company or institution that monitors its employees. Everything that "Y" writes, including email, is accessible to corporate network security; the company automatically monitors computer use and fires people based on this surveillance. While companies give lip service to tolerance for diversity, Y asserts that this is hypocritical; in actuality, prejudice is rampant. Someone in a present or future workplace could innocently or purposefully google Y's name. A coworker, manager, or potential employer could have instant online access to intimate details revealed in a memoir. According to Y, survival in the business world is related to anonymity.

My first reaction to these objections was to think that Y is paranoid and these are not realistic possibilities. But I was ensconced in a cozy tenured position in a stable educational institution. Most people are far more vulnerable to losing their jobs for reasons that are often difficult to understand and entangled in complicated workplace relationships and rivalries.

Disguising the names of family members can minimize the dangers of search-engines digging for dirt. Yet often it would not be difficult detective work to link a story to an identifiable person. There is also the audience of people who know my family, especially in the town where I grew up. I can't describe how other lives influenced mine without giving details that identify them to people who know our family.

"Who cares what people think?" This is easy to say when it is not my private life that is displayed. But it does matter. In interpreting how my sister's family background shaped her understanding of her vocation as a therapist, I quoted her description of her work. Blair didn't like being quoted in this way, for although I rendered her words accurately, the quotation nevertheless simplified into a few sentences wisdom gleaned from many decades. Trying to be empathetic, I imagine how I would react if I had to give my philosophy of teaching or scholarly writing in a nutshell. I would likely cringe if this statement appeared in print; I would want to qualify and explain what I meant about an endeavor so important and complex. In the case of my sister, a published remark about psychotherapy might also affect her ability to attract new clients or be hired by an employer. I deleted references to relatives' workplaces, though I've described—too briefly—their sense of vocation insofar as I see a connection to conscience.

"T" was a victim of sexual abuse as a child. When the abuser was arrested, the police asked former victims to come forth. Although the statute of limitations had passed and T could not testify in court, T's evidence supported the credibility of the young person making the accusation, helping prosecutors to decide whether to press charges against the alleged abuser. Had T been in slightly different circumstances and directly involved in a trial, it is not hard to imagine a defense attorney trying to discredit T's testimony by researching what can be known about T. A memoir that explores psychological problems, trauma, or relationships could be used to damage T's testimony. Even membership in a little-known political or religious group could be presented in a way that would undermine T's credibility and subject T to painful scrutiny. A public record of someone's past is potential evidence to discredit testimony in a legal case.

When the Memoired Protest

The most pointed protest of my memoir took the form of a satire "Q" wrote and sent to me. It was a fictional book review of Q's imaginary memoir, which was entitled "Skeletons in Our Closet." The book depicted my family as dysfunctional and a shameful incident in my past. When the fictional book reviewer asks Q about the ethics of the memoir, Q responds with words that echo my own assertions: "The events of a person's life do not just occur to that person but have a profound effect upon the entire family. Readers may benefit from understanding our family." Q claims to have analyzed the ethics of the project, asked the most difficult questions, and spent sleepless nights pondering these matters from all sides. This fake book review made me cringe. My ethical arguments didn't seem as convincing to me when what was revealed was my own secrets. This satire helped me to imagine what it would be like to be one of the "memoired," whose intimate life is revealed in someone else's published work, however high-minded the author's intention or potentially valuable for other readers.

None of the readers of my manuscript from outside the family thought that I was being malicious, settling old scores, or revealing things that I shouldn't. But many family members, especially those in my generation, were very upset. I may think their need for privacy is excessive, their desire to control information obsessive, or their skin too thin, but they are my family, the only one I've got, and I'll be interacting with them long after anything I write will be forgotten by a shadowy audience of unknown readers.

I try not to confess the sins of others or expose their failures to practice what they preach. A cousin told me: "The key to making a memoir is that you have to be willing to make yourself look like an ass. If you make somebody else look bad, you must make yourself look worse." Yet even when I tried to do this, some members of my family saw me as judging them. For instance, when I mentioned one person's alternative title for this book—*Conscience Schmonscience*—I was admitting that not everyone in my family takes an exalted view of my capacity for virtue and truthfulness. This person was angry because she thought quoting her remark portrayed her as unsupportive and critical.

Even when I state the objections of the memoired to what I've written, trying my hardest to render their perspectives accurately and fairly, I represent and simplify them. How should I respond to their protests if they are not to be either dismissed or allowed to paralyze writing?

* * *

In 2010 I put an earlier version of this manuscript in a cardboard box in a closet. I decided that I could not publish a family memoir without permanently damaging my relationships with my siblings and spouse. At the suggestions of my brother, several memoir writers, and fellow scholars of autobiography, I wrote a fictional version of one part my story. As I said in the Author's Note and Acknowledgments in *Renunciation: A Novel*, I transformed the raw materials of my experience into a story true only in imagination.[7] This fiction described the relationship between two brothers, one of whom, Will, converts to Bhakti Dharma, a new religious movement influenced by Hinduism and Sikh tradition. My portrayal of this group was based on my knowledge of 3HO, the group following Yogi Bhajan with which I was involved in 1973. The story is narrated by Peter, Will's older brother, who is a graduate student at the University of Chicago Divinity School. The novel's central theme of renunciation is directly connected to conscience. Peter studies early Christian asceticism partly to try to understand why Will's religious devotion drives him to acts of fierce mortification and self-punishment. Peter sees the desire to overcome self as highly ambiguous, revealing yearnings for service, sacrifice, and devotion and also dangerous and self-destructive urges. Although most of the situations and incidents depicted in the novel are fictional, the emotional heart of the novel comes directly from my own life: the charged relationship of two brothers who are estranged partly because of their very different religious orientations.

My father had advised me that to understand my mother's conscience I should read her journal from the 1948 German work camps. I got more and more interested in this document and its historical context. Bolstered by the encouragement and boundless enthusiasm of Yogi Reppman, a German historian I met at my father's funeral, in 2016 we coedited and published *Toiling with the Defeated: American Diaries from the Ruins of World War II; Deane and Ian Barbour in Hamburg and Münster, 1948*.[8] I wanted this book to honor my parents and show their ethical and religious perspective, and it did not explore the darker aspects of conscience.

In 2019 my thoughts returned to the abandoned family memoir project. I told myself that I would focus only on my grandparents and parents and leave out living relatives. With that limitation in mind, I made research trips to Yale University's Divinity School Library, the University of Cincinnati Library, and The Imperial War Museum. I read through several cartons of family papers that came to me after my parents died. When my uncles and aunt died, I felt freer to discuss previous generations.

7. John D. Barbour, *Renunciation: A Novel* (Eugene, OR: Resource Publications, 2013), xi.

8. John D. Barbour and Joachim Reppmann, eds., *Toiling with the Defeated: American Diaries from the Ruins of WWII: Deane and Ian Barbour in Hamburg and Münster, 1948* (Northfield, MN: Stoltenberg Institute, 2016), printed and distributed by LuLu.com and available on Amazon.com.

I had given myself permission to write about my ancestors, but a fundamental question haunted me. Why do these dead people matter? I couldn't explore that topic without interpreting at least some of their ongoing influence on later generations. As I put together a new version of family history, I tried to limit discussion of living relatives to depicting how certain patterns and preoccupations continue and how individuals responded in different ways to our moral inheritance. The compromises that limit full disclosure of family history veil certain kinds of truth. Yet telling this story of the story discloses other truths about the workings of conscience in my family.

There is no single understanding of conscience among us, but rather ongoing dialogue and debate about certain recurring questions. I see family resemblances, not identical portraits. We don't sing the same song, but certain motifs are repeated. Our disagreements and dialogues about the ethics of life writing show not settled conclusions but conscience at work on a recurring issue in my family's history: how to balance and reconcile openness and truth with respect for privacy and boundaries.

Epilogue
Who Is Speaking?

So everything is wrapped up and tidy? Are you feeling swell about yourself, virtuous and smug? Think again. We're not done here. You shut up now, and I'll do the talking. I will interrogate, accuse, or let you off the hook—for a while.

You started with Everett and your relationship to Deane. Ian's side, the Barbour story, had always been told and celebrated publicly. There was no mystery in that story, it seemed at first, and no reason to write about it. The secret that you needed to understand was Everett's tragic death and the destructive afterlife of suicide. You had to transgress a taboo to exorcize his ghost. Then you could see another side of his legacy as a positive influence on Deane and your family.

Deane's sensitive conscience was at once a source of her goodness and a cause of suffering. Ian's rational and intellectual approach to life is a bequest that both empowers and limits you. Each parent is more complex than you realized: each made conscientious moral judgments and was shaped by obscure influences and needs. You are all swayed by a family conscience that is sometimes stronger than conscious deliberations. It runs in the family; it has a will of its own. A family conscience knits you all together even as you each try to loosen the fabric, create some breathing room, find the right distance.

Do I make you conscientious and responsible or drive you crazy? Are my unrelenting demands a sign of moral seriousness and integrity or neurotic, narcissistic perfectionism?

You try to break out of the family, at least enough to see it from a detached perspective. You disclose family secrets, violate others' privacy, and probe the limits of rational deliberation and your academic,

Epilogue

intellectual perspective. In the old days, when David, Blair, and Heather struggled with their relationships to the family, you thought that if they were as independent and disengaged as you were, they could get on with their adult lives. They simply broke away before you did. Your memoir is a long-delayed adolescent rebellion, a feeble attempt to bust loose. At the same time, it is an act of filial piety, a ritual commemoration of ancestors. Although Dorothy would have expected something more purely celebratory, she would approve.

When you began this project, your sons were leaving home, both emotionally and geographically. They wanted out. You grieved the loss of intimacy you had with them when they were children; you didn't want to let them go. You wanted to hold on to Graham and Reed, yet you knew that they must find their own ways in the world, make their own decisions. From their moral inheritance, they will choose what to keep. As they departed, you wondered how you influenced them, and that was another catalyst for writing a memoir.

You think about how you did as a son, sibling, spouse, and father. Maybe you seek forgiveness, a later-day John Bunyan who hopes salvation will come to a confessed sinner. You do what you wish Ian or Deane hadn't done: kick yourself for missed opportunities to have done better. Ian called it regret, not guilt, but you can't tell the difference. Don't get stuck in useless remorse but learn something and move on. You can't listen to another person while you are arguing with me.

You want intimacy and also to disengage, to be apart from others but able to return. That is why you wrote a book about solitude, too. You want to be alone, but not too alone. You want a conscience that is independent, yet responsible to others and part of a community.

Your portrayal of conscience leaves out so much, even given your focus on the family. You don't say much about experiences with friends, teachers, students, or ministers. Or how girlfriends, marriage, and sexuality trigger deep feelings and judgments about right and wrong, shame and joy, what you do and don't do. You seem only fitfully aware of political events and issues such as the Vietnam War, racism, the women's movement, poverty, and the environmental crisis. What will your trivial ponderings matter in the long run? The things that you obsess about display the privilege of a certain economic class and social position: you have the luxury to worry about nuances of family relationships while

Family Conscience

ignoring the crucial moral challenges of your era. Your scruples reflect a peculiar and myopic sense of how people are harmed.

Most of what you show about conscience is its negative side: how it curtails passion and enthusiasm, worries about trivia, or inflicts guilt and shame. According to you, I keep you confined in a cramped cell, gnawing on those bits of bone, your scruples. There is a more positive understanding of conscience, as Ian, David, and Graham point out. What about the joy of doing good, as opposed to the duty of doing the right thing or fear of harming others? Looking to the future, I can be affirmative and exuberant. I live in you as generosity and striving for justice; I call you to commitment, vocation, and love. I invite you to heed the call of the other, and sometimes the Other, God. My tests and challenges offer the possibility of clarity and integrity, so that you can live and act with confidence and enthusiasm. Sometimes I speak with passionate intensity. Yet sooner or later, you feel the uneasiness of skepticism and doubt, like the slight touch of a knife's edge, reminding you not to move too quickly or carelessly. You never forget the dark side of anything, including me. To see only the happy and optimistic side of conscience would leave out the conflict and struggle of the moral life.

Still, there is too much self-punishment here, as if making yourself miserable were proof of a serious conscience. As if a furrowed brow justifies whatever decision you make or atones for mistakes. You're like the prisoner who pleads, "Sure, I killed the guy. But he's dead now. I have to live with myself! So let me go!"

A friend of yours asked: "Do you have a free conscience or a conflicted conscience?"

You replied: "Why would anyone whose conscience was light write endlessly about this topic?"

"Yes, of course," she said. "What is it with you Protestants? You are supposed to be free of guilt and to live by grace, but you are burdened with a heavy conscience. Luther said we Catholics are preoccupied with works and anxious about their value, but we are free of your problem. When I go to confession, I come out clean. It's like magic. I don't obsess."

In you dwells the Protestant need to confess sins outside the confessional. This impulse can lead to egotistical self-indulgence, to honest disclosure, or to both at once, hopelessly entangled.

Your emphasis on the guilty, backward-looking conscience reflects the Protestant notion of salvation by grace; you need to repeat ritually

Epilogue

the recognition of sin that precedes turning to God. But you're like Rousseau: although he wanted the guilty pleasure of confessing, he chose trivialities and kept silent about more important matters, such as abandoning six children.

All this fussing and fretting is Protestant angst, and it's just human. Every religious tradition and community has yea-sayers and naysayers. Those who look hopefully to the future and those who linger regretfully over the past. Careful thinkers and exuberant lovers. Big-picture dreamers and nitpickers. There is a larger human conscience beyond your family and your religion, a gift and curse of evolution.

Some people think that guilt is useless, wasted energy, water over the dam. With Nietzsche, they reject regret, want life to be all affirmation and celebration, and see conscience as a killjoy. Granted, you could lighten up a little. But they protest too much. It is a fantasy to think you should live without looking back and sorting out what you affirm and what you would have done differently. For you, to regret nothing would mean to forget what you learned the hard way.

Nietzsche asserts that you should affirm your fate, whatever it is. He said that a test of character is whether a person would choose to live his life repeatedly forever. Well, you could walk down your road ten thousand times, and always you will end up here, listening to me and wondering if I'm right. Don't lament my role in your life. We were made for each other. You don't need to work so hard at reconstructing events or trying to be right. I'll do it for you. Relax. Let me carry your burden. Regret nothing. I'll do it for you.

Part of a memoir's truth can be checked or confirmed by others and some cannot. You hoped to discover yourself outside yourself, as if documents and family members' words were a mirror. But the deepest truths lie inside. You haven't gotten there yet. You can't discover yourself by analyzing ancestors, siblings, or that boogieman called family conscience, if there is such a thing.

You try to resist the temptation to confess the sins of others or expose their inconsistencies and flaws. So it's not just about yourself that you withhold crucial information. You don't show anyone else's hypocrisy or rationalization, which reveal so much about conscience. You protect others and caricature yourself as a neurotic worrywart, but you don't tell the whole truth about anyone. Your cousin said that when you make someone else look bad in a memoir, you must make yourself look worse.

Family Conscience

If you have to do that, how truthful can you really be? Admit it: you are performing for an audience. You aren't really this obsessed with picking at your scabs. Most of the time you don't even listen to me.

When you sought the approval of family members, was it because of genuine moral concern or just anxiety masked as a scruple? You are still walking on eggshells, wanting to please others, but you can't write a book using the Quaker method of consensus. You sacrificed a lot of your own truth by trying to satisfy everyone in your family. You need to be careful, because representing people is a form of power. But the individuals in your family are stronger than you give them credit for. Protecting others can be an excuse for not going deeper and a failure of courage. And scruples about writing aren't much of a story.

People get pissed off when you talk about conscience. They see you as smug, self-righteous, or judgmental. You have seen similar reactions outside your family, for instance in the battles of college faculty when disagreements about the curriculum or hiring for a new position create moral rhetoric worthy of a noble crusade and then a backlash of disdainful cynicism. Appeals to high-minded principles, virtue, or conscience often trigger not just disagreement, but outrage based on knowledge of the speaker's flaws. Sometimes, too, people get angry or defensive because of what is triggered in their own conscience.

You experienced the anger and hurt of people who felt caricatured or disfigured. A memoir claims to tell the truth but reduces others' lives to a few incidents. It diminishes the complexity, richness, and depth of lived experience. Writing about other people inevitably distorts them, no matter how much you try to be fair or careful. You aren't writing a family memoir, but a disguised autobiography. Other people are bit players in your drama or ghosts in your personal myth about the family, assigned roles they did not choose. No wonder they get angry.

The literary form of your memoir is ambiguous, even duplicitous. You tried to be fair to others by quoting their own words, using documents and tape-recorded interviews, and asking them to respond to drafts. On the surface you are deferential to others and often give them the last word. The underlying truth is the egotism of autobiography and the struggle for power within the family. You don't really want to get across others' perspectives, but rather to show yourself as concerned about their feelings. You are always in control, and even your self-criticisms, like this one, are a way to beat the reader to the punch.

Epilogue

You lurk behind the stories of others, so your creepy consciousness pervades the whole book. A ventriloquist speaks through everyone in your family. You hide behind the roles of interviewer, editor, and biographer. It's hard to use the first person, isn't it, when a bossy superego tells you to suppress your ego? "Down, Vanity!" This suppression is the source of your writing, for your ego disguises itself and comes out dressed up in others' words. A family memoir is a game of hide-and-seek.

Admit that this ploy—ending with my speaking to you in the second person, mostly asking questions—is an elaborate way of avoiding the truth that you have no story of your own and can't come to a conclusion about anything.

Where has the writing of this book taken you? You are still searching for the truth. Are you finally at peace? You think you have greater clarity about your family's problems and gifts and a firmer sense of who you are. On certain days, you are more comfortable in your skin, serene about your family's legacy, and confidant about what you choose to disclose and withhold. You think you passed my little tests with flying colors. Don't get too comfortable, laddie. A cheerful or quiet conscience may just be asleep or dormant. Give up on trying to portray the right kind of conscience, whatever that would mean, and yourself as having finally arrived there. That literary project, as well as that kind of life, is an exercise in self-justification and self-congratulation.

You would like to nail me down, put me in a box, come up with a theory to explain me. But I elude that effort, I'm too many things, and I'm free. I'm your father's rationality and logic, your mother's intuition and imagination. I echo your Puritan ancestors, the doubts of skeptics and agnostics, and Buddhist insights. I demand that you speak the truth boldly and then warn you to be careful you don't hurt anybody. I tell you to break away from others, take responsibility, and stand on your own feet. Yet you are made of bits and pieces of the people, books, and communities you've known, all jumbled together and arguing with each other, with no one in charge. It would be nice to have a theory that would make me more predictable and manageable. But I say what I damn well please.

Often you know me as a stab, a gnawing sensation, a heavy burden, or paralyzing self-doubt. These things are not me but your symptoms, your reaction to my challenges. Sometimes when you feel like my admonitions are threatening or your angst is unconscionable, you turn

Family Conscience

away or plug your ears. You don't trust me much, do you? But you'll listen to me soon enough. I distress you but you can't live without me. I am a voice outside yourself that is central to your consciousness. I express the doubleness within, the spirit negating the past and striving to move on. I speak for all the ways in which history bears down upon you, yet I evoke your capacity for choice. I can be a blessing or a curse, crippling or creative, depending on how you respond to me.

I'm a voice, not a verdict, and I question more than condemn. Am I the deepest part of you or alien to your authentic being? Do I hold you helpless and squirming, or am I the source of your freedom? Is my role in your memoir and your life only a complicated form of narcissism, or do I move and motivate you to self-transcendence?

Whose voice am I? Am I the deepest and most authentic part of you or a shadow self that you will leave behind? When I preach to, accuse, or acquit you, who is speaking, and to whom am I speaking?

www.ingramcontent.com/pod-product-compliance
Lightning Source LLC
Chambersburg PA
CBHW032051220426
43664CB00008B/961